From the Galaxy, with Love
a Lightworker's Textbook

By Max M. Rempel, Ph.D. and James Ernest Charles

CONTENTS

ABOUT THE BOOK

This is a textbook for lightworkers who don't need convincing. It is unique because we don't argue with anybody, we just summarize the vast knowledge on aliens, alien worlds, spirit worlds, dimensions and ascension in a simple systematic way. It is a book for insiders and open souls who believe and want to know more. We choose to focus on the positive and put in positive information. Negativity is also mentioned, with love and respect, but without too much attention.

Our focus is on alien worlds, their life, families, emotions, galactic history and modern galactic politics. The information comes to us first hand via a continuous dialogue with aliens, angels, and spirits. We are in a wonderful privileged position since we have a researcher, Max, who has had a continuous weekly dialogue with aliens, angels, and spirits—via Jim—for over four years, asking important questions, comparing notes, and researching available outside sources.

During our sessions, we frequently ask fundamental questions such as: *How do you see God? How do you bring up your children? What makes your civilization proud? And, Why are you interested in us?* Importantly, from start, we published our dialogues on YouTube, created a channeling community (hashtagged Hucolo, which is short for Human Colony) with weekly live online webinars, also published on youtube, helped many other lightworkers to become energy healers and channelers and connected with many other channelers such as Shawn Swanson, Roxanne Swainhart, Karen Newmann, Jonathan C. Martin, Louise Kay, Ivan Teller and many others. We share similar values and work diligently to heal the world and bring about the Disclosure, the Open Contact, and Ascension.

The book's narrative is concise in style and comprehensive in scope. The major topics are illustrated with the selections from the original transcripts of our channeling sessions. The narrative and transcripts are represented in about equal proportions, so the reader gets the best of both worlds—the precise factual information and the authentic vibration of the transdimensional dialogue.

Our hearts are pure, we co-create a peaceful reality and invite you to share a journey together.

THE ALIENS ARE FROM ANOTHER DIMENSION

This volume is intended as a textbook about friendly aliens and Ascension. Although the subjects are complex and dramatic, I will keep them simple and focus on the positive side.

This book is the result of seven years of research. I think that the emergence of aliens and hybrid children is the most important event happening to humanity which, awakening to these transformative visitations, gives us great hopes for our collective future.

The first source of information about the aliens is experiencers. Experiencers are humans who have met the aliens face to face, conversed with them, visited their ships and planets. Another source of information is channeling. In these sessions, a channeler enters a trance state, connects telepathically to an alien and mediates the dialogue between them and the audience. This allows discussion with the aliens, i.e., ask questions and receive answers.

Transcriptions herein are based on the channelings of James Ernest Charles, co-author, as well as other channelers listed in the Acknowledgements section at the book's end. In these pages I will summarize what I learned, and illustrate the main points with selected quotations from the channeled sessions.

Most of the aliens visiting Earth and interacting with humans are from other dimensions. That means they exist in a different reality, are invisible to us, yet have the technology to materialize here as physical presences. Many of them can exist on our planet only for a few hours before they must return to their dimension. In their ships the aliens can take humans to distant worlds, and many experiencers have indeed taken such journeys, limited usually to only two weeks. Any longer, human physiology will adapt to the alien reality and, upon return, readaptation will be fraught with difficulty.

The world from which the aliens come is usually called the 4th Density, 4th or even 5th Dimension when a different numbering system is used. The aliens who speak through Jim call our reality 3D and theirs 4D, so throughout the text we will use this numbering.

The experiencers who visited 4D commented that they feel much healthier on alien ships, and their illnesses cease until the return to our reality. Clearly, life in 4D is different from ours. The most notable difference is that 4D beings are telepathic. Many possess psychic and telekinetic abilities allowing them to talk with spirits, and use their minds to manipulate matter. The fundamental perception of 4D is that it is lighter than human 3D. In 4D even linear time is flexible; some 4D aliens have the ability to shift back and forth in time by a few hours. Our 3D reality permits only forward temporal movement, whereas the inhabitants of 4D are able to shift their consciousness back and forth and clairvoyantly glimpse fragments of the future.

ASCENSION

Ascension is the process of shifting to a higher density and dimension. In this way, many civilizations in the universe shifted from 3D to 4D. Humanity too has begun Ascension, and currently is at an early stage, with but a few—mostly from aboriginal cultures—individually ascended. The timing of collective Ascension is uncertain, dependent on our collective awakening and presently making slow progress. Although the massive Ascension is predicted to occur some 180 years hence (circa 2300) during our great-grandchildren's generation, there is much hope that humanity's collective awakening will be hastened by Open Contact with friendly aliens. Humanity then could possibly ascend in our lifetime. Currently, the 4D Earth (Tara Ha) is sparsely populated; its population entire roughly one million people, the majority aliens from the Pleiadian and Yahyel cultures. Among them are scattered Reptilians and some ascended humans.

It is predicted, however, that not all humans will ascend. Ascension is a conscious process, requiring an adult person's willingness. Some will ascend individually; some as families and other groups. The crucial requirement is desire to ascend, and a certain level of spiritual purity, which can be attained through meditation and positive intent. It is further predicted that fewer than fifty percent of the human population will ascend, with the rest remaining on the 3D Earth.

For each individual, the Ascension process takes about one 3D-Earth week, during which the physical body transforms to a light body. This can be assisted through meditation and prayer, and is a conscious process of transformation, the body disappearing from 3D Earth and shifting into the 4D.

The decision to leave this reality and shift into a new realm is tremendous; much work is required in order to properly disseminate information about Ascension. Effort on the spiritual level too is needed to guide the human collective into acceptance—and commitment to—the idea of Ascension. In this learning and collective acceptance, we receive help from aliens, angels and spirits. The information comes in the form of channeling, dream work and direct contacts. Once alien contact becomes open, the process of learning and collective awakening will quicken. As the human collective dawns to the idea of Ascension, there will be much discussion, and communication with the aliens will expand. When the wave of Ascension surges, all will know what to expect.

New visitors to the 4D Earth will have much assistance. In about one month, their physiology will accommodate the novel reality. Here, a person goes into Ascension by themselves, but on the other side receives much support with the process. Children will ascend with their parents, pets with their owners.

Physiologically, Ascension involves activation of the DNA, nervous system, and energetics—similar to the Kundalini awakening—of the body. Those of aboriginal cultures who reach spiritual maturity are currently ascending slowly. A tiny percentage of Westerners ascend: those in a positive state of mind and health; those consciously working on ascension. The current rate of ascension is very low, as only a few hundred people ascend per year. At present, the majority of ascended humans are accommodated by 4D Earth's existing alien population. As the rate increases, the newly ascended humans will develop their own culture.

The 4D reality is not new to humankind; ancient Earth experienced it during a global catastrophe that wrought planet-wide descension from 4D to 3D. This fall of humanity is recalled by many ancient traditions, including the Bible. According to Ashayana Deane and David Wilcock, the fall from 4D happened about 500 million years ago. After that, the human civilization was several times rebuilt, and again destroyed several more. According to Bashar and other sources, the last and major destruction of Atlantis happened about 23,000 years ago. This fall caused a loss of culture and technology. Some of the Atlantean knowledge has been kept by secret societies and priests, and now some of it is resurfacing.

Among major advantages of 4D life is richness of spirit, and enhanced connections between people via telepathic communication. Life there is much lighter and happier, lessons clear with a higher vibrational nature. There is, of course, drama, challenges and instructive events in the 4D, but these are of a higher level. Ascension is like graduating from middle school to high school; the lessons become more complex and interesting.

The idea of past downfall and approaching Ascension is central to human culture, and threads through religions and spiritual texts worldwide. In addition, the Ascension was predicted by many prophets, including Jesus (Yeshua). Ascension is a central idea in many current channelings and teachings. Much work is needed from us to help humanity awaken and prepare; much is being done by our higher-dimensional friends from 4D and higher spirit dimensions. Ascension is a process guided by the Creator.

Ascension can be compared to a major upgrade of a computer's operating system. Consider also a computer game analogy: Ascension would correspond to reaching a new level in the game, where at each step one earns new powers—and faces fresh challenges.

At this time, only a fraction of society is aware of ascension. An even smaller number desire to Ascend. Many humans are stuck in the 3D drama and fear the unknown. Many are frightened even by the *idea* of aliens and spirits. For humanity to ascend, a major awakening will be required.

ANGEL GAHIL ON ASCENSION

Channeled by Jim

I am the Angel Gahil from the Nine Realms.

Your world comes under attack daily from outer forces, but you are being protected. Sometimes these negative forces come through. What you should do if you feel this negative force is thank God—your Creator, the white light—the energy that created us and flows through all of you. You must call on Him immediately, as a group, when you feel [negative forces].

As soon as you feel, you will be connected to all others who [also] feel, and be connected in light when you thank Him for relieving the problem.

This is what I needed to come and tell you, because all over your planet the vibration has fallen [due to] these depressions, and we would want you to pick that back up again, with great love, great power of unity. There is so much power in your unity. You grasp together, souls and spirits which have so much power. The body is nothing compared to the energy within you. Do you understand?

Blessings to you. Gather together. Become a force of light. Do not be foiled by negative attack. Together, even when you do not see each other the bonds are strong. You needed to hear these things. These words were given for your continuation.

OPEN CONTACT

The key step in the collective preparation for Ascension is Open Contact with the aliens. Incidentally, contact takes place every day, but has not yet signalized—or become conspicuous in—global awareness. Individuals and groups, however, are in daily contact with the aliens. This takes many forms: some people are visited; some ferried in ships to the stars; others communicate telepathically and/or speak to aliens via channelers. There are aliens living on Earth, some with families comprising humans and hybrids. Each year, the public is getting closer to realizing that contact is possible, and at some point will be ready to invite the aliens to openly speak. The friendly aliens are eager, but restrained by a so-called First Directive and cannot show up until invited by the human collective.

Many channelled communications predict Open Contact will happen soon, likely within 10 years (before 2027). This is determined by the collective awareness and desire of the Earth's people. Official opposition can be found in the form of politicians who find it safe and profitable to delay Open Contact as long as possible.

Top levels of Earth governments are aware of the aliens, take regular meetings with them, yet delay overt disclosure for fear of losing control. If the public learns about extraterrestrial presence and technologies, support of ongoing wars, armies and the military industry would end. The politicians realize that Open Contact likely would spark revelation of many shameful secrets, and inspire worldwide redistribution of power. Nonetheless, the process of Ascension already has begun, and it is absolutely essential for the population to become aware. Delays in the process would be detrimental to our civilization. Since meeting the aliens face to face would greatly boost collective awareness, we, the lightworkers of Earth, advocate for Open Contact to be organized as soon as possible.

Furthermore, we advocate for disclosure including worldwide governments publicly releasing from deep classification all information relevant to their interactions with the aliens. We advocate for Open Contact in which the public and governments invite the aliens to come down and openly begin consultations with both. Until that happens, we continue to communicate with the aliens on an individual level and share our experiences online.

THE LYRANS

The first galactic humans who appeared in our Milky Way galaxy were Lyrans. They are referred to as Founders. Until the arrival of Lyrans, the galaxy was populated by Reptilians and Insectoids. The Lyrans came from outside the spiraled Milky Way, and settled on a planet called Lyra - "rock" or "soil" in the Lyran language. The ancient Lyran home star is not located in the familiar constellation known as Lyra, but in a different sector of our sky, northeast of Alpha Centauri.

The Lyrans developed a peaceful civilization and advanced culturally, technologically and spiritually until a tragic day when their planet, Lyra, was destroyed by the Reptilians. The Lyrans knew in advance that the Reptilian ships were coming, evacuated much of the population before its destruction and took many treasures of their culture with them into space. Plant life, animals, books, technologies and even pieces of buildings accompanied them as they scattered through the galaxy. The diaspora of refugees created several new subspecies and Lyran cultures as they continued to evolve on other planets. This is how galactic humans came to exist and populate our galaxy.

The Lyrans cherish their ancient culture and language. An average Lyran is about nine feet tall. They are feline humans; like lions in a tall, humanoid body. Bone structure and other features are predominantly feline, but the overall form resembles that of an Earth human. Lyrans are very strong, proud and kind—ancestors, and friends of our civilization.

Many Lyrans are incarnated as Earth humans, some of whom carry in their DNA ancient Lyran bloodlines. The presence in a human of Lyran DNA grants strength, emotional power, telepathic and psychic abilities. To some, Lyrans serve as spirit guides.

Like us, biologically the Lyrans are placentals and mammals, give birth to their children and feed them with milk. The mammaries of Lyrans are much smaller than humans', and (as in lions) of reduced volume when not in use. Lyran faces are covered with hair; women presenting longer, leonine beards and deeper voices than males.

The Lyrans do not find humans sexually attractive, and humans feel the same toward them. We are otherwise sufficiently similar, so Lyrans and humans can become friends who easily hug. Given their exceptional strength, it's advisable before hugging a Lyran to request gentleness.

Lyrans are spiritually very advanced, psychic and clairvoyant. Their chakra system and spiritual powers are exceptionally developed. They are powerful healers. The Lyran culture places a special value on emotional power and spiritual integrity. They are wise and serve the progress of galactic humankind across the universe.

TEKKRR ON LYRAN HISTORY

Channeled by Jim

Tekkrr: Greetings. I am Tekkrr.

Max: Hi, Tekkrr. Welcome. We would like to invite you to dictate some of the information for our planned book.

Tekkrr: What kind of information are you looking for?

Max: The most interesting question is the origin of Lyran Civilization. Can you give us a little introduction to this?

Tekkrr: Yes. The origin of Lyrans is very ancient. We used to have a planet called Lyra, of course. That was the earliest name. It meant—just like your name, meant a rock or earth—but was an early term from the Lyran people, that we came from the rock which has since been destroyed. Where it was in space is now questionable. It's been that long ago. However, it was not the Pleiades. We know that for sure. If you were to look at your sky, do you pick out Alpha Centauri? To the right and to the north—northeast of Alpha Centauri—was where the Lyran planet was supposed to have been.

It was destroyed by Reptilians many, many millennia ago because they felt they were being cheated. You see, it was like an Adam and Eve scenario there, where life was very beautiful like paradise, and people got along, and the primitive elements of life were not as evident as they are today in most civilizations. And God had smiled on our civilization because we had been getting along so well. Therefore, the Reptilians did not like this and started to come around and act as if they were being cheated. Therefore, yes, we had some technology back then and things we could do to fight back, but we were not a warlike people. And so, we could see we were not going to win a war against these particular beings.

The next step was to find a way off the planet, because we heard rumors that they were going to destroy it. Indeed, they did eventually, but not before many thousands of ships left the planets and scattered across the galaxies. And that is where we are now. We are all over the place, actually. We are happy to say that even though our planet was destroyed, we made our own, we created another in the Pleiades—about twice the size of your moon. That is where the Lyran culture is now based. Is there another question?

Max: Yeah. Other participants, prepare your questions about the Lyran culture. First, why is the Lyran culture called Lyran? Was it initially on a star called Lyra?

Tekkrr: Yes. That was the name of our original planet. It means earth, or rock. It has changed meanings over the years to infer the civilization living there. Originally, though, they believe it meant simply "earth" or "rock."

Max: We have a small constellation named Lyra. Is this where we, or your civilization, is from?

Tekkrr: No. That is what humans have called the Lyra constellation. We had nothing to do with that.

Max: Ah! That's an important mistake—which we caught.

Tekkrr: Yes. The human culture can have no idea where we originated. There is no written history about that on your planet.

Max: So, the constellation Lyra has a star—Vega—which is the fifth brightest in the sky. Okay, that's not where you're from.

Tekkrr: Exactly.

Max: Second important question. What did the first Lyrans look like? Were they feline humans?

Tekkrr: Yes. We started as a cat-like civilization. We are still a cat-like civilization. It was very different back then, of course. The tails were still intact. The ears were still intact. But as time has gone on, evolution has taken the tail down to almost a stump. The ears are no longer obvious on the outside of the head. The reason for this is telepathy became part of our culture. We no longer needed to hear as much and we did, nor listen, because we started to speak in psychic languages. However, we do still have a verbal language, but there are times when we use mental telepathy to communicate.

Max: Thank you. Staying on the topic of the felines, were their bodies and the present Lyran body more like the human form or a lion's body?

Tekkrr: More like a lion's.

Max: So, the structure of your legs is more like that of a lion than a human.

Tekkrr: They are now similar to human legs, but originally were not. Of course, there's a [vestigial] bump on top of the knee to remind us where we came from, but the way the legs move also is different in some ways. We are much taller, and need a lot more support. And so, the thigh area is very large.

Max: Our kids can climb the tree using only nails. Can the Lyrans do the same?

Tekkrr: We still have a form of claw, if you will, but it is not now much used. But we do trim them, as you trim your nails. Therefore, they are not sharp like they used to be, but they do hang over the fingertip—if you could call it a finger or paw. We use hands [similarly] as you.

Max: [Using claws] can you climb trees?

Tekkrr: I'm sure that I am still capable of climbing trees on my planet.

Max: Wonderful. Audience, do you have questions? Please raise them up.

Brian: Yes. This is Brian. Hello, Tekkrr. Greetings.

Tekkrr: Greetings, Brian.

Brian: My question, my friend, is was it through just the Lyrans' own natural evolution they became bipedal, more-human looking, in the legs? Was there actually more hybridization or, rather, species eventually like the Nordics, the [0:09:01][Inaudible]?

Tekkrr: As I told you originally, we went off to different sections of the galaxies. And so, we landed and became part of other cultures. There was interbreeding with some of these cultures, when it was able to be done. And so, yes, we are a hybrid culture in many areas of the galaxy. In this part, where we are now, we are, yes, hybrids with other species from thousands of years ago. But within the last 1,000 to 1,200 years, we have not been interbreeding with any other species. So, the way we have brought forth our changes were from long ago.

Actually, you have to understand that when you live in a certain culture, a certain atmosphere or a culture that is not exactly the same as where you came from, there will be— Eventually, changes come about. And that is what happened with us as well. Of course, we were in a more telepathic region of space, with telepathic beings. Therefore, we were able to develop that skill much quicker than some other Lyrans in other parts of space, because we were able to understand and grasp ways to do things that catapulted us beyond some of the other sex, if you will—other of our species. Of course, just like your planet, we were not all exactly alike. And so, some Lyrans look very much different than we do at this point and still have ears, tails, and longer fur. We are related to them from millennia ago. But we have run into them in our space travels and we are still friendly, and speak about the legends of our planet from the very beginning.

We do take our culture with us wherever we go. One of those things is that we did have a binary sun or a twin sun. And this was something that was part of our culture for many, many years since early on. They were named Econ and Oshunda, and were mated as they were our creators. Those were the earliest thoughts about Econ and our civilization. So, we still all have that in common. We take that memory, if you will, along with us and the memory of what our planet was like. We took parts of the planet with us. Some of us took trees and some of us took animals. Others preserved pieces of the culture: stone, brick, to remind us of home because we were sad to have to leave. We took as much of our homeland as we could. Not that we were going to live in the past because we knew that was not possible, but we did bring it along because it was part of who we were and we wanted to remember. Our songs, our dances from that time were written and stored in libraries on each ship to remind us of our early cultures and what they were like. And the instruments that were being played at that time, although they are very different today, they are still in what you might call museums. And there are thousands of museums all around the galaxies with different artifacts from the original Lyra planet.

We all took our particular things along, of course, many similar things. What a peaceful and beautiful culture it was. We're very proud, in the sense that we have not ever been a warlike people, that we have developed into even a more peaceful fourth-dimensional culture. We are moving eventually into a fifth-dimensional culture, within the next few hundred years. Just as you are moving into fourth dimension, we are moving into the fifth.

Max: You mentioned that you limited hybridization with other species in the last 1,000 years. How is that possible without limiting personal freedoms?

Tekkrr: It was a choice of the people. It was not that they were forbidden, but they chose on their own to stay within the confines of the 80,000 or whatever population that we had when we moved. Right now, we're [counted] in the billions of people. And we are developing a second Lyran-made planet. So, it is a beautiful thing. They just decided they wanted to remain culturally pure. Not that we are prejudiced against others, but we wanted to keep our culture alive in a very pure way.

Max: Wonderful. And wait, another question from the audience.

Tekkrr: Yes.

Max: Did you always know about extraterrestrial life on the Lyran planet?

Tekkrr: No.

Max: How did it all begin to happen on your world?

17

Tekkrr: We did not know about extraterrestrials until the Reptilians started to attack. We were actually a rather peaceful culture. And we had developed technology of course. We have come from a very wonderful beginning, and God has blessed us very much. At the very start, there was a lot of confusion about who we were as a people. And we had many decisions to make, but we decided early on that those decisions were to be made as a group, as a planet, and we would bring ourselves together because our planet was not small. It was actually a very large planet, since we are still very large creatures. We found it worthwhile to bring together our cultures, share thoughts of who we are and were, and that we could understand we needed to [live] a certain way to survive.

The cultures were brought together that way, and it was decided we did want to search the sky for a better place to live because, of course, we were using up the fossil fuels and things of that nature that you have discovered on your planet. So, we came to a point where we were running low, looking for new places to gather fuel, but we had not really been invaded by any other species. Our planet was very large, but sort of isolated as well because it was in the corner of a galaxy and there was [minimal] life outside our planet and three others in our solar system. There was no life on those planets. And we were sort of in an isolated area, which is just the way it was. And so, we were not visited by anyone, which is unusual because I think most civilizations at our point would have had many visitations, much interference. But I think those interferences are some of the reasons why there are warlike cultures, and civilizations that do not get along.

Perhaps because we were left alone we developed into a peaceful culture. So, therefore, the other thing is after discovering the Reptilians, of course, we knew they were a warlike culture, and that actually solidified us even more into a peace-like culture 'cause we did not want to be like them. There were those who thought we should fight them, but logic won out in that discussion—plus love and peace, because it was spread through our culture. Do we want to be like them [we asked ourselves], or separate ourselves?

It was then said, "But they're going to destroy our world." The elders responded: This world is worn out. We need to move on anyway. So, let them take this world if they wish, and let us find greater pastures in the sky because we know that with all these millions of stars and galaxies there will be found something for us, [including] fuels that could last for thousands of years. So, let us take these synthetic things and move on. Let them have our old discarded world.

We didn't realize they were going to blow it up, but we knew it was profoundly used. Therefore, we did move on, but decided to do so in many different places instead of just one. Some headed out for places we called Senda—a heavily populated part of space with many stars. Some of us went to the Furna side, where burned a sparse number of suns. And others simply set out for wherever they felt God was leading them. So, it was very much individualized where we settled, but we took our families with us. We maintained contact for many, many years, and are in contact still with many of our specie and their various ships, but we lost track of some.

Max: Was Earth part of your initial migration?

Tekkrr: Yes. And some of them were destroyed by the Draconians, Reptilians, and other species they ran into because they did not even have onboard weapons. We saw Earth, [and] there were some who went there. My portion of the population did not—we went to the Pleiades.

Max: Were Lyrans ever involved in aggression, like war?

Tekkrr: I am sure there [is] some evidence that Lyrans were involved in wars in other places because they were attacked, but most were destroyed because they had no weapons—and some did develop weaponry, if they decided to protect their planet. But I do not know if any of them are warlike at this time.

Max: So, the Lyrans were the first humans in the galaxy, which gave rise to all other humans.

Tekkrr: Gave rise to what?

Max: All other humans in the galaxy.

Tekkrr: You mean Lyrans?

Max: Are Lyrans the ancestors of all other humans in the galaxy?

19

Tekkrr: No. No. There are many species in the galaxy that are older than us.

Max: All humans.

Tekkrr: Humans are actually younger than us. So, we did not develop humans, but we did have something to do with their seeding at some point, but did not stay on Earth for long. Perhaps a few hundred years.

Max: Oh, I'm using humans in galactic term. There are galactic humans, which I think are all descendants of Lyrans.

Tekkrr: Oh yes, like the Nords, Pleiadians.

Max: And Aryans.

Tekkrr: Pleiadians are the ancestors of humans, yes.

Max: So, are Aryan humans also your descendants?

Tekkrr: Yes. There are some Aryan humans who are also part of the ancestry, as well as Arcturians, and other species that had given some hybridization to the Earth. Now, let me explain something to you. You realize that there are missing links in your evolutionary patterns. Therefore, that is when quick change was happening and when other species were changing the life forms, causing gaps in the actual evolution of humankind.

This was different than with any other species, in which you'll be able to find what they would call a missing link. But on Earth, there are definite missing links that you will never find—they were evolved so quickly because of hybridization and seeding from other planets. This [Earth] that you are on has been the object of many, many visitations because of its role in the prophecy of the universe. The planet has been mentioned many times, now in a very clear and interesting way, which I cannot presently go into. But your planet is very important to the growth of the galaxy and the universe.

Max: Thank you. Carolina has a question.

Carolina: Yes, hi. My question: are different types of feline classed as

Lyran, for example lion beings or the tiger beings. Are they Lyran?

Tekkrr: Yes. They have Lyran in their background. Yes. And they are hybrid breeds of Lyran. Yes. This is true. There are many hybrid breeds of Lyrans that did interbreed once they moved out of the Lyran stage as we can call it, and moved into other galaxies and made their various homes. Some of them found worlds that were very primitive, with breathable atmospheres, and they could simply inhabit it and become the population there. Not that they kicked out any part of the [existing] flora or fauna, but simply adapted to it.

Carolina: Right. So, which feline on our planet would you be most close to?

Tekkrr: Well, if to be honest, we are closest to the lion. But if you realize, if you go back, lion is a missing link as well. They have no idea where lions began. It is because they came from other worlds.

Max: There is a belief here that Lyrans donated lions to us, and that Sirians donated dolphins and dogs.

Tekkrr: It is possible, but I cannot tell you if that is true or not. But it is very possible because we do have an animal very similar to a lion that is not Lyran, an animal kept as a pet similar to us as your monkeys are to humans. This pet is similar to Lyrans, but is not intelligent or advanced like the Lyran population.

Max: We've run out of time. We have many more questions. So, I suggest we pause for now and continue when Jim has time.

Tekkrr: Very well. It was good to speak to you.

Max: Thank you very much. Nice talk, Tekkrr. Thank you.

Tekkrr: Perhaps we can talk more about our culture next time, and what things we do for rituals, what things that are happening annually, as you might put it, that are pertinent to our traditions.

Max: Absolutely.

Tekkrr: Someday soon you will truly understand that you are just energy, and see it is really no different than walking from one room to the next. As natural as breathing as it is to come and go. And there was only pure love, light, and comfort. Just as we experience when we are feeling the channeling essence within us of source energy, and the high frequency of those beings we feel in our heart space. It is just like walking into pure love. And they are here very strongly. Sending their love. Namaste.

Max: Namaste.

TEKKRR ON LYRAN HISTORY

Channeled by Jim: Jan 6, 2017

Tekkrr is of Lyran race. She joined Girk Fitneer alliance in 2012 working as a secretary, then organizer, of human settlements in Girk Fitneer. Later as a Girk Fitneer communication representative to Earth governments. Jim—James Ernest Charles—is the main channeler and leader of Hucolo community. This book is based primarily on Jim's channelings.

Tekkrr channeled by Jim: Greetings, I am Tekkrr.

Max: Greetings. Hi Tekkrr, welcome.

Tekkrr: Ah, I hear Max's voice but I do not see his face.

Max: Can you see the blue and orangish images of Arcturians on the screen?

Tekkrr: Very lightly, they are very pastel-colored.

Max: Right they are. Do you mind commenting on what species these are?

Tekkrr: These are Arcturians.

Max: And the orange one is part of Girk Fitneer?

Tekkrr: One moment. Let me look a little closer. There are parts of both of these species in Girk Fitneer. It is a group called the Arcturian Group, but there are several different kinds of Arcturians. At least three, anyway. Both of these are within the group here.

Max: Can you ask them if they will give us the names for these orange and blue ones?

Tekkrr: You mean a name other than "Arcturians"?

Max: Yeah, just a subspecies.

Tekkrr: Ah, a subtitle. One moment, and I will speak to them. [speaks Lyran] They will ask them and she will get back to me. I asked Sengi to get with them.

Max: Wonderful, thank you. The last time we talked about the book we asked you to tell us about the origins of the Lyran race. You mentioned that you also wanted to speak about the culture of Lyrans and many other things.

Tekkrr: The cultures and the rituals. I do not know if I spoke about any of the cultures or the rituals. Did I?

Max: Not yet.

Tekkrr: There are different Lyran cultures, and now they are even more diverse because they have been scattered across the galaxies and some, of course, have taken all the traditions with them. Others maybe have picked up or dropped some earlier, or more ancient, portions of the traditions due to the fact they are evolving, or feel that it's no longer meaningful.

But there are different feasts, as you have feasts on your planet. Ours are for the remembrance of various occasions, just as yours are. However, they are a little different, and include only one particular kind of food for each feast. There are three separate feast days in what you call a year. We have one at the beginning of the year, taking in the seasonal foods grown around the center of the planet. You see, the center of the planet is where most of the crops and things that are natural or organic are from.

Yet they have three different seasons, while you have four. Your equator has only one or two seasons, I believe, but on our planet the equatorial area has about three seasons because of the wobble of our planet's axis. Or of the original planet's, I should say. It was in an elliptical rotation around our Suns and provided different seasons for that central part, and for the entire world.

The first season was the cooler. Not cold, not wintry like any of your seasons, but cooler. This provided more of the Semion. Semion were the fruit groups, and so the first feast celebrated them during the end of the season when the harvest is taking place. The fruit group would have its own kind of festival, and all the different foods that were made from these fruits would be eaten. No other kind of food would be eaten at that time because we were celebrating that harvest. Remember, this was from the original planet of Lyra.

The second feast celebrated another third of the year, the Sembion group. The Sembion group were the meat-eaters. Therefore they celebrated by eating only the animals most plentiful at that time. You see, that was the mating period at the end of the fruit group; then they started the animal group which was the mating season for them and that is when we celebrate the Sembion group. That is mostly what they are in that festival, in that feast.

The final group was vegetable-oriented—the Kelly-kahn. The Kelly-kahn group was when more vegetables were grown than at any other time. Of course, there's intermingling of these different things happening all at once. It wasn't just fruit, then animals, then vegetables. However, those are the majority of the festivals in these three groups. Does that make sense to you?

Max: Yes, thank you.

Tekkrr: Three food groups were celebrated during the year. Now, I know that you have dairy and other groups in your culture, among other things. Yet we did not celebrate those because they were year-round things. The foods that were year-round were not celebrated in their own right, but the seasonal ones were because we felt fortunate to be able to have those particular crops at that time. And that originated with the ancient Lyrans.

Also, many traditions about unions and marriage have changed over the

24

years, just as in your culture. Getting married has changed in several ways. Our final stage of that resulted because we became semi-communal, in the sense that different parts of the family of course were separated. Yet it was very free and open, and we celebrated the family in many ways. The times of birth and the times of death. The times when children reach maturity, or when someone was ill. There was always the semi-community, which took care of these particular situations.

Now, you may say, "We go to the doctor for our needs when it comes to illnesses," but in our culture we have evolved to take care of our own illnesses and needs in that regard. There is always one person in the community who will take care of sick family. You may run into some families that have died out, or are down to only a few members. And sometimes those small family units are adopted by a larger family, and that is also fine and very much acceptable. Are there any questions about that? I know this is very general.

Max: Yes, thank you. Last time you mentioned that you are a peaceful race. Can you specifically tell about the wars you participated in?

Tekkrr: Yes, well, the original Reptilian confrontation was the war that we refused to fight. We left the planet, and the planet was destroyed. However, with that we had resolved as a people that we were not going to fight because that would only create a greater war, greater source of aggression in the galaxy. Instead of fighting the Reptilians, we left. Now because of that it made us even more peaceful, because we felt we had done the right thing— and took no negative action.

And so I do not know about all the species of Lyrans that have gone forth from that time. But I know that the ones from our area who have moved forward and made this planet and lived on several other worlds, have always been peaceful and friendly. I know that we have not always been met as friends by other species, but soon after we arrive and let them know who we are, they understand.

News of us travels far. We are a very peaceful civilization. I do not know of another species that has not been involved in many wars. Our earliest development had some negativity, but we realized that that was not working for us as a planet. You see, we came together as a world, not as fragmented regions. Somehow we were able to maintain contact with each other over time and space, were able to get together and communicate peacefully. And even if there was a disagreement, we would not rest until it was taken care of.

This is how we have always managed. All I remember is that if there was a disagreement in the family, or between families, or even between planets we would not rest until it had been resolved. If their idea was to fight, then we would move on. We would say, "No, that's fine, we will take our things and move away." We are not going to fight for the planet, for ground, for "matter"—that does not work for us. Because what you have fought for is tainted by violence.

Max: There are no professional warriors among Lyrans, is that right?

Tekkrr: We do not bring up warriors. We raise our children to be peaceful, and we talk to our people in a peaceful manner. That does not mean we do not have disagreements, or there isn't some trouble at some places because people have a tendency to disagree and to want what they want. However, it is always compromised, or always met in one way or another. We hold a council. If things get too out of hand, we take it to the council, and they will make the final decision. Then the people will live with that, because they realize the council is made up of wise men and women and they will live with the decision, even though they may not agree with it. But it usually never gets that far out of hand.

Max: What is the type of government you have?

Tekkrr: We have, there is a government, there is a council ... um, that is the central form of our government. We usually govern our own family units, without any problems, because there is always someone—or more than one—in the family designated to keep the peace. There is always someone too for medical purposes. The family is a self-contained government, and some families are very large. We have our own little, uh, way of handling things within our own family units and communities. But if things get out of hand it is taken to the council.

Max: If you look at the human society and culture, what parts most resemble Lyran?

Tekkrr: We do not see any particular area on your planet that reminds us of ourselves, except in the guise of Tibetan and Franciscan monks. They are very peaceful, quiet and to themselves a community. They venture out rarely to purchase things they need. You see, we don't have the money unit here so we barter with other clans and other communities for things that are important. And we mingle during festival times.

Max: I understand, thank you. I would like to let Kaan ask his questions.

Kaan: Hello, Tekkrr, my friend.

Tekkrr: Greetings, Kaan.

Kaan: I have some drawings for you [to view]. Do you have any thoughts on that?

Tekkrr: I love your drawings. They show various species from many areas of the galaxies. This particular picture is of a Lyran descent. It's not from our particular area of space. [Golden Lion head] This is from the Alpha Centauri area. Because they grew up on a planet more similar to Lyra than where we grew up, they remained in appearance similar to the ancient Lyrans. We have adapted and evolved into a shorter-haired species with shorter tails because of where we have lived, and the different atmospheres we have breathed over the millennia. We share some facial features of course.

[next picture shows a short-haired, gray-colored Lyran] Yes, this looks almost like a Reptilian, but I cannot see the mouth. Ah, yes, this is a species from Andromeda. Similar to the Eli-a shawn di zendi (spelling?), probably coming from the roots of their descendants, but very similar. The Eli-a shawn di zendi have bigger muzzles, sharper teeth and look a bit more reptilian.

[next picture] This is another species from Alpha Centauri. I'm wondering if they've changed any part of their name. I think they still go by Lyrans.

[next picture] Lyran as well, definitely. This reminds me of the species in the Arcturian space, far behind what is actually the Eli-kondo space. They have a species of Lyran that looks very much like this.

Max: Tekkrr, what is your subspecies?

Tekkrr: We call ourselves Lyran. Many of those from the planet Lyra have their ancient roots there, and call themselves Lyran. There might be a few groups who have slightly altered their names.

Max: Do you have a name for your variety of Lyran?

Tekkrr: The El-kondo Lyrans and the Alpha-Centauri Lyrans. They usually take their galaxy name.

Max: But which is your race?

Tekkrr: Mine are called Lyrans from Pleiades.

[next picture] This looks like a priestess, or priest, from the ancient Lyran culture. They would wear the third-eye symbol, which did glow like this. I'm not sure if there's anything like this at his time. Kaan, I have a question for you. Did you pick this up in your recent thought process as a being existing today?

Kaan: Actually, I'm thinking you're right. I feel it looks ancient.

Tekkrr: I feel it's from the original planet Lyra. I have a picture similar to this in some of my ancient history books.

Kaan: What was the name of the first Lyran Planet? Eden?

Tekkrr: Yes, some called it that because that is how the Reptilians perceived it. Many saw it as an Eden because it was so peaceful, blessed by God in many ways, and the reptilians thought it was cheating them out of something—so they fought with us. They wanted to destroy this planet, because they thought it was an unfair representation of life in the galaxy.

[next picture] This is a Reptilian species, from the Andromeda area also. Many of the earliest Reptilians and Draconians came from this sector.

[next picture] Also in the Andromeda area.

[next picture] This is a different species. You may think it's Arcturian, but it is not. It is actually an early version of Yahyel. Notice the blue eyes. Arcturians rarely have that color. Their eyes can be blue, of a lighter tone than this. Or they can be lavender, silver, or other pale colors. This is an early Yahyel look. They developed into a very human-appearing creature.

[next picture] That is hard to see. A sun?

Kaan: Yes, a sun being.

Tekkrr: Yes, there are beings in the sun. Let me tell you that the older the sun is, the more chance it will have a sentient life form within it. Especially red dwarfs and suns that are [profoundly] ancient. They keep their suns alive as much as they can. But when they go supernova, the beings take the opportunity to return to the oversoul. Some sun beings are very advanced. It's hard to communicate with them because they do not speak a language that is well-translatable. We understand a few things, because they try to speak the galactic languages. Other than that, they remain mysterious and we do not know how they live.

Kaan: That's all. Thank you, Tekkrr.

Tekkrr: You're welcome.

Max: Thank you, Kaan. Wonderful images. How many Lyran individuals are involved in the solar system project?

Tekkrr: You mean in Girk-Fitneer?

Max: Anywhere.

Tekkrr: Girk-Fitneer has about 1,800,000 involved with this project.

Max: Wow. Can you comment on how the Lyran family differs from the human?

Tekkrr: Well, we're much more communal. Your families seem to be separated. There are very few family units we have studied on your planet that are close, and if they are it's only four or five of them per unit. For us, it's more like 50, 60, 90, 1,000. We can have some very large family units—like a whole city, with their own governments and laws and run very well.

Your units seem very small and often disjointed. They do not eat together or talk much—in fact, there is a lot of fighting. Seems like a lot of anger, especially when the children reach adolescence. When ours reach that stage, separate themselves but in a different way than your children do. This is done in order for them to learn what is happening to them, and why they are feeling changes in the body. It is a very short separation, like one of your classrooms for about three or four weeks. When they come out they are very aware of the things they may want, feel or desire, and it makes for a much more peaceful transition into society.

Max: How many children in one birth? Is it like kittens?

Tekkrr: An ancient form of birthing had three or four at one time. In this day and age it is possible for that still to happen, but for the most part it is one or two.

Max: Do you breastfeed them?

Tekkrr: Yes, we do have feeding ways for the first six weeks of life.

Max: And your births are not technological? They are born naturally?

Tekkrr: Yes, but there is technology that helps with pain. They are very easy births for the most part. We found that the less traumatic a birth is, the greater chance for a child to be happier for the first few years of its life.

Max: Do you have two genders?

Tekkrr: Yes, male and female, just as you have.

Max: Can males give birth?

Tekkrr: No, males cannot. There are some species where males can give birth, but they are usually not humanoid.

Max: How much technology is present in the daily life of a typical Lyran family?

Tekkrr: In my work, I have a lot of technology to move information quickly from one place to another. In the family life there is technology to help keep the habitat clean. Sometimes we use it to cook and to read. When we do our exercise or working out, we prefer the more natural. We've found that machines do not recreate nature as well as natural movement.

Max: Do you have plants, gardens and things like that?

Tekkrr: Of course. Plants and gardens are what some of our people devote their lives to. The study of plants and animals—even for food purposes—is for some a specialty. It takes much time. These people might work a ten-hour day in your time [measure].

Max: How psychic are Lyrans? You are all telepathic and fourth-dimensional, right?

Tekkrr: Yes, we are fourth-dimensional, telepathic, and many of us know psychic language. Meaning we talk to each other without actually speaking. The reason we do verbalize is out of consideration for our fellow creatures who lack telepathy or psychic languages—such as the friendly Reptilians.

Some Yahyel do not yet have psychic language. The thing is, psychic language can still be misunderstood if you do not speak the tongue of that particular species. So, we use galactic languages and speak aloud most of the time.

Max: Thank you. Do you have telekinetic abilities?

Tekkrr: Telekinesis has been nurtured in some of our people, but we do not actually like them because they can get out of control. The area of the brain that controls telekinesis can be automatic. You may start moving things here to there automatically without being aware of it—very disruptive, especially if a group of these people are in a room together. It became a social disruption and now is used strictly for certain rituals and meaningful activities.

Max: Do you use natural teleportation?

31

Tekkrr: Yes, it's much faster and easier to move people and things around. It is in its advanced stages now, a stable technology. There have been terrible accidents in the past, but now the energy is constant there is no issue.

Max: My question is complex. Do you use natural teleportation as I understand Yahyel to have this ability—as a learned skill?

Tekkrr: That is astral teleportation. They can bi-locate, meaning appear in two places at once. They have developed this because they are very empathic creatures, and that quality has made bi-location easier. Let me explain. The first forms of bi-location experienced occur when someone else is in trouble. Someone bi-locates to help them. Or someone is dying, and they bi-locate to be with them.

The Yahyel have this incredible empathic ability so they can feel what is happening within their world and families. This allows them to bi-locate more easily than other species. Therefore they have developed a greater sensibility about bi-location than any other species. Not that other species don't bi-locate, because they do. The Yahyel are probably best at it because they can bi-locate to more than one place at a time if there happens to be a need.

Max: You do not bi-locate?

Tekkrr: I do not.

Max: I mean as a species.

Tekkrr: There are some in our species that can bi-locate, yes, but it is a developed skill—not natural to us.

Max: When a Lyran is born, do they remember past lives?

Tekkrr: Not immediately, no. It is the same with any child we have studied. Born rather like a blank page, and I believe that is the way God intended. Are we saying that they share our ideas about "God" because... think about it: If you were born with all kinds of information in your head, would it not create problems immediately? Learning about who you are and your surroundings is much better than having it forced on you in your thought processes—that could cause psychosis. You must come into life, so to speak, as a blank sheet of paper and learn who you are and why you are, instead of having all that information immediately thrust upon you. It would be maddening.

Max: When would you normally become aware of your past lives?

Tekkrr: When your chakras ignite, and you discover that you know who you are and understand your physicality. When you understand that your body has spirit and life, that there is a God presence, then the chakras ignite. You can discover more about yourself through past-life revelations, but you cannot understand these experiences without spiritual understanding of some sort.

Max: Do Lyrans normally communicate with the personalities of past lives?

Tekkrr: There are a couple rituals that include connecting with past lives, yes.

Max: So it's not an everyday thing?

Tekkrr: No, it is not. It's something very special to us.

Max: What is your idea of reincarnation? Is it linear, as in going from one life to the next, to the next? Or is there more branching? Can you choose a new past life?

Tekkrr: There are species that can do that. We cannot choose and go there at will. The Chakkani can. We understand it is something we will evolve into.

Max: Let me explain: my question is sophisticated. Basically, as I understand it, you create your past. Can you also create a past life?

Tekkrr: We can, but it is forbidden by the time-keepers.

Wendy: Have you evolved to the point where you can instantly manifest, and if so, do you still use the procreation process?

33

Tekkrr: We are only fourth-dimensional and cannot procreate by thought, if that's what you mean. We can recreate by technology, yes. We have developed devices that can recreate many things—clones, for instance. Some of these things we do not use very often because of negative outcomes. However, we cannot organically manifest objects—have them appear before us, but we can technologically.

Wendy: I understand. Do you still use things like we do to enhance your experience, such as scents, clothing, aromatherapy, and meditation?

Tekkrr: Yes, we find that clothing is essential protocol in many situations. And we find that meditation, prayer and things of this nature do enhance the lifestyle we want to lead and are necessary for our continued growth. You can learn things and intellectually grow, but there is a spiritual aspect to each individual. For that to grow, we need meditation, prayer, understanding and learning of what spirituality is and how to control it, because telekinesis, like we spoke of before, has a spiritual element and can be of negative or positive intent.

It can be automatically controlled negatively or positively and therefore we limit the learning and use of it. If someone has developed it automatically from birth, for example, it is sometimes necessary for us to go in and remove that talent or skill, because it becomes dangerous not only to themselves but others. It is spiritually motivated at points.

Wendy: Yes, I understand that. We as humans strive to understand our multidimensionality and our lack of separation. Are you already completely aware of your multidimensionality, so that you don't have the challenges that we do, that we are not individuals necessarily, but part of a whole?

Tekkrr: Believe me, we do realize our multidimensional nature, and that creates more questions than answers.

Wendy: I completely understand that.

Tekkrr: And that creates more problems than solutions, so we do understand how to manipulate some forms of dimension, especially moving backward in dimensional thought. Forward is much more difficult, because you have the blockages or realm separations, if you will.

Comprehending the dimensions also changes how you think about your own dimension, about who you are there because you want to be moving steadily forward, yet see that each dimension will bring greater questions and challenges.

Wendy: I completely understand that. I am experiencing that very thing myself, so thank you, I needed to hear that.

I was surprised to hear how many were mentioned in the Girk-Fitneer project. It's more than I thought. How many of you are actually communicating with us telepathically or through the light languages?

Tekkrr: No, there is a select group allowed to communicate with Earth. Let me explain. There are so many Lyrans, so many Yahyel, so many of this and that because they need to keep control of the information incoming to the planet. If they had random people just doing channelings to the Earth, then the information would be even more confusing than it is already.

There is so much information heading toward the Earth from so many locations, it is very confusing for many and misconstrued by the channeler—sometimes that causes the information to change. Many times the person who is the channel hears something quite differently in their head than what is trying to be said by whoever is speaking, so the message will come out in a very different way because the mind of the channeler has altered it. They do not actually comprehend or understand where the information is coming from, or even why they are communicating it.

Therefore, it is best to be as uninvolved in your channeling as possible, to let the purest form of the message come through even if you don't seem to always understand what it is. The message will come through and come out as close as possible to the original, if you let it go. It's very difficult for it to be perfect, because many words and phrases from other languages are not [parsed] the same to Earth people.

We had much difficulty communicating exactly what we meant at first, because it would be changed. You thought we were meaning this, and you let it come out as that. We've learned how to control that somewhat better, but it is still one of the great reasons there is so much adverse information

35

on your planet. And some things are coming through encrypted as well, and this can be a problem.

Wendy: Thank you for that. I completely understand. How is that relationship developed? How have you and we co-created who will receive that information? Is this done on a higher contact level?

Tekkrr: Yes, in some fashion. There are those who will get the entire world and those who will not, because they cannot channel properly. They will be what you call a flash in the pan. They will start to channel, gain an audience, and then all of a sudden they are gone—taken away because the messages coming through were not what they were meant to be, so they had to be stopped.

They will not be killed, or anything of that nature, but their message will be stopped because it is against what we are trying to do. Against what all, or 90%, of the alien species out here are trying to communicate. So you have seen that some people have started but never continued.

There are some under negative control, and they will continue because they have those negative controls and their messages will be dark and foreboding—even true some of the time. However, when we put out a message from here we want a positive slant into it, so that it may come onto the planet as beneficial in the most possible way, even though it may not be an uplifting message. Our hope is that people may use it in a positive way, not for darkness, negativity, or anything other than what it was intended.

Wendy: I understand.

Tekkrr: There are many problems right now on your planet in this regard, but those of a good, true nature will thrive.

Wendy: Thank you. I appreciate that and know there are many of us with that desire—to bring through the most pure message.

Tekkrr: Absolutely.

Wendy: If someone puts out an intention that they wish to communicate with your species, telepathically or through channeling, how do you receive that information? Do you receive that telepathically from us?

Tekkrr: We have certain technology that can pick up empathic thought processes and mindwave things. If the thought process is strong enough to get onto these particular monitors, activate and let us hear them, then it is worth it for us to give them a chance to channel.

Wendy: Thank you very much, I appreciate that.

Tekkrr: There are those who will wish to channel all their lives, but their frequencies are not open far enough for us to get through in a valuable way, and therefore it would be impossible to help them. They may be picked up by someone else, but for us we're looking for certain positive vibrational channels.

Wendy: I understand. That's what I was going to ask you, [whether] it really just boils down to frequency.

Tekkrr: It does.

Wendy: Do you keep the same partner throughout your time? Do you have more than one?

Tekkrr: We are permitted to have more than one partner. If you have only one, it is a sign of great loyalty. We are allowed, on our planet and in our world, as many as three at one time. But those who are most well respected have only one.

Max: Thank you all. It was a wonderful discussion.

Tekkrr: I hope you learned a lot from this. I certainly enjoyed speaking with you.

[next picture] This is a light-being from Sirius.

Max: There is one more question from Kaan. We asked before about orange and blue Arcturians. Did you get their subspecies name?

Tekkrr: The pink (orange) one. Well, if you really want me to tell you you'll probably not remember them.

Max: We are recording.

Tekkrr: The pink one is Des e fem pondia.

Max: Des e fem pondia.

Tekkrr: Yes, you said it correctly, I think. And the blue, Oretendi.

Max: At this point I have to close, but let's continue when we have the next opportunity.

Tekkrr: Have a wonderful day.

PLEIADIANS

The Pleiades (or Seven Sisters) open star cluster in the Taurus constellation is associated in northern latitudes with winter, but visible from the north pole to southernmost South America. The Pleiades resemble a small misty dipper, and are easily located by scoring Orion's three-starred belt with a line, extending it to the right until reaching a V-shaped pattern whose center flares with a red star—the Bull's Eye, Aldebaran. Another easy method to locating the Pleiades in the night sky is to first find Cassiopeia which looks like a "W". From there, go down and to the left and find the Polaris (North) Star. Finally, go in the same direction down to the left, and the Pleiades will be there.

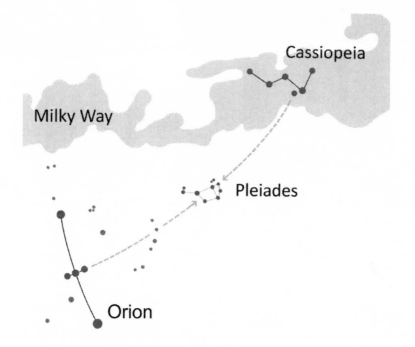

The illustration by Heather Eilrich

I also recommend a smartphone application (Star Chart), which provides a search feature for stars, planets and constellations, using your device's compass and gravity meter to properly orient you. Learning the constellations is good preparation for Contact. In general, the closer stars often are neighbors, and knowing their locations helps us understand stellar histories.

The Orions from the eponymous constellation came to our planet long ago. The populace of ancient India and Europe called them Aryans. Orions lived on Earth for a long time, and eventually departed for the Pleiades. Our planet is therefore the ancestral home for many Pleiadians. The migrations unfolded in all directions: from Earth to Pleiades, Pleiades to Earth.

While on Earth, the Orions-Aryans contributed to the creation and evolution of humankind. Since our civilization was wiped out and rebuilt many times, Orions and Pleiadians hugely contributed to our current society and are our ancestors, and we are the Pleiadians' ascendants—a two-sided process. Across time, the Pleiadians frequently visited the Earth; some stayed and formed colonies, while others married into humanity, thus enriching Earth's progeny with fourth-dimensional genetics. Another benefit was cultural exchange: the Pleiadians shared their knowledge, and in turn were influenced by human culture. We now are closely related, with continuous migration in both directions. This is why Pleiadians often present themselves as our galactic brothers and sisters—they are.

In the Pleiades, there are two stars closely related to Earth, Taygeta and Maia. Both Mayan and Taygetan civilizations are now in fourth density. Maia and Taygeta are inhabited by several different alien species known collectively as Pleiadians.

PLEIADIANS: THE MAYANS

Earth's Mayan civilization originated on a planet orbiting the star Maia in the Pleiades cluster. In ancient times the Mayans visited Earth and, for a while, thrived there before returning to their distant world. It is not clear why their civilization failed, nor why they journeyed back to the Pleiades, although likely this was due to moral failure and practicing dark magic. The primary civilization residing now in the Maia system is very advanced, spiritual and enlightened. In recent years, they have started to channel to us wonderful, illuminating messages.

PLEIADIANS: THE ERRANS

The civilization orbiting the Pleiadian star Taygeta likely most resembles Earth's appearance and culture, and their main planet is called Erra. It is no coincidence that Erra, the star's third planet, recalls the Latin name (Terra) for Earth. Regarding culture, divine path and divine origins, our planets are sisters. Erra is populated by several alien races, and by Earth humans— some of whom migrated in the distant past, fleeing the destruction of Atlantis, while others arrived during the Roman Empire. Involved in many galactic activities, Erra also hosts settlements of Earth-human-Pleiadian hybrids.

The Errans are technologically, spiritually and culturally advanced. Modern Pleiadian culture is different from Orion culture, and the Earth is gradually moving from the Orion model to the Pleiadian. The Orion model is based on the ideas of empire, hierarchy, control, domination and wars, ideas brought to Earth in the distant past by Aryans from Orion. Since then, the Pleiadians have developed the ideas of democracy, equality and compassion. Pleiadian society is more horizontal, less structured and in many ways akin to a tribal society structure. You can see now that the ideas of equality and non-hierarchical communes are gradually becoming more popular on Earth.

Earth humans who have visited the Pleiades say the culture in many ways resembles that of the tribal aliens portrayed in the movie *Avatar* (2009). Despite possessing advanced technologies, they build their lives in harmony with nature. Numerous Errans incarnate on Earth as humans, while many Pleiadians work in our solar system to protect it from invasion and help humanity to evolve and ascend.

Even though usually taller than us, Errans often appear human and, accordingly, could pass muster on Earth. They can utilize a technology that allows them to quickly reduce their height. Most aliens of the fourth dimension live extended lives, upwards of 300 to 1,000 years, and Errans employ body-modifying technologies in order to appear more youthful, heal various injuries, alter skin color, hair and general appearance—all carried out quickly, comfortably and reversibly.

Errans have families, and raise children in a community. One of the advantages of the 4D is that its denizens are psychic, thus easing reconnection with their past life identity, skills and experiences.

Like humans, Pleiadians enjoy leisure time by way of celebrations, holidays and games. Since they are telepathic, deception is not a big part of their culture; therefore, sincerity and respect are at all times authentic. When I watched the movie *La Belle Verte* (1996), I cried tears of remembrance— what a wonderful introduction to the Erran culture.

Errans have a government headed by a king, which is comparable to a president. The Erran king's name is Kenjin. He has Earth-human genetics and looks like a human. In the past three years, Kenjin has spoken to us often through Jim and other channelers. Kenjin consults the Erran elders on many questions of government, and its involvement in the lives of Errans is much lighter than on Earth.

Erran culture is open to the galaxy, and the planet itself receives many far-flung visitors who in turn spread that culture's influence through the Milky Way's starry spiral. Enhanced by quick travel, communication, technology and telepathic abilities, Erra enjoys a unified, tightly connected culture. Moreover, the populace is closely connected to certain locations in the Andromeda galaxy, likely via a system of wormholes.

Pleiadians have been involved in hybridization with humans, and there exist many human hybrids on Pleiadian planets and space settlements. Pleiadian-human hybrids develop their own culture based on Erran mores, ethics and society. Too, they study Earth culture, are eager to consult with us concerning possible solutions to our ever-mounting challenges, potential entrance into the galactic community, and are ready to visit whenever we extend a collective invitation.

Some Pleiadians look like Scandinavians. Others have brown or black skin and resemble Central Africans. There is great variety in their appearance, even more than among humans. Since ecology is important to Pleiadians, they have developed a technology that allows them to absorb sunlight to generate energy in their bodies via photosynthesis of glucose. This technology infuses their skin with chlorophyll, rendering hues of green and blue.

Genetics and transdimensional manipulation enable Pleiadians to modify the body; their surgical techniques are radically advanced. They can access inner parts of the body transdimensionally without damaging surrounding tissues. Time too can be manipulated: compressed in the body during surgery, and dilated throughout recovery to hasten regeneration.

Although Pleiadian medicine is levels and levels beyond ours, similarities can be found. In addition to bioenergetic, dimensional and genetic medicine, they use advanced pharmacology. This is somewhat unexpected, since we, the lightworkers of Earth, have lost trust in chemical pharmacology and prefer herbal, naturopathic and energetic medicine over synthetics. Yet Pleiadian medicine, among other means, does utilize pharmacology.

Many children on Pleiades choose to speed up their growth (and studies) using time-manipulation technology. Since there exist no side-effects to interfere with naturally long lives, this is considered normal. Accelerated childhood can take much less time than on Earth: years of studies can be compressed into a few months, and the child becomes a grown-up packed with knowledge. Advisers assist the children in choosing studies. This truncated childhood/jump to maturity and bypass of dependence, protected play, childhood limitations, restrictions, etc., makes Pleiadians quite different from Earth humans. Therefore, the hybrid children who intend to learn about humans and work with them in the future sometimes choose to experience slow growth and learning in childhood, including our games and children's culture.

On the other hand, our childhood on Earth is almost always loaded with repression, abuse, psychological trauma and violence. Even if the parents are enlightened, in school there is plenty of repression and violence. Pleiadians have no experience, or model, of that thus rendering them even more harmonized and uninhibited.

The Pleiadians are allied with other civilizations friendly to Earth, including Arcturians, Lyrans and Yahyel. These help the Earth in a coordinated fashion and protect the solar system from intrusions by aggressive aliens connected with Orion—Nordics, Reptilians, Draconians and Zeta Greys. Not all alien individuals from these races are negative towards humans, but the above-named races are more frequently involved in hostile and repressive acts.

The main agenda of the negative aliens is control of the Earth, and slowing our ascension. There are many galactic alliances friendly to Earth, and these protect us from such intrusions. Primary benevolent allies are Galactic Federation of Light, Ashtar Command, Girk-Fitneer, The Council of Nine, Arcturian and Andromedan Councils. Pleiadians are compliant with all of these.

In the old days, the presence of Pleiadians and other aliens on Earth was commonplace. People in the ancient world would not be surprised by aliens striding along the streets and residing in temples. Nowadays, the Pleiadians visit the Earth in disguise, using technological adjustments of the body to mimic humans. Some of them come simply to learn about our life. Others are secret operatives actively working to boost our progress. These covert alien agents are called Progressors.

PLEIADIANS: THE CORIATORIANS

In addition to those from the Mayan and Taygetan star systems, another Pleiadian culture in communication with us through channelings are the Coriatorians. Known to the American military as The Blues (there are, in the Pleiades alone, many blue races), this specific race identified themselves as Coriatorians after their home planet, Coriator. In early channelings, Coriatorians were represented largely by Lakesh.

Coriatorians are in many regards quite different from humans, especially biochemically. Coriator's atmosphere, by Earth standards, is toxic; Coriatorians are short, five-feet tall and broad—picture a "cookie man." Their highest-caste members don't commonly walk, but float in the air. Rarely do they leave their home planet, and avoid complicity in galactic politics. This political neutrality must rely on other species for protection. Coriatorians communicate with other worlds, and explore the universe, via tech-enhanced telepathy and holographic projections.

We have been channeling extensively with the Coriatorians, and they have helped us to understand many details about alien life. Due possibly to their neutrality and non-involvement, they were able to share more information about sensitive alien secrets than many other channeled sources.

Lakesh told us that the Coriatorians contributed during World War II to the downfall of the Nazis and, further, that the Nazis were aided by the negative Sirians. Other sources claim the Third Reich was aided by the Nordics and Reptilians from Orion. In either case, the Coriatorians holographically projected to the German Nazi leaders, presented evidence exposing the deception of their alien partners and revealed similar information to the American Military. As a result, the Germans' alien allies withdrew their support and flipped the balance of power.

ON PLEIADIAN PLANET ERRA, BY YIRA

Channeled by Jim

Yira: Greetings.

Max: Greetings. Are you Yahyel?

Yira: No. I'm Pleiadian.

Max: Yes. Thank you for coming.

Yira: You might have called someone from there. I am not sure what the reasoning you're calling us was.

Max: I just wanted to learn about Pleiadians, about the life on Erra.

Yira: There are many different cultures just on your planet. The culture that I live in is hundreds of miles from the hybrid area, which you probably know most about, or at least that's what I would assume. We are in the larger cities. And we do the greater work for the planet. The largest cities are all connected except for two that are on the other side that are in a slight quandary about who they represent. And so, until they find out their own personal identities, we cannot be a part of it. It would be too confusing. They either want to join us or not. But right now, my culture, the one that I live in at this present time, is full of technology and full of discovery. Our people are very happy in the sense that they are satisfied with what they are receiving from Erra itself; the government if you will. We work on privilege and education. There is talent that is not considered intellectual but is considered valuable such as music and things of this nature. Therefore, some with these kinds of talent and artistic, etc., will gain privilege through their work in this area. I will gain privilege, and honor, and acceleration through my work with education and business. Now, that is just a small portion of our culture. My family life is much different than other places on Erra as you might guess. We have a tight family unit. We are allowed to marry more than once. We are not declined any kind of relationship. And it is a very free and open society. Most meals are spent together because this is traditional, not only traditional, but it has a meaning for the culture. We have to make our conversations at least once a day over at least one meal. This way, it continues to bind us. A binding ceremony every six months is part of our culture. And the family will be bound together once again. It is a wonderful thing. And we do not take each other for granted. We celebrate each one's talents and performances and are equally happy for one another. What is it that you really are searching for? I do not think that an arbitrary statement of our culture or description is going to be satisfying for you.

Max: Thank you. Is it true that... I just heard that story recently that Pleiadians actually came from Orion through Earth? So, basically Orion first came to Earth and then Orion came to Earth and then to the Pleiades.

Yira: Some of us came that route and that is true. There are other parts of our civilization that came from the Orion area and have mixed with us because we were so similar. But yes, there's some of us here that are originally from the Pleiades as well.

Max: Oh.

Yira: Our ancestors came from Orion. Actually, if you go back into history even farther where some had been star travelers from the Pleiades many millennia ago.

Max: I'm talking about ancient history.

Yira: Yeah. That is what I am speaking.

Max: So, the main path was from Orion to the Pleiades directly or through the Earth?

Yira: Some of it was direct, and some of it was through the Earth. There were more than one Exodus.

Max: Uh-huh. And when your ancestors were on earth, which historical period was that? Would that be before Atlantis?

Yira: Just before Atlantis. Yes. And actually, we were there at Atlantis at some point afterward, but we did not stay.

Max: Thank you. So, how do you look? What's your height? Like what's your height distribution on Erra?

Yira: There are many different heights. My particular height is about 6'4" tall. A little larger than human, but not much.

Max: Which race would resemble closest the race of Erran Pleiadians? Which earthly human race would resemble your people?

Yira: Those from the continent of Africa. Many of those have the same structure in the face. The color may be slightly different, but we do go into dark shades, and greens, and silvers, and blues depending on the chemical atmosphere. The chemical makeup of the planet in certain areas changes the skin color. So yes, around Congo would be some of the greatest examples. The central portion of Africa.

Max: Uh-huh. And the height distribution, what is average height on Erra?

Yira: Since there are several different species, I suppose you are talking just about Native Errans.

Max: Okay.

Yira: The average height is actually larger than me 6.7, 6 feet 7 inches.

Max: How about other races on Erra?

Yira: There are some Yahyel. There are some Fendorian. There are some other species of course. So, their heights vary between 4 foot and 7 foot.

Max: Uh-huh. Can you describe Fendorians a bit?

Yira: Fendorians?

Max: Uh-huh.

Yira: Well, similar to Arcturians, the Fendorians are shorter. At least a certain portion of their species is.

Max: Are they related to humans at all?

Yira: We have never done that DNA test. But yes, there is some Fendorian and some people on your planet.

Max: Well, I mean, do they look like humans at all? What do they look like?

Yira: Facially, a little bit, but not very much. Body wise, more. The body looks more human than the face. Although the body is small, the organ's positions are very different. Also, the brain is divided into three portions and not into two.

Max: What Earth species would they be more related? Are they bird-like?

Yira: Fendorians and Arcturians look more like your Japanese and Chinese population.

Max: Oh. So, they at least look like a human. Right? They're not birds, right?

Yira: They are not humans, but that is the closest to your resemblance table that I can find.

Max: Uh-huh. So, they're not birds.

Yira: No. Arcturians and Fendorians are not birds.

Max: Okay.

Yira: Fendorians are short. Arcturians have more of a triangular body with broad shoulders and a small waist. The Fendorians, on the other hand, the body is not as triangular. They are more square in the body. Broad shoulders and just go straight down and more of a turn in toward the legs. It's hard to describe. A picture would do better.

Max: That's okay. Thank you for describing at least because we talk about them a lot, but we have very little understanding how they look. So, what color are Arcturians?

Yira: Arcturians are more orange and green.

Max: And Fendorians?

Yira: Fendorians have many colors as well as the Arcturians, but the Arcturians have the orange color, which the Fendorians do not have. They both have a rather silver shade or shininess of the skin in some places. There's a place above the ears for the Pleiadians, that there is a symmetrical shiny place, which is actually very handsome.

Max: Okay.

Yira: Now, the Fendorians have a similar kind of shininess on the sides of their heads.

Max: Okay.

Yira: Now, they do not have the orange color. They have darker shades than the Arcturians. As I was mentioning, they can be dark like the Africans, but they're also lighter shades as well. And some of those shades are in the green and blue categories or in the deep reds.

Max: All of the above, are you guys all in the same dimension?

Yira: We are in the same—Well, no. Actually, we aren't. We are 4th dimensional in the Pleiades. The Fendorians and the Arcturians are 5th dimensional, but we see them many times in the 4th dimension because they can come back and be seen in the 4th dimension. They cannot live

49

here permanently, but they can live here long periods of time.

Max: Okay. Have you visited Earth?

Yira: Personally, no. I have studied Earth in some ways and find it very interesting and very curious, but I have not been.

Max: How much do your people know about the Earth in terms of culture like population culture? What is known about Earth? What's the information?

Yira: Most of the information that we know about your cultures are coming from the larger cultures such as the people who have gone to England or different portions of the United States, and Canada, and South America. So, finding the different cultures and the different ways people live is interesting. We have found that within the last 20 years there is a greater closing of the gap, if you will, of cultural differences in some places especially South America and places that are getting technology in faster, more efficient ways.

Max: Wonderful. I still don't understand how much you're informed about Earth. So, how many of your people have visited Earth?

Yira: Oh, hundreds, but not recently.

Max: Okay.

Yira: There have only recently been about 30 because they are not allowed to appear as humans.

Max: Okay.

Yira: They are only allowed to be in the 4th dimension and do their studies. Studies are much greater when they can interact with the people. Learning is much better.

Max: Okay. Continue.

Yira: But in the last 50 years of your country, 57 to be exact, we are not permitted to come physically.

Max: Okay. How does the 4th dimensional Earth look like?

Yira: The 4th dimensional Earth is interesting because it does reflect the 3rd dimension in many ways. It has many of the same attributes as the 3rd dimension. A lot of hybridization qualities still exist in 4th dimensional Earth. And so, therefore, it is noted that the hybridization that was given unseeded through the millennia is still very evident when you move to the 4th dimension and the 5th. There are some 5th-dimensional elements of the Earth at this time as well.

Max: I have very little clue about the population of the 4th dimensional Earth.

Yira: In 4th dimensional Earth, the population is very small. I do not know the exact number, but there is less than a million.

Max: Okay. Less than a million. What do they do?

Yira: Correct.

Max: Do they live, or are they visitors?

Yira: They live there.

Max: What culture are they?

Yira: They are different cultures. That is just the point. They are all over the planet even though there are only a million or perhaps slightly more. They populate different places for different reasons and live out their cultures in their own ways.

Max: Are these humans or others?

Yira: They are. Some of them are. About 20% are actual fully human.

Max: And who are the rest? What's the dominant race on 4th dimensional Earth?

Yira: There are some mostly Yahyel and Pleiadian.

Max: Ah. Are they technologically advanced?

Yira: In some ways, yes. They're advanced, but yet they seek connection. That is the best word. We are not connected with some of the other portions of the galaxy. It's because they choose to advance first and not communicate at this point.

Max: So, it's not galactic culture. It's isolated culture?

Yira: Yes.

Max: Weird.

Yira: But it has some galactic overtones, of course, because of the people and species that are there. They bring their own thought processes, but it is a wonderful place to develop. That is what they are doing. They are developing the planet in the 4th dimension.

Max: Do they have a government?

Yira: It is a global department. Because they are advanced, they can communicate with one another very easily. And they can transport one place to another very easy. So yes, it is a worldwide government that is working very well because they each understand their differences.

Max: Excellent. Are they permitted to speak to us? To me?

Yira: I would imagine they are if they choose to do so.

Max: Okay. Now, how do they call the 4th dimensional Earth? What's the name for it?

Yira: They have given it the name of Terra Ha.

Max: Again?

Yira: Terra Ha.

Max: Terra Ha.

Yira: Which means the next evolution of Earth.

Max: Yeah. Okay. So, they are progressive.

Yira: Yes. Terra Ha is the next evolution of the planet.

Max: And they will accept the waves of ascension sometime from now?

Yira: They are helping as much as they can, but of course they are involved in their own societies and do not help as much as they once did. They are waiting for those, and there are those daily that come into the 4th dimension from the 3rd, but that will happen in a greater amount over 100 years of your time.

Max: So, what's the rate of humans popping into the 4th dimension, ascending?

Yira: Very slow at this point.

Max: Can you explain?

Yira: It's probably one every 12 days.

Max: Oh, it's substantial. That is some progress. So, do these humans disappear from the third?

Yira: The ones that are disappearing are the ones that have very little contact with society, but there are some in the big cities that are disappearing as well.

Max: So, if a person pops into the 4th dimensional Earth, Terra Ha, do they have to disappear from the 3rd dimension or do they kind of bilocate?

Yira: Well, let me describe how it works.

Max: Okay.

Yira: It takes at least 24 hours to a month for them to change physicalities from one density to another depending on how advanced they are. Those that are very advanced will only take a 24- to 48-hour period to move from one dimension to the other. But for the most cases, it takes about five to six days for the average 3rd-dimensional person to move into the next dimension and disappear from the Earth.

53

Max: So, the disappearance, how does it look? Is it controlled? Are there other guardians who guard that process?

Yira: They realize what is happening because they have been planning for it all their lives.

Max: Okay.

Yira: For many of them, they have been seeking the transference from 3rd to 4th dimension all of their lives.

Max: Okay.

Yira: So, therefore, when it starts to happen, they know what is happening. And therefore, they go into solitude—

Max: Okay.

Yira: …as though it didn't happen.

Max: Is it an assisted process? Or, does the person do it by themselves?

Yira: They by themselves. They go on their own.

Max: And when they appear in the 4th dimensional Earth, and Terra Ha, what happens?

Yira: They have to be acclimated. It takes several days in 4th-dimensional time for them to acclimate to the 4th-dimensional density. It is very difficult for some of them because they are used to do such a stranger density and a stranger way to survive than what it is there. But once they get used to it, they're very happy.

Max: Are they being assisted on the other side?

Yira: They must be assisted. Yes. We have been able to detect when someone is coming through. There will be assistance for them when they make it.

Max: Uh-huh.

Yira: I should say they will make assistance. We can detect it from here if we are monitoring it—

Max: Okay.

Yira: …because we can monitor that kind of thing. However, I personally do not monitor it. I have little interest on those that are coming in except to know that they will be doing all right.

Max: What spiritual practices accelerate the transition? How do people prepare for that shift?

Yira: The Tibetan culture with the monks there have a great deal of understanding.

Max: Right.

Yira: Yeah. It is not they that go through the quickest, but they do happen to have a great deal of people in the 4th dimension.

Max: Which people pop in right now from which cultures?

Yira: Mostly from Native American Indians that have kept their culture pure and the aborigines of Australia.

Max: So, currently, that transition is done mostly by those people. Right?

Yira: Correct. The aboriginals from Australia seem to be the quickest to come through.

Max: Would any of the lightworkers of Western type make it currently?

Yira: Yes. But only those that are not soiled by the negativity of society.

Max: Uh-huh. Are any families coming through?

Yira: Any what?

Max: Families?

Yira: Do families come all at once? It's very, very rare. Sometimes 1 or 2 members of the family may go, but it's rare to see an entire family move to the 4th dimension in a short period of time.

Max: I'm talking more about couples of people.

Yira: Couples. Every now and then.

Max: So, do the people get citizenship or something when they arrive?

Yira: Citizenship is not an issue. They are part of the 4th dimension and part of the all that is.

Max: So, they are free to go in the galaxy anywhere?

Yira: They are free to be who they want to be. Now, it takes some time for them to acclimate to the 4th dimension. With this, then you understand that it takes a little time for them to learn how to move about properly and easily.

Max: So, if someone wants to travel the galaxy, they're free to go.

Yira: They are free if they wish.

Max: Does it actually happen?

Yira: There are occasions, but most decide to stay with the population.

Max: Wow. So, the current population is largely Pleiadian, Yahyel, and 3rd-dimensional humans who made the transition?

Yira: There are other species there as well, but those are the majorities.

Max: How many are Reptilians?

Yira: About 5%.

Max: How many are Draconians?

Yira: About 2%.

Max: Thank you. I've run out of time, but the conversation was very helpful. We discovered a layer of knowledge, which was—We weren't aware of that. At least I wasn't aware of much of it. So, thank you very much for—

Yira: It is one perception of it. Yes. This is how I perceive it and how it is written about in my culture. So, therefore, yes, this is one perception of it. I'm sure that there are other perceptions—

Max: Okay.

Yira: ...perhaps similar to this or perhaps, maybe, very different depending on where they are looking at and how they are experiencing it.

Max: Excellent. Last question. So, do we have like news about Earth? Is there something like television or some sort of updates about—

Yira: There is always news about your planet because it is such a thriving culture. And so, therefore, there is always something interesting about your culture to read about.

Max: So, how many Errans are following?

Yira: Many. Probably several million.

Max: Can you give a percent?

Yira: Pardon?

Max: Can you give a relative ratio? A percentage of Errans.

Yira: 21.4%.

Max: An estimate would suffice. Okay. So, about one fifth. Do Errans follow Earth culture and what are the latest news?

Yira: The latest news is about your presidency, also about the Russians how they are moving to take over this area in some ways. [the dialogue was in Dec 2016]

Max: Oh, I was thinking that there are some other kinds of news which are of importance.

Yira: Oh yes. There are also those news things about people that have done extraordinary things in the 4th dimensional Earth and the 3rd dimensional Earth.

Max: Uh-huh. Okay. I ran out of time, but thank you very much, and it was very helpful. Is it okay to publish your interview?

Yira: Yes.

Max: All right. Thank you very much. Do you have a nickname which you could take?

Yira: Call me Yira.

Max: Are you male or female?

Yira: I'm male.

Max: Okay. All right. Thank you very much. Have a good day, Yira.

Yira: Thank you. Be well.

Max: Thank you.

Yira: It was interesting speaking to you, Earth person. What is your name?

Max: Max.

Yira: Mix.

Max: Max.

Yira: Max.

Max: Uh-huh.

Yira: Interesting. I will write it in my journal.

Max: All right. Thank you.

Jim: Okay. That was interesting.

Max: Thank you, Jim.

Jim: You're welcome.

THE YAHYEL

As members of Pleiadian culture, the Yahyel are an advanced extraterrestrial race friendly to humanity. Among the galactic races, the Yahyel are closest in their DNA sequence to humans: over 95% identical. Akin to speculations on humankind's origins, there are several conflicting threads weaving through stories about Yahyel lineage. Some are human-like in appearance, and would pass unnoticed on Earth's streets, while others resemble light-skinned Tall Greys. There are even Yahyel in whom are expressed both human and Gray attributes. Bashar maintains the Yahyel are one of the composite Zeta/Earth human races created by Zeta Greys. Pentim, a Yahyel channeled by Jim Charles, claims the Yahyel are *not* Zeta descendants. What might conceivably solve the contradiction is the possibility that the Yahyel and Zetas have a common ancestor.

The Yahyel, and other extraterrestrials, have been visiting Earth since ancient times. In general, various human races have been seeded as hybrids by different extraterrestrials. It is likely that the ancient Jews, Arabs and Assyrians were seeded by the Yahyel on Earth as Yahyel-human hybrids.

Psychologically, the Yahyel are less emotional than humans. Their emotional spectrum is narrower and less nuanced, displaying emphasis on kindness and caring. They are known for empathy and non-aggression. Seeding life across the Universe is their calling and passion.

While many Yahyel live on planets in the Pleiades cluster, others live on ships traversing the great spiral arms of the galaxy. These ships, and Yahyel physiology, have been adapted for long-term life in deep space. Few Yahyel procreate like humans. Most multiply artificially, fetuses grown in incubators. The majority of Yahyel don't have families, but instead are raised in social groups similar in principle to our daycare centers, kindergartens and schools.

Yahyel have exceptional telepathic abilities. Unlike Zetas, who are plugged into a hive mind, each individual has an independent mind, though it is likely that Yahyels may connect to their collective consciousness as we do with the internet.

The Yahyel have profound intellectual abilities, live for more than 700 human years and—upon reincarnating—develop metaphysically and recall past lives. The Yahyel, deeply spiritual, have strong psychic, telekinetic, and organic capabilities of mind control and bi-location. It is normal for them to be working simultaneously in multiple settings. Transportation is carried out simply by materializing and dematerializing from a given destination to another. Again, this is done without technology. Also, the Yahyel well understand human medicine and are strong healers and doctors.

Since the Yahyel are genetically similar to humans, hence resemble them, they have been designated by several extraterrestrial races to establish first Open Contact with humanity.

The Yahyel are a part of the Girk-Fitneer alliance (extraterrestrial-friendly races: Lyrans, Pleiadians, Arcturians, and benevolent Reptilians the Lashunda and Fendorians). Augmenting this status, Yahyels are hosting a voluntary hybridization program and settlements of Yahyel-Human and Pleiadian-Human hybrids. Abiding accepted volunteering principles, this program accepts genetic material from Earth humans only—who provide informed consent.

On March 13, 1997 Yahyel ships openly passed over the city of Phoenix, Arizona to attract public attention, but the numerous sighting reports (known in ufology as the Phoenix Lights) were repressed by the media. Currently, under the auspices of the Girk-Fitneer Alliance, the Yahyel are promoting to major human governments ideas of Disclosure, Open Contact and offering consultation on these and other matters. Unfortunately, these earthly governments have so far elected to keep these contacts secret.

Some Earth humans carry ancient Yahyel genes, while others are recently emerged Yahyel hybrids. Again, and importantly for any success negotiating with authoritative human power structures, the qualities of the Yahyel hybrids include expanded intellect, reduced emotional range for aggression and anger, high capacity for kindness, healing, psychic and telepathic abilities, empathic link with other Yahyel hybrids and faculties allowing influence-at-a-distance over the minds of others.

THE HISTORY OF YAHYEL BY PENTIM

Channeled by Jim

Max: You said you are busy. What kept you busy?

Pentim: Well, we are redoing some of the colonies, updating all the time, because the Fendorians and Sirians are the new members of our group and they have made some great improvements.

Max: Which of the Sirians? There are tons of them.

Pentim: Yes, well, this is a group of several hundred thousand that have joined us because they support our cause. It is not the whole Sirian race.

Max: Is it Sirius A, B, or C?

Pentim: Sirius A of course.

Max: Which culture is that?

Pentim: It's not the aquatic, but more the light-being portion; very light beings close to sixth dimension but still in the fifth. They are similar to the Arcturians and the Fendorians. They are where Centia's group is from.

Max: Ah, okay. Do they have a name?

Pentim: They just call themselves Sirians; they do not want to be diversified.

Max: Okay, do they look like humans?

Pentim: No, not really. They are very, well, they do have…they are bipedal but they are not…ah, they are very light and have a lot of light to them, a glow. Their features are a little washed out because they do not…they don't have the exterior like we do. It's invisible; you can see through them.

Max: Are they related to earth humans—to dogs and to dolphins?

Pentim: In the distant past, yes.

Max: We have a country called Syria. Are they related? Were they in Syria at its origin?

Pentim: No. That's, well, actually they have been there, yes, but the country named Syria is not because of them.

Max: Oh, not?

Pentim: But they have been there, yes. I do not think it's named after them. You see, the country was named Syria and the star system was named Sirius, so it was…there are two different verbal beginnings. One is Latin; the other is Greek or something. I am not sure. But they have different language roots.

Max: The Dogon tribe from Africa say they are from Sirius.

Pentim: Yes, they are more related to Sirius.

Max: And would this be the same, or a different race?

Pentim: That is a different portion of their population. However, it is definitely related to them.

Max: So dogs and dolphins are coming from the same world?

Pentim: Yes, there are some from the same area of space.

Max: Same area of space…all right.

Pentim: And we will send energies for that, and positivities. There are those on your planet—we have picked up on several hundred—who are ready to move into the fourth dimension, but we cannot let them move into the…well, they will move in at their own pace of course, but it would not yet be right for them to move into the fourth dimension. So we are actually trying to keep some from moving there, because it would cause a scandalous time on your planet…but definitely an interesting time. There are those who are ready to move, and those far, far from ready.

Max: What are the symptoms of being ready?

Pentim: You'll feel lighter, constantly in a positive frame (almost constantly) and you will be able to communicate and see into the fourth dimension, feel its energies, and also be able to bring back information vital to yourself and others. You will be able to talk to those in the fourth dimension about moving into it. There are several hundred who are in this particular way, and their vibration is over the five or six points necessary for this kind of movement. But yeah, you can move up to (most people can) a twelve-point vibration, but for some with that high vibration it's not necessary—it can be reached at lower vibrations, with the right thought processes and positivity.

Max: When they are that high in their vibration, does their three-D life become easier or otherwise?

Pentim: Yes, in some cases it does and I will tell you why. Because they are moving through the third dimension and not really dealing with the density part—not dealing with the harshness of that dimension as much as they used to. And so, when these harsh things happen, they become easier to move through and do not lose their positive edge. [People] move through

63

these things with only a slight bit of drag—if you know what I mean. They don't fully feel the negativity of it, but they understand it for what it is and how it can be used in a positive way. They take negativity and push it into positive realms.

Max: Is Jim one of those who is ready?

Pentim: He is on the verge, but he is not going to leave.

Max: Is he in the proper state?

Pentim: Yes, but he has a mission, so there is no room for him to translate into the fourth dimension because he knows he has to—and will—stay in the third.

Max: My question is different, it's not whether he will leave or—? The question is, looking at Jim, could we recognize the traits of being ready?

Pentim: Yes, about eighty-five percent.

Max: So, it is not a question that people would have no information? People will be informed, when they have to decide to go, or not to go, they will be fully informed about the move, right? Because they will...

Pentim: Yes they will. In many ways, they will be informed because there will be something instinctive within them that will have to get the information—they have to know what is happening, because many of them will question what they are feeling and why so differently than ever before. They will seek an answer, and we will definitely give it to them. There is no way they will not want to know what's happening.

Max: But, why do you need to give it to them if they already have the ability to see through? So they can see the details, right?

Pentim: We will speak to them and let them know what all this entails. We need to let them know that, even though they are ready for fourth dimension, we prefer them not move that way for a little while yet.

Max: Are you able to visit the surface of the fourth-dimensional Earth?

Pentim: Yes.

Max: That is fully open for you?

Pentim: Yes, that part is fully open to us—we are allowed to visit the Earth in the fourth dimension, yes, but not in the third.

Max: So your ships come down?

Pentim: We have several ships around, but not as close as we used to because of the anomaly. They're about nine-million miles out of Earth's atmosphere at this point, but we are getting closer. We've moved three-hundred-thousand miles closer within the past few days, and expect to be moving another few hundred thousand closer toward the tenth of January [2017], because the anomaly is getting smaller. As it's moving through it's getting smaller at the end portion. You might think it would get bigger but it's actually more voluminous in the center.

Max: Do Terrahaans have ships, spaceships?

Pentim: Yes, they do have ships.

Max: So they can leave whenever they want, right?

Pentim: Yes, and they don't have to interact with the third dimension at all. Same as we don't have to interact with you if we don't wish to. If we do not have the right technology turned on, we cannot see you at all. But within our technical scope, we can find the third dimension easily, but we do not have to. We can pass right through it if we wish.

Max: My question: after people shift to Terra Ha, what are the open communities—I mean galactically open? Do they have the ships, and can they travel through the galaxy as they wish?

Pentim: Yes.

Max: Are there bad guys on the fourth-dimensional Earth, on Terra Ha? Are there cabals, as they are also known, on Terra Ha?

Pentim: There are some Qarabal on Terra Ha, yes, absolutely.

65

Max: Thank you. So another question: are there Earth military active on Terra Ha? The three-D military—American three-D military. Are they present on Terra Ha?

Pentim: Yes, in some ways.

Max: Is there a conflict going on there, or is it all formalized?

Pentim: It's not a conflict, not at this time. It's hard to explain, but they…there are some from your third dimension who know how to move to the fourth because of alien technology, therefore they have gone there. They cannot stay there, but they can go.

Max: Okay, so when they come, do they have certain status?

Pentim: Yes, they have certain status that you call temporary. They cannot stay for more than so many days without starting to dissolve.

Max: How many days?

Pentim: Thirty-four. Most of them do not even stay thirty, because you start to feel the effects of it before you dissolve of course—it's not a good feeling. You start to be disrupted, feel nauseous, achy. You'll feel many things before you dissipate.

Max: Sounds familiar. All right, switching to the next question. I am writing a book with Jim and others, about our friends, and of course Yahyel are on top of this list. I was even thinking of naming the book PLEIADIANS AND YAHYELS—something like that. In any case, let's start collecting more information about Yahyel, whatever you can put in a book. That transcript, you can possibly simply transcribe and put it there as is. Can you give us an introduction to Yahyel civilization? Like a ten-minute description of history and current state?

Pentim: Well yes, all right. This is a book that's already been thought of?

Max: Right.

Pentim: Yes, what you would like to do is make a small recording from each of the people? Each of your main characters who are alien, such as

Tekkrr and Lakesh, have them tell a little about themselves and their societies and what they do. Thereby bring some interest to sections of the channeling they are involved in. So, to preface the chapter featuring Tekkrr, you might want her to tell a little about herself, her people, and culture. Then have the channeling transcribed. Also she could give them a little more understanding of who she is, and why she channels the way she does. Then Lakesh—the same thing, you would have him do a brief history of himself; who he is, why and what he does, something about his culture. Do some Lakesh transcriptions, and see how that adds color to what he has to say.

Max: Excellent. Can you please answer a specific question? I am still confused, since understanding of the origins of Yahyel is very limited. Where did you come from?

Pentim: We are very ancient, so we have come from…our origins actually are not even in the Pleiades, but from the Taurus area. Do you know where that is? [The Pleiades star cluster is in the Taurus constellation.—ed.]

Max: Of course.

Pentim: We are from the Taurus area and our beginnings were very…what is your word? Humble.

Max: Ah hah.

Pentim: And we did look like humans from very early, and our planet was not seeded quite like yours. There was, of course, some seeding in the very beginning, but in our case we developed the human look more naturally, so appear more human than any other species. But your human form was developed by many other species and very many other hybridizations. Even though we are like ninety-seven percent of your DNA—we have about that much similar—some of that is coincidental because of how hybridization took place on your planet.

And that is something very curious; something we have been looking in to for thousands of years. There is no reason for your DNA to be as close to ours as it is, except by natural selection, and the kind of planet that you have, which is similar to our beginning planet. Natural selection, Earth's

67

atmosphere, distance from the sun, gravity, have all brought you to appear similar to us. And then, of course, there was one point where we did our own hybridization program, thousands and thousands of years ago on your planet and it happens that your appearance did not change that much, but we are...you did become a little closer but there are many, many mysteries about our two species and we are wondering if there is some even more ancient connection, because we do not understand how, in some ways, we are so closely related.

Max: Who, as a race, are your ancestors?

Pentim: The ancestors are not called Yahyel, but the Fenzie. You've heard of the Fenzie, I am sure, but they are no longer in this—or any—galaxy that we know of. The Fenzie have disappeared from space, unless they are now somewhere several hundred galaxies away. We have not heard of them for several thousand years.

Max: So from which star were they?

Pentim: The legends or speculations that they came from the Andromeda area are scattered. Some say Andromeda, some Alpha Centauri. Others claim they came also from the Taurus area, but it is not...we do not believe they came from Taurus. Definitely not. That has been proven over and over. Even though some of them still claim they are from Taurus, but I believe...my thought process is that they are from Alpha Centauri, but not this galaxy. The next one over, which I do not know how your people name, the next one behind the Milky Way.

Max: Okay. By the way, what is the name of our constellation, of Earth's solar system?

Pentim: You mean our name for it?

Max: More like the Galactic name.

Pentim: Oh, Kaleasausan.

Max: Kaleasausan?

Pentim: Yes.

Max: What other stars are included in this constellation?

Pentim: You mean in the galaxy?

Max: Yeah, like when you look at say our constellations, we assume...we know that the stars there are kind of together because they are about the same size or brightness. So when you look at our solar system and neighboring stars, possibly it is a constellation? What stars are included?

Pentim: Oh, there are seven, no... Yes, there are seven stars in the constellation, from our perspective. Your sun is called Kaleasausan, but the constellation is Pirem.

Max: Pirem? So I can say that I am from the Pirem constellation, star Sol, third planet Terra—right?

Pentim: Actually, if you look at the constellation, it resembles a half-circle with a line over it, so it's five stars and one in. You are on the circular part of the third one from the right.

Max: Okay.

Pentim: Third star from the right.

Max: And it would be third star from the left, as well?

Pentim: Yes.

Max: Okay, all right. I think you've already answered this, but I would ask to repeat. Is it right that the Jews were seeded, or created, on the planet as Yahyel? So basically, it was Yahyel who mixed with Earth's humans?

Pentim: That is what... Yes, there is a great deal of evidence that points to the Jewish people being more Yahyel than any other species on your planet.

Max: Are there any other races who have elevated Yahyel, any other human races?

Pentim: There is... Well, the Asian people have a lot of Arcturian but there is Yahyel there also. There is Yahyel also in Africa in the very southern portion, and Yahyel also in South America near where the Nazca lines are.

Max: Aha. So which tribe in South Africa would it be?

Pentim: I do not know the name of the tribe. It would be in South Africa—the northern part of South Africa.

Max: Would it be blacks, African blacks?

Pentim: Yes, it would be, they were dark-skinned and lighter in South America—lighter skinned.

Max: Aha, interesting. So there is a story that Egyptian pharaohs, at some point there were foreigners who conquered Egypt and there was a series of Egyptian pharaohs who were outside of Egypt and there is a belief that these were Jews, and I wonder if Yahyel civilization was involved?

Pentim: As a civilization we were not. They travelled on their own, but were Yahyel in some ways, yes. Anyway, one moment please I am having some technical difficulties.

Max: All right.

Pentim: We have lost your picture.

Max: That's okay. It's the connection. It's okay.

Pentim: All right, can you still see us?

Max: Yes.

Pentim: That is interesting. That you can see us and we cannot see you.

Max: Ah yeah, that race had a name, and there was a period in Egyptian history which had that name. Hyksos. They were called Hyksos.

Pentim: Yes.

Max: So I wonder if Hyksos were Yahyel?

Pentim: Yes they were, but they travelled on their own—we did not land there or, we were not that much part of the Egyptian culture. But we did travel there; some of the people that were created were travelling there. Actually Egyptian culture has much to do with Jewish culture as well, especially in early portions of it.

Max: Aha.

Pentim: They did have a lot to do with the Jewish people.

Max: Also there was a story that Jews were present, or Yahyel were present in Bengal [Bangladesh], that Bengali were Yahyel?

Pentim: Yes, that's fine. There are several countries that have many Yahyel people in them.

Max: Ah.

Pentim: Many Yahyel beginnings, I should say. I would not now consider them our people. They are more humanized.

Max: All right, so what is the relation between Yahyel and Zetas?

Pentim: Zeta Greys?

Max: Yeah.

Pentim: There is a great difference. Although it is believed that most Greys have a [same] beginning [with Yahyel] in culture, I think we were more advanced than the early Greys. They did not evolve quickly. It took them a great deal more time than us to evolve. The Zeta Greys are still negatively charged, or at least a great percentage of them are very primitive concerning survival instincts. They feel that everyone is out to get them. They are paranoid, therefore must conquer before *they* are conquered. And so they feel that everyone…even though they do work with the Reptilians, they feel the Reptilians to be secondary to them, that they are smarter. Although there are some Reptilian species I believe are even greater—intelligence-wise—than the Zetas, but they find them to be good workers [and cooperate] with them because they feel they are smarter and can in some respects handle them.

71

Reptilians also find Greys repulsive as far as flavor, so they don't eat them. So um...they can work together, not be hostile toward one another, and still do many negative things. So the Zeta... Reptilians and Zeta Greys work together. They definitely are from the Andromeda area; there's a great many of them.

Max: Historically, they came from there?

Pentim: I believe so, yes.

Max: Ah.

Pentim: There especially are a lot of Reptilians in Andromeda, and a lot of Greys—probably more Reptilians than Greys in Andromeda, but of course you have to understand that your culture has named twelve different Andromedas. When I am talking about Andromedas two, three, four, five—those four Andromedae have definitely a lot of Greys and Reptilians.

Max: Are you talking about stars or galaxies?

Pentim: Galaxies.

Max: Wow, okay. So Bashar mentioned that Yahyel are one of the hybrid races made by Zetas, is that right?

Pentim: Well, that is something that we always questioned. There seems to be some hybridization that comes from that area, yes. We will say that we do share some DNA with Zetas, but it goes back very, very far, so to answer that correctly I would have to gather more information.

Max: All right, that's sufficient. But since then don't you partner?

Pentim: We are not partnering, no. Their ideals are different from ours. We have grown apart—if we ever were together—in the way that we react to the dimensional shifts. We changed our thought processes on negativity and positivity. We've learned to cope with survival in a much different way, learned to become friendly with the galaxy, instead of fearful. So we have developed in a totally different way than they have. They have seemed to continue to reproduce their negativities on every generation, and no one and nothing has seemed to come of that—except the survival and paranoid instincts taught to them. Now I am sure there were some who tried to break away from that, but it's so strongly ingrained they probably were not successful, or I can see they have become part of another Grey species of which there are several—some much more advanced than the Zetas.

Max: Okay, I have to clarify. It looks like... Ah, I think I remember that the initial hybridization program of abductions on Earth about fifty to twenty years ago were done by...a lot of that was done by Yahyel and Zetas, right? And it's like your involvement was close to half of that abduction?

Pentim: Yes, we did do a lot of that, that's true, it was for scientific, ah...but we were not the cruel ones. Zetas did the cruel things with their abductions and [while we did] more psychological exploration, we understood the physiology of humans so we wanted to do more psychological portfolios.

Max: Were you working together? What are they like? Because there were reports of tall Greys and short Greys being in the same room. Were you the tall Greys?

Pentim: We were not in the same room with them, no. We are actually the medium-size... (Laugh)... I am a more medium-size. But there are, of course, shorter and taller Greys. The shorter are not necessarily Yahyel. A shorter portion of our population *is* Yahyel, but I do not think they would be seen with the Zetas.

Max: When I interviewed one of the abductees, they said that short Greys are Zetas—biological drones. Not very smart, and the tall ones *are* very smart, wise, and actually very humane. So the tall ones were humane and the short ones were very clumsy.

Pentim: There are some other Grey species that are humane, other than the Yahyel.

Max: Aha, so it wasn't the Yahyel in the same room with the...?

Pentim: No, it was not. Not with the Zetas. The Zetas would try to get rid of us, as they might want to get rid of that other species in time because

73

they are very paranoid. Unless they have some kind of contract with them—that they are working together. But I cannot see benevolent species collaborating with them.

Max: I've run out of time, so I have to let Jim go. Thank you very much for your answers. I hope to continue that discussion, but I think we covered essential, initial questions we needed to be answered.

Pentim: Very well. It was very nice to speak with you again, Max. I haven't spoken to you for a while.

Max: Nice to speak with you as well. I wish we could speak more, but life here is so dense with events.

Pentim: Yes, I see that. Have a wonderful day.

ABOUT YAHYEL: BY DISDOO

Channeled by Jim

Disdoo is from the Yahyel race. His full name is Disyakabudisduda. He is captain of a scientific research ship of Girk-Fitneer, working on stabilising our planet's climate and preventing disasters—axis flip, major earthquakes or oceanic stream reversal.

Disdoo: Welcome, everyone. I am Disdoo from the vessel over North America.

Max: How old are you?

Disdoo: In Earth years? 137.

Max: So you are very young?

Disdoo: Yes.

Max: I think you live about 500 to 600 years?

Disdoo: Yes. But I moved quickly up the ranks because of my ability to communicate.

Max: Back in the 1940s, the Roswell incident in New Mexico? Can you tell us a little about that?

Disdoo: I can tell you some, but not a lot, because your government knows everything about that. They were Yahyel in that accident. They were Greys, and they were friendly.

Max: Were they Greys or Yahyel?

Disdoo: Greys are Yahyel, but a different species than Yahyel. Yet they look very much the same. There are five different Grey species.

Max: Earlier, you talked about abductions. There are no more forced ones, as that was a while back. Can one be still abducted in the dream state?

Disdoo: Yes, but our species and [others] in alliance with us do not [conduct] any form of abductions anymore. There are species that still do, but we are not of them or allied. However, yes, they still do that.

Max: Can you tell me about your religious practices, and connection to God?

Disdoo: We do much meditation when we can, but even our work is our religion because we are helping move people up into a greater vibration. We are working at a spirit level with humanity.

We are also working in a physical, natural level but our intention started when it was spirit.

Therefore, our religion is helping you, if perhaps you needed help, which you do at this point. Yet, you help us as well with your prayers, thoughts and positive actions, as well as encourage us to do our job better.

Max: Are you praying using words? Are you in contact with the Angels and maybe some higher consciousnesses?

Disdoo: Angels choose when they want to come into your reality. It is the same with us. If they want to be in our reality, they make themselves available. They give us the message, and let us know what they want us to know.

Max: Do we know, or have something in common with, your gods or higher consciousness?

Perhaps we also know their names. You are in connection with them, and give praise?

Disdoo: Oh, yes. God would be your name, and Allah is known in the Universe. Yes, we pray to God, Allah and Ra.

Max: Is Ra a separate being from Allah?

Disdoo: Yes, but slightly underneath—that's all.

Max: Are you in connection with Ra?

Disdoo: Correct.

Max: Ra Material is very much correct, right? ["Ra Material" was channeled in the 1960s by Carla Rueckert]

Disdoo: Yes.

DESTRUCTION OF ATLANTIS

Earth is a relatively young planet, was visited by Galactic Humans over a million years ago and even during the time of the dinosaurs. Our evolution involved not only spontaneous processes based on random mutation and natural selection, but upgrades by spiritual and alien genetic engineers. Among the spiritual beings, important roles were played by angelics, elementals and other celestials. Thus, our evolution was shaped by three parallel processes: natural evolution, targeted evolution directed by the spirits and intelligent manipulation by extraterrestrials.

76

Prehistoric man developed very slowly. For a long time—perhaps several hundred thousand years—only rudimentary tools were used, which evolved with humankind's intelligence. Earth was a refuge to some alien races.

The Lemurian civilization, more advanced than prehistoric man or modern humans, existed here likely over 0.5 million years ago. Lack of archaeological traces can be attributed to that civilization's higher density. Following was the Atlantean civilization, with its highly developed technologies, cities and large population. Both of these cultures were openly visited by extraterrestrials, and Earth's climate was artificially controlled with a grid of temples and artificial satellites. The Atlantean civilization, however, misused genetic engineering and practiced dark magic. They exploited advanced technologies for military purposes, and as a result suffered a series of wars and catastrophes, the last and biggest some 23,000 years ago destroyed Atlantis and Lemuria. The enlightened Atlanteans, though, managed to escape before the catastrophe and settled in the Pleiades cluster, Andromeda galaxy and inner-Earth (subterranean) cities. Still, the surface civilization lost its culture and population, while the remaining humans continued developing from a basic level.

FINYET ON ATLANTIS, LEMURIA AND ORIGINS OF HUMANITY

Channeled by Jim

Max: The recording has started.

Finyet: Greetings.

Max: Hello, and welcome.

Finyet: Thank you. Did you want to speak about Atlantis?

Max: Yes, my main question is about the genetics of humans. I just realized that Atlanteans weren't Homo sapiens, they were some other species, right?

Finyet: They were. They were not humans, correct.

Max: Are you one of them?

Finyet: I am one from the continent of Atlantis. It was really not a very big continent; more of a large island, but they called it a continent because it had all the makings of a different kind of lifestyle than had ever been seen before on the planet.

Max: Will you introduce yourself, if it is appropriate?

Finyet: Finyet.

Max: Okay, Finyet, and are you a spirit?

Finyet: No, I'm simply one of the elders.

Max: Are you one of the spirits, or are you living now?

Finyet: I am not in physicality at this time.

Max: Thank you for coming. So, first question—were the Atlanteans giants?

Finyet: No, we were not. Large, but not considered what you would call a giant. I don't think seven-feet-tall is a giant.

Max: I see. Did you have elongated heads?

Finyet: We did have, some of us. There was more than one species on Atlantis. Many welcomed from different areas of the galaxy, and those welcomed from Egypt and some European areas if they could get here. We would actually go to them more than they would come to us.

Max: And the ones from Egypt also weren't humans, were they?

Finyet: There were some humans in Egypt, but also non-humans. The bloopy aliens and some reptilian species. There were several other species there, but not all at once.

78

Max: Which ones were Nephilim?

Finyet: Nephilim were Blue Avians—the essence of Blue Avians. They did not all look alike; they did not take on the [appearance] of humans completely. But some did. Let me correct that. Some did take on the look of humans when they wanted to go in and talk to them, and give propaganda. Then they became more human-looking. However, you will notice that some of them did not look human.

Max: I see. So Nephilim are blue avians?

Finyet: Yes.

Max: I see. That's easy. What's the name of the species with elongated heads which protrude backward?

Finyet: The ones with elongated skulls?

Max: Yeah.

Finyet: The Porendition.

Max: Say it again?

Finyet: The Porendition. They are no longer around.

Max: We hear they exist in the Vatican, they live [there] and wear long heads too.

Finyet: They are far away at this point. The Porenditions were very harsh with humans, actually, and were not a kind species. At least not when they arrived, and we were around.

Max: Okay, so I found…

Finyet: They were really not that welcome on Atlantis, because they caused a lot of trouble.

Max: Right, I got it. Were Elohim a physical species?

Finyet: Elohim were never a physical species.

Max: I see.

Finyet: They were always a God species, an angelic kind from somewhere off-planet. Their density was much less than that of a human, or anyone who would be considered corporeal.

Max: How about Yahweh?

Finyet: Yahweh?

Max: Yeah.

Finyet: He was a God.

Max: I see. He was present in Atlantean terms?

Finyet: In some ways yes, spiritually yes, he was called many things. Yahweh was only one of his names.

Max: One fact I need to put in historical perspective is that modern human geneticists found that all humans share one originative mother and father. The mother lived much earlier—thousands of years—so it wasn't a couple. There must've been a kind of a bottleneck, and then one person gave rise to all humans. All of us modern humans arise from one person. And not only from one, but we had a major mother and father, roughly 150,000 years ago—putting it in Atlantean times.

Finyet: It would be the seeding of the human population; you realize that there were different errors [because] they brought forth evolution quickly, and some of the early seedings resulted in Cro-Magnons, Neanderthals, etcetera. So [that is the reason why] there was such fast evolution— experimentation. But that wasn't from the Atlanteans. Those were other species that did that, but during the period of time of Atlantis there was some great experimentation with humanity going on.

Max: Did Atlanteans contribute to modern humanity, and are we relatives?

Finyet: In some ways yes, we did contribute [our] DNA to help with more successful evolutionary traits.

Max: How much of that DNA is yours, percent-wise?

Finyet: Well, that is hard to say. I believe that at the time it was only about 15-20%, but now I believe it might be even higher. The numbers were not available for all the things that was going on in the secret society of Atlantis.

Max: Thank you.

Finyet: So, you see, the scientific community was advanced, and the elders were [predisposed to] the spiritual level and not interested in scientific advancements. We thought spirituality was more important. However, there was much going on in the scientific world during the Atlantean era.

Max: Got it. Which of the human races would [resemble] Atlanteans?

Finyet: Well, I know octoroons resemble Asians. They got some of their genes from the octoroons. Those considered to resemble Atlanteans would probably be of maybe Scandinavian [descent].

Max: How did the Atlantean species die? Did they actually just die out, or did they [evolve] into humans? After the destruction, how did it happen?

Finyet: How did what happen?

Max: How did the Atlantean species vanish from Earth?

Finyet: The Earth of that time was disruptive and volcanic, with a lot of earthquakes still going on even though we found it to be a beautiful place. In many ways, there was still too much going on. We left after a great earthquake and tsunami. They decided to leave the planet and so the Lumerians moved to a different place. The Atlanteans moved out from the planet all together, gathered up their technology and moved on.

Max: So, not many Atlanteans remained, and humankind started to grow instead?

Finyet: Yes. The continent of Atlantis as it is called was pretty much destroyed by earthquakes and tsunamis, so there was not much left of it on the surface. This caused part of the continent to sink, and they realized the [whole island] was going to sink, so departed.

Max: Was Atlantis at the same density as we are? Was it the same?

Finyet: Yes, we were higher third dimension. We did come from a third-dimensional place outside of your world. Many now believe we were higher-dimensional, because the technology was so strong and the legend persists that it was far beyond anything the earth had ever seen—which is true. We could not, however, survive directly if we were of a different dimension.

Max: Where did the Atlanteans come from?

Finyet: We came from a couple of different places. You mean what part of the universe?

Max: Yeah.

Finyet: I'm not sure that I am allowed to tell you that. We are still a few galaxies away from here. We survived and still exist.

Max: Are you part of modern history? Are you involved in our development?

Finyet: There have been some Atlanteans involved [by] reincarnating into humans.

Max: Physically?

Finyet: Physically, but only in the tenth and eleventh centuries. These are the last times Atlanteans were on Earth physically.

Max: Is there any way to recognize an Atlantean?

Finyet: They disguise themselves. We did at that time look like humans, but we were much taller.

Max: So, if I say "tall person," it does mean an Atlantean, right?

Finyet: That does not mean they are Atlanteans, but pre-aliens. They are nubs. There are others of your planet who are tall as well. You will know the nubs by their blond hair, blue eyes and strong physiques, but they are also very tall. They are very charming, too, but don't anger them.

Max: Okay, thank you. Where are nubs from?

Finyet: They are from the V80s.

Max: I got it. Not Aryan. How do you tell them apart?

Finyet: No, the Aryan ones have a different temperament completely.

Max: What temperament?

Finyet: They are very stoic. You see, the nubs are very friendly and charming. The ones from Aryan are very straight-laced, disciplined, and anger easily. So you will know them. They anger easily only because they expect that everyone knows as much as they, and do not tolerate any stupidity.

Max: Thank you. I got it. The story has it that Atlanteans continued some of the colonies after the destruction of the continent—some in Egypt, the Americas and maybe other parts of the world.

Finyet: Well, they moved to a couple of different places. Especially the Lemurians. They moved to places in North America, New Zealand and areas near there. Also to Crete, because it once was connected to the continent of the Atlantis that moved out through the middle of the Mediterranean and close to Portugal. So it was a very long, windy, curved island. Part of Atlantis still exists as the Greek islands.

Max: How different were Lemurians from Atlanteans? How can you tell them apart?

Finyet: Well, it's more of how they behaved, but the Lemurians were not as tall as the Atlanteans, and were much more interested in the crystals and the energy of technology. Their religions and spirituality came from the stones and from the different elements they could control. They were thinner, serious types.

[They] were a very loving species, very much more interested in materialism connected to spirituality because their crystals meant a lot to them. They would tell fortunes, and were able to see things in the future through the crystals. They were very valuable.

Max: Which of the Earth's cultures might remind you of Lemurians?

Finyet: Let's see, the Lemurians were darker-skinned, so there are some Africans that resemble Lemurians.

Max: In terms of general culture, which in today's world would remind you of Lemurian traditions?

Finyet: Actually, if you go into Australia, the Aborigines remind me of a shorter version of the Lemurians.

Max: What's the difference between Lemurians and Lumerians?

Finyet: I don't think there is any difference; I think it's a pronunciation.

Max: And we tried to figure out whether Mur was a continent, or a series of islands. Lemuria is derived from Mur, right?

Finyet: Yes.

Max: And Lumer, I think, is a planet or star?

Finyet: Yeah. Lemurians existed long after the Atlantean culture left, stayed a lot longer on your planet—at least a thousand years. The Lemurians settled in many different places, but eventually left the Earth because their home planet was in danger.

Max: Which star was their home?

Finyet: Their home star was Selibus.

Max: In which area is that?

Finyet: Selibus is in an external galaxy not commonly named by your scientists, but given a number.

Max: So... the Greek history and gods are very interesting, so...

84

Finyet: Yes, Zeus and all those.

Max: Yeah. Does that originate with Atlanteans, Lemurians, or elsewhere?

Finyet: The Greek mythologies came from a different species all together, not Lemurians or Atlanteans. The ability to throw lightning as Zeus was able to do was not common among Lemurians or Atlanteans, but was among other species at war traveling through the galaxy. Two species were [at war], and they would find planets to fight on, but were nomadic. They fought because one had stolen a planet from the other, and they continued to war. Moving from planet to planet, they would extract much mineral content, or take things of value to them—but the war went on.

Let me explain. They had many battles in Siberia, Scandinavia, and also Greece—higher terrain over there. There are still remnants of their battles, scarred earth and elements found in Siberia today are from other parts of the universe. I'm not sure if you're aware of that.

Max: No. Is there a name for those species?

Finyet: We did not introduce ourselves. They were worrying among themselves, passing through. They on Earth only for a matter of a year, but they caused a lot of damage, and developed quite a reputation with the people. They appeared as gods. Humans were transfixed by their appearance, because they were human looking in some ways except their bodies were much larger, and differently colored—orangish in nature. Some were golden, and they could change at will because they were emanating energy fields. You could see through these, to the being, who would appear to be glowing orange, yellow or gold.

Max: But Greek mythology is much deeper, and it can be picked up in one year, it is the whole history, very…

Finyet: Yes, well, humans decided to make a whole culture around it.

Max: Well, it feels very different; it feels like somebody had given it to humans. Who was that?

Finyet: Yes, they gave some of their history to humans—that is true. And interacted with them as it was. They were there for a year, or, gave them a great deal of history of their past and of how they have existed, but they fought a lot of battles in the meantime.

Max: Thank you.

Finyet: But the people were transfixed by their appearance and stories, and they celebrated them constantly. They loved that, by the way, and were very happy humans thought they were beautiful, that they thought they were elegant. They were quite a beautiful species.

Max: So, the transition from Lemurians and Atlanteans to Homo-Sapiens . . . how did it happen? When you left, how many humans were on Earth?

Finyet: There were thousands.

Max: Did humans interact with Atlanteans and Lemurians? What was the status of human culture?

Finyet: The human culture was rather barbaric. It was rather simplistic, but we were able to help them along with certain things. We taught them about arms and things of that nature and they would come to us. They did not know how to make cuttings out of cloth, so we taught them.

Max: Were humans used as slaves and workers?

Finyet: They were at some point. Yes.

Max: Because there is a history of humans being engineered as workers.

Finyet: Yes, they were used as slaves at first, but we elders decided that was not what should be happening. So we released them. Many did stay on Atlantis. But they did not live in the cities. They lived outside that culture.

Max: Was there an intentional transfer of culture from Atlanteans and Lemurians to humans when they left, or is it just...

Finyet: We thought it was not right to leave them with a culture they could not understand. We did teach them what we could, but when we departed they were on their own. We did not leave them anything. We felt it was only right they should evolve on their own.

Max: Was that the ideal from the prime directive, or something like that?

Finyet: Well, the prime directive was to not interfere with the culture they were developing. We were there when they were being worked on, and things like that. They knew about us. They were interfering with your culture anyway even before it was an intellectual one. It was primitive, but intelligent.

Max: Final question: there is a story that Atlanteans were given a choice—either submit to being reduced in bodily stature, or leave the planet. They chose to leave. Is that right?

Finyet: That is not why we left. We did so because of the size. You see, the continent we were inhabiting—Atlantis—was perfect for us in many ways. We had developed and brought it into our own sort of utopia. When things started to fall apart physically as a city, an island, a continent, it was time to move on. There was no other place on the planet for us. We wanted to go somewhere that didn't present as much danger as your planet had.

Max: Thank you very much for the conversation.

Finyet: It was good to speak with you.

THE HYBRIDIZATION PROGRAM

The destruction some 23,000 years ago of Atlantis, and the Ice Age this wrought, left humankind dismal and fractured. Surviving tribes, as if lost in an existential swamp, were mired in a low vibrational level of life. Various alien races contributed their genetics to boost the development of our civilization. As a result, modern *Homo sapiens* was created, and has evolved as a hybrid between Earth humans and the aliens. We are told that humanity is comprised of approximately 22 alien races, although it is not clear in which order the hybridization occurred. Most likely, each of the modern human races was created by different aliens through hybridizing the DNA of Earth humans and galactic humans. These races and tribes have since intermixed, thus creating the modern *Homo sapiens*.

Primary races who contributed to the modern human gene pool are Lyrans, Pleiadians, Yahyel, Orions, Sirians and Annunaki (Tall Whites with human-reptile-insectoid genetics). Other races likely to have contributed are Reptilians, Andromedan Humans, Martians, Non-Zeta Greys, Zeta-Greys, Fendorians, Arcturians, Ubsilo and otherworldly entities (sometimes referred to as ultraterrestrials) residing on our planet: Sasquatch and Agarthans. Though it is unclear whether Elohim (mentioned in the Bible) augmented our genome with their own DNA, they are likely higher-dimensional humans (literally, "the ones who came from the sky") who had a hand in genetically engineering modern *Homo sapiens*. We can conclude that most Earth humans are descendants of the above-mentioned races. There were times when Earth's population was minuscule. Across time, war, and migration the human genome has become thoroughly nuanced and complex, though there remain isolated groups resistant to intermixing.

In the old times, open alien visitation of Earth had the various races worshipped as gods. Humankind simply had no model, nor alternate perspective, in which to frame what must have been a jarring experience comprising terror, exaltation and psychic overwhelm. In more recent times [see Dr. Jacques F. Vallee's groundbreaking PASSPORT TO MAGONIA: ON UFOs, FOLKLORE, AND PARALLEL WORLDS—Ed.], the aliens were perceived as supernatural and fairy-tale beings which—hailing from non-Euclidean dimensions—they essentially are. This ambitious hybridization with humanity has sustained itself since time immemorial. Some of these infusions were performed via genetic manipulation; periodically, galactic humans would find refuge here and establish families with Earth humans.

Dedicated alien settlers taught us technology, art and philosophy. Some became priests *and* teachers. Numerous talented people of the current era came from the alien bloodlines. As recently as 1954, the hybridization program received a boost when the aliens obtained permission/official sanction from a scatter of Earth's governments. An alliance of Zeta-Greys, Reptilians and Orions negotiated with the intelligence agencies established by these same, mainly English-speaking, governments to exchange the secrets behind technologies such as propulsion, free energy, teleportation and mind control. Soon, and tragically, both parties in a myriad of ways violated the agreement, thus rendering it invalid. Nonetheless, the aliens continued their hybridization program.

At certain stages, the program ran jointly between the negative aliens and human counterparts. Civilians were abducted, brutalized during nonsensical alien medical procedures, examinations and hybridization. The abductors were negative humans, Reptilians, Orions, Tall-Greys and Short-Greys, working in the same facilities—both on Earth and off-planet.

For an unlucky many, the first 50 years (until roughly 2005) of this phenomenon were fraught with trauma. The program's initial failure rate was high, thus hybrid children frequently were deficient. Too, the founding purpose of the overall program was negative. Zeta-Greys and Reptilians created the hybrid people; disbursed their DNA back into Earth humans, thus furthering hybrids unaware of their own nature. Subdermal implants track these hybrids on Earth, and possibly for mind control (sinisterly effective, as anyone reporting interaction with non-human entities—"They forced an implant into me!"—is dismissed as delusional). The overall purpose of hybridization was to take control of Earth. Zeta Greys are known in the Galaxy for employing sneaky tactics to dominate other civilizations: they use time manipulation and transdimensional travel to quietly spread Zeta genes—predisposing new hybrids to mind control.

As far as I know, this plan was stopped around 2006-2010. Human-friendly alliances—The Galactic Federation of Light, Girk-Fitneer and the Ashtar Command—increased their protective military presence, forcing the negative Zeta-Greys, Orions, Annunaki and other Reptilians to leave the solar system. Historically, the Reptilians and Orions controlled the upper echelon of our military and financial structures. Since that time, the planet has been protected from takeover attempts, and administration returned mostly to Earth humans.

Although the hybridization program began with negative intent and means, positive results have been obtained: hybrid human-alien bloodlines possessing advanced telepathic/psychic abilities, and enhanced compatibility with the 4th density. New human-alien hybrid races (such as Shakani) have been created and seeded elsewhere in the galaxy. These hybrids live in the 4D, enjoy the riches of galactic culture, and are eager to assist and advise our civilization.

In addition to the negative hybridization program, there was also a positive voluntary effort carried out by friendly aliens, including the Pleiadians and Yahyel. Relationships were cultivated with human individuals, who would be taken aboard ships for visits to the friendlies' planets and invited to assist the program.

The hybridization process involves several steps requiring human participation: genetic material—sperm cells and eggs (ova)—are obtained. Next (and keeping in mind that even with alien technologies, it is difficult to grow human fetuses in incubators; the mother's energies and nutrients play vital roles in early development), women are taken to the ships, impregnated with hybrid embryos and returned to Earth. Since the impregnation is done transdimensionally via teleportation, this should be considered as immaculate conception. If the child is to live off-planet, the embryo is allowed to grow for a few weeks before being taken away for transfer into an alien or hybrid mother selected to give birth.

Alternatively, some hybrid embryos are grown in incubators. Reported cases of women losing an early-stage embryo usually are interpreted as miscarriage. Yet, these cases are reminiscent of the "Rumpelstiltskin" fairytale. For some, donating an early-stage embryo to the hybridization program could be voluntary and purely practical: (1) The parents might not have adequate material resources; (2) Desire to provide the child an opportunity to live in a 4D reality, with advanced technology and freedom of space travel; (3) Ambitions to spread their genes to other stars; (4) Having a relative in the free galactic world could entitle the parents to visitation—akin to those who obtain the right to emigrate to the United States to rejoin their children. The fourth consideration, although selfish, could become quite practical especially in the later years when Earth is predicted to become a member of the Galaxy.

The third place where humans participate in the hybridization program is in helping to nurture hybrid offspring who remain off-planet. Children born in alien space feel estranged; the aliens would bring human volunteers to serve as babysitters and teachers. In this way, the children feel human warmth, become healthier and better-adapted to Earth-human traditions.

A majority of abductees were subjected to memory manipulation to prevent conscious recollection and trauma. Infrequently, years later, fragments and even full recall of the experience resurface. Representing scarce glimpses into alien worlds, this information is valuable to the abductees and humankind.

The hybridization program by the friendly Yahyel and Pleiadians continues to this day, but now utilizes consensual human volunteers. Hybrids live in the alien space as full-fledged members of society, enjoy freedom of movement and access to alien information.

These hybrids grow up in the Pleiadian or Yahyel cultures, but also choose to learn Earth culture and are eager to visit as soon as they're permitted in order to serve as advisers. Their scientific and practical knowledge of galactic life is highly valuable. Numbers of hybrids are physiologically capable of prolonged residency on Earth.

The aliens that work with humans in the hybridization program have developed an understanding of empathy and compassion. They have even modified themselves to experience our emotions in order to better comprehend human psychology.

By now, the hybridization procedure and technology has been improved and humanized: the program takes only volunteers, who are treated kindly via comfortable methods. Failures and complications occur less frequently than in human medicine. The hybrids are healthy, and enjoy rich, creative lives.

As I mentioned, one of the positive outcomes from the hybridization program is that Earth-human genes become spread throughout the universe. Yet, surprisingly, many descendants of Earth humans live in our Milky Way and in the Andromeda galaxy. For example, before the destruction of Atlantis, many Atlanteans escaped to the Pleiades and to Andromeda. Another group of humans was taken as slaves from the

91

ancient Roman Empire by the Pleiadians to the planet Erra. Since that time, the slaves were liberated, emancipated and became full citizens of Erra. Even Kenjin, the current King-president of Erra, is genetically an Earth human.

It is remarkable that natural Earth humans with unaltered genetics can live comfortably in the 4th density. They are fully telepathic and capable of being citizens of the alien worlds, and are treated as equals. This means that, biologically, we are ready for Ascension and travel into the Galaxy. Only our politics prevent us from awakening, Ascension and entering the Galaxy.

Another positive result of the hybridization programs is the appearance on Earth of starseeds, indigo and crystal children. "Starseeds" are humans seeded from the stars, and usually comprising some percentage of alien genetics. Also, some of us have alien past lives, and often are linked to the stars both genetically and on the level of soul.

"Indigo children" are usually defined as those whose aura is colored indigo, which corresponds to a heightened level of spiritual development, connection to higher densities of the spirit worlds, and greater development of the body's upper chakras/psychic abilities.

"Crystal children" is another variant of newly appearing humans with advanced design of the spiritual body, the chakras, and psychic abilities. The world *crystal* symbolizes the idea of purity and harmony.

While it is often said that indigo children are not compliant and have trouble fitting in with society, "crystal children" are known to be well socialized. Indigo children could behave like revolutionaries and troublemakers, while crystals would change reality through peaceful evolutionary ways.

Although slightly different, these terms (starseeds, crystal and indigo children) often are used interchangeably. They indicate an idea that humanity is currently evolving into a new species, which has been prophesied throughout our history. One of the clearest examples is that given by Russian-born theosophist Helena Blavatsky in her book THE SECRET DOCTRINE (Theosophical University Press, 1888). There, she comprehensively outlines the Lemurian and Atlantean races, and extraterrestrial role in developing new genetic design of Earth humans via hybridization, which she called "the 6th race."

The recent appearance of starseeds, crystal and indigo children is well aligned with ideas of the prophecies that humanity will develop into a new species. Furthermore, channeled alien messages explain that the primary quality demanded of this New Humanity will be telepathy—essential for profoundly enhancing, and quickening, our communication on individual and collective levels.

With telepathy, our persistent capacity for deceit will become impossible. Though many consider "cunning" a positive survival trait, deception driven by self-interest is in fact suicidal for humankind—an engine of war, plunderer of economies, breaker of trust between nations, and fuel for political tyranny. The entire advertising industry—regardless of market crashes and lesser fiscal woes—remains enduringly successful because it combines deceptive business practices with psychological insights hijacked wholesale from the lie, cheat and steal departments of global intelligence agencies (particularly the CIA's infamous MKULTRA program). Not only is deception a ruiner of international scale, but of family relationships, sex life, education and upbringing of children.

Most importantly, vital information about the aliens and Ascension fails to reach mass consciousness. The development of telepathy will heal many societal ills, spark collective awakening and Ascension itself.

Nowadays, crystal newborns are more frequent, children possess psychic ("psi") abilities, and their upbringing generally is less repressive to the development of these so-called wild talents and telepathy. It is predicted that in a few generations humankind will acquire telepathy, linking us in the manner of numerous alien races, and ascending to the 4th density. That connectivity will develop the new level of consciousness; impossible without telepathy.

This expanded consciousness will conclude the transformation, and be the main tool for Ascension. Therefore, the hybridization program and infusion of alien genes is priming humankind for the development of telepathy, collective awakening and Ascension.

ON HYBRIDIZATION PROGRAM BY KENJIN, THE KING OF ERRA

Channeled by Jim

Kenjin: I am Kenjin. I've just come for a moment because I have not spoken to you for a great while. There are a few I have spoken to, but only in private sessions. I want to bring news from Erra: the wars are nearly done. The things of peace are happening now. Events are developing that are much pleasing to all those on the Erran world.

Some of you have visited the Erran nurseries for hybrid children. Thank you for your visitations, and understanding that it is important for them to have human contact. Although you may not recall (some of you remember, some do not), many of the ladies (there are a couple of men) do come to the nurseries. We bring you there astrally, but we know those of you who are nurturing, who want to be seen with the children, hold and give them the energy of your species. Your hybridization is a wonderful thing for the universe. You do not even understand, as of yet, what good you will be doing. You will not be doing any harm to anyone, and will not be ruining or conquering any species. Your participation will unfold as a thing of love and understanding.

We realize some of you are concerned that some things given in peace turn into war. We understand that. But our intent is to ensure that all hybridizations that have come to our planet, are here growing, and meaningful to us are those of great understanding. Prosperity, in the sense that will encourage and strengthen the galaxy. Your deliberate presence here is so useful, and saves many species that would otherwise end. Your immune systems are vital to some species dying of maladies that cannot be cured within their own environment. They can no longer integrate and benefit from curatives, because they have gone through and adapted to so

94

many medications. Their bodies no longer are taking anything in them for healing purposes. They have expired, or exhausted all the various medicines. Do you understand?

Through hybridization, your immune systems will save the galaxy. Their properties are strong, able to make a difference to species that have developed immunity to what once worked. Now, you might say, "Why haven't they used the natural? Why haven't they done that?" They have; but In order for it to have been useful, they would have had to use it before the poison tainted the system. They understood the natural was better, but it was too late. The natural could not defeat the unnatural, in the sense that it was toxic. Yes, they can pull out some, but it was too much a part of them. Therefore, your immune systems will be used in a greater and more wonderful way than you can ever imagine. It will give them a new start; enable the use of their energy system.

Now, I give you this knowledge with the understanding it will not be used in a negative way. Many of you are learning how to treat your bodies in a more sensitive, healthy way. This is so much appreciated. Your health, exercise, comprehension of the value your energies bring have thankfully manifested in time to save your civilization, and its timeline—if no one blows it up. But you have the right things. Development of good food, removing toxins from it. You will now cultivate processes to rid your food of all toxins, because you've made timely discoveries, in the right era of distance. Be assured, you can do this.

This is the whole of my message: that you develop health and understanding. And many of you are very aware, and very much teaching the world how to move forward in a more beneficial manner. Your energies will be greater; your immune systems will enter into a profound state of effectiveness. Those of you now giving your DNA to the hybridization program are healthy even if you feel as if possessing flaws, and have no idea what the galaxy is suffering from, nor what diseases are out there afflicting the universe.

Thank you very much. I am Kenjin, King of Erra.

ON HYBRID CHILDREN BY SANGI (FENDORIAN)

Channeled by Jim

Max: Hello.

Sangi: Greetings. I am Sangi.

Max: So nice to meet you, Sangi.

Sangi: Yes.

Max: It's a pleasure to have you with us today.

Sangi: Thank you.

Max: Are there any messages you would like to give us?

Sangi: Yes. I am now in charge of hybridization children and hybridization specimens. Those who come to you to take the specimens, I am not necessarily in charge of. They do bring me the information on what they have done, and I do record it. The recording system of all the hybridizations has changed a little bit since I have been in charge. We have much more documentation. I would like to see much more of this between humans and their children. If you do have children in the hybridization program, we would like to hear from you will give you the information as quickly as possible. I will note that you have been inquiring about your child, and what data have been shared. This is helpful to know that the program is moving on in a high, integral way. I'm not sure I said that correctly, but I think you understand.

We would like to make it a very close program in the sense that nothing beyond protocol is done. No inappropriateness is any longer tolerated. Still, there have been some inappropriate sample gatherings, and hybrid children created because people have not been telling the truth about how they got permission, or why they want the children. Now, this will stop. We will have an integral program of high standards. The children will be taken care of, you will know everywhere they go, and you will be part of their education and upbringing. If you would like to give suggestions for these things, it is very much appreciated. We would like them to be aware of their human culture, as well as their alien cultures, and those species and aliens around them in this world as well. Your input is very valuable. Cultural suggestions are most helpful, because [the children] will someday be coming to earth to visit their human counterparts, although your percentage of the child is much less than that which is conceived by the parents on this side.

It is a great responsibility you have given. Much of the time, it's between 5 and 12 percent of your human DNA that is shown at birth. Therefore, it is important that if there is any percentage of humanity shown within the hybridized child, you would have some say and it would be beneficial for you to do so. Are there questions?

Sheer: Hello, Sangi. This is Sheer.

Sangi: Sheer. Greetings.

Sheer: On behalf of the human colony, I want to welcome and thank you for all you're doing.

Sangi: Thank you. I have just begun my mission. It's only been a little while since I have taken over this very large responsibility, but already I believe we have it under control in a much greater way than it was before. Not to say anything against Tekkrr, or the way it was run before, but she had too many responsibilities. And now, the program will be a lot tighter and more responsive.

Sheer: I see. The first question is about the visitation of us with the hybrid children. How many times do we see them a month, if at all?

Sangi: Well, we come to you. This is another portion that is being set up at this time. We will come to you and ask if you would like to come visit them. We will set you up on a schedule. Now, some people will just ask to see their children out of the clear blue sky, which is fine. If we can accommodate that, we will. But usually, scheduling a time for you people to visit children will probably be more beneficial and much more able to be— information will be better tracked. If you would like to visit your child, we

97

will do our best to accommodate you.

Sheer: I see. So, first of all, any time that they can come, I would like to visit my hybrid child.

Sangi: And they are most grateful. You have to understand also that sometimes the parents are not able to receive at that particular time, so scheduling makes it much easier for them to know when you are going to visit.

Sheer: I see. And next question, if I have hybridizations, a couple of them, and I'm making the hybrid child, does he get the other infusions with the DNA or just the human DNA?

Sangi: That is up to you. If you decide that you wanted only a human specimen, then they will remove the other hybridization scientifically.

Sheer: Okay.

Sangi: Usually, we only do human-to-species hybridization because it's purer, and we can get a better result. We can get an understanding of how well it works together and see a purer form of hybrid child.

Sheer: Okay. Thank you very much.

Sangi: You are welcome.

Max: Okay. Michelle, did you want to ask next?

Michelle: Yes, please. Much love. I was told by Tekkrr that I have a hybrid son. Pleiadian.

Sangi: Yeah.

Michelle: And it happened two years ago. I'm not even sure that I knew about Girk-Fitneer two years ago.

Sangi: No. They were taking DNA samples from higher-vibrational beings even before permission was granted.

Sangi: So, we're taking samples even without their permission two years ago. The program did not start until after that. Your child is two years and six months.

Michelle: I'm curious who took the samples without my permission, and how.

Sangi: We have many gatherers on each of the ships.

Michelle: Is this all Girk-Fitneer then?

Sangi: It is now. Samples taken from beyond Girk-Fitneer sometimes were given to us. That's a gift. An exchange for technology and things of this nature because it was of very great interest to us. We do not do that any longer.

Michelle: So, where is my child now?

Sangi: He's on Erra.

Michelle: He's on Erra?

Sangi: Yes. The educational system is taking care of your child. He is beautiful and is learning very much. His interests are in science and biology.

Michelle: And how do I connect with him?

Sangi: You simply ask.

Michelle: Okay.

Sangi: In your astral form, we will take you to visit him and his family. And you can give them instructions. Some have instructed that they want the child to be held more, or given closer attention as far as touching, or cultural information, pictures or facts about Earth that they might not have originally wanted—elements the original family might not have wanted them, so early, to have—but it is partly your child. And so, you can give instructions and they will be obeyed. There may be discussion with the parents. Usually, though, things are amicably done.

Michelle: Are his parents Pleiadian, or another race?

Sangi: They are of his race. Yes.

Michelle: They are Pleiadian?

Sangi: Yes.

Michelle: Okay.

Sangi: Yes.

Michelle: Please send them my love. And yes, I would love to meet with them. Thank you.

Sangi: You are welcome. Please formulate questions for the parents before you go.

Michelle: I will. Thank you.

Max: All right. Dan, you had a few questions?

Dan: Yeah. There are a lot of questions from the group. It stirred up quite a thing here. Many people are wanting to know if they have hybrid children. Really, over a dozen people are asking me.

Sangi: Have them write.

Dan: Write to Jim?

Sangi: Yes.

Dan: Okay. So, Jim can be contacted at jimreiki@gmail.com. I'll post it here on the things. Some of the questions about the hybrid program are not going to be able to be approached during this webinar, because there are other things that we need to do too.

Sangi: Also, do not expect a lengthy answer if there are going to be many inquiries.

Dan: Yeah. And there are. There are so many because the whole thing just lit up. I got people coming from all over. And we're not going to be able to answer these questions today. So, I would ask the hybrid questions be directed to Jim's email, and Jim will get to them as he does or as he will.

Sangi: Have them write to me. I do not know the ones that do not know because that information is not available to me yet. If you do not know if you have a hybrid child, please give me your name so that I can check. If you know that you have a hybrid child, then I can give you information. But there are many children who the parents have not checked on as of this time. Probably about 60 or 70. Therefore, I know that some of the parents did not give permission, and some [children] are now. But there are some still very young who have not had inquiries from their parents. It would be good if you did inquire, and we will give you that response. That way, my records will be more complete.

Dan: Okay. I see it's being suggested on the side, and this is expanding quite quickly that we need somewhere on the website to have just a hybrid section that deals with this kind of thing, so all the information can be found in one place instead of it being all over the place. So, that would be a nice thing if we could—

Sangi: That will be the responsibility of your side.

Dan: Yes. We'll handle that. I think we can do something. Thank you, Will, for those ideas. But otherwise, it's gonna get quite out of hand. That's all I have for right now, because it's too large to—

Sangi: Very well.

Dan: ...handle at this time.

Sangi: If that is all the questions, I will be going for now.

Max: Oh, hold on one second. I do have a question.

Sangi: Yes.

Max: This is from Sabrina. She asked what is meant to happen with all these children.

Sangi: They do have parents, and these children are loved and nurtured by parents in the alien forms. And they're to be brought up as outstanding

101

citizens of Girk-Fitneer. Some of them are made into ambassadors to different worlds, the United States, and other countries. I would hope that you would understand it is only beneficial that they are being raised. It's not a random thing, that they are not going to be taken care of or looked after.

However, some have ignored the human portion of the hybridization, and that is shameful. And we would like to include all those humans that have been part of the hybridization program. It is a wonderful program and I sense that you are feeling that it might be irresponsible. Do not feel that way. These children are going to be brought up in a very, very loving and wonderful home and to be given wonderful tasks. And they have great abilities in many cases. So, do not be discouraged by that or disparaged by anything. Please keep a positive attitude toward these children. They are not orphans.

Max: Okay. Also, on that same note: the humans here who have hybrid children—are they responsible for those children?

Sangi: If they would like to be, of course. They have a great responsibility if they want to be that parent. If they were unaware that they gave their DNA for becoming a parent, then they do not have to accept any responsibility. It would be lovely if they did, but they do not have to. Their parents are taking care of those children. Their mother and father in this realm are taking care of those children. And if you did not want that child, it is all right. They still have loving and caring parents.

Max: Well, that's wonderful to know. Okay. Just letting you know I'm gonna jump out now, and Sabrina is gonna come in because she would like to talk to you personally, if that's okay.

Sangi: Very well. Are there any other questions while we are waiting?

Max: I have one. If you didn't know you had a hybrid child, and say you were not interested in having one child—

Sangi: Correct.

Max: Let's say that's the case. Wouldn't the hybrid child know that on some level, and feel?

Sangi: It will be explained to the hybrid child that the donation of your DNA was given without permission, and that their parents accepted it, but were not aware your permission was not given. Therefore—

Max: But wouldn't that make them feel unloved?

Sangi: No. Because they have a set of parents that love them very much.

Max: Okay. Thanks. You are additional parents. Their hybridization parents are in addition to the birth parents. You understand that. Of course, the child will feel usually a greater connection with the birth parents than with the hybridized parents. However, there are some strange situations where the hybridized child feels closer to the human parent. Now, this is unusual, but it is to be expected in some cases.

Sangi: Yes.

Max: It looks like Sabrina is having a hard time coming in. Fendorians are relatively new to Girk-Fitneer, and I don't think we've heard much about you. While we're waiting, can you tell us something about your race and species?

Sangi: We are a very high species, and are usually in the fifth dimension. Those of us who are working on the ships have come down to the fourth to work here, which we find very important. We have sacrificed the fourth dimension for this occupation, and are helping in the ships in many different ways, engineering scientific advancements, creating new thought processes, spiritual development, advancement of some of the programs that are already in order. And we are very welcome by Girk-Fitneer and the Octorian culture that runs and makes the final decisions. Therefore, we are here to help humanity as well.

Angie: A question.

Sangi: Yes, Angie.

Angie: When we want to talk, or get information to our hybrid child, do we just say it out loud? Do we send an e-mail? I mean, how can I connect with my hybrid child without going through the internet? Is there a way I can do that?

Sangi: We are working on ways for you to communicate, without any form of technology on your end. On ours, there will have to be technology, but we are trying to connect you through vibrational means—translators—by giving them a source, a communicator that will pick up your energy signatures. This is not in place yet. But give us some time. We are working on an advancement of the hybridization program. I was not going to speak about that yet, because I'm sure there will be a lot of questions. However, since it has already been brought up, there will be a communication system attached to the hybrid child so that whenever the hybrid parents, or parent, speaks they will be able to get a translation eventually.

Angie: Thank you very much.

Sangi: This program has not yet been completely developed, but I would like to see that happen. I think the connection between human and hybrid child, and hybrid child's parents and human, is very important. We are wondering how we could do this also for the parents. We will have to have some councils on how they are to be involved in this process. Did Sabrina make it in?

Sabrina: Yes, I'm in. Hello.

Sangi: Very well. Hello.

Sabrina: I would first like to make a comment. I know it doesn't refer to you, that this happened previous to Tekkrr even, but I have to say that the way the DNA was acquired before, I find it very unethical. I think that needs to be said because some humans are flabbergasted by this. So, I need to note that not everybody—

Sangi: We have already made you aware of what has happened and for what reason.

Sabrina: Yeah. But it was done—

Sangi: I understand there are people who are not happy about it, but saying something of like that does not help.

Sabrina: But it needs to be noted, because it's the feeling of some people.

Sangi: Let them speak to me, and I will help them.

Sabrina: So, it needs to be acknowledged. Now, about the children nobody knows were created—'cause, see, I remember—this didn't just happen with me—but I remember, from before anyone might ask "do I have any?" Which means they didn't know it had happened. So, I am glad—

Sangi: There is a different protocol now.

Sabrina: Exactly. I'm glad that you're there now and you're tightening how things are done, that they're done in an appropriate way. And then the question is, yes, they have their own parents, but the issue is that they also have human in them, which it's in a different basket because we're very different. So, it was done this way. You know, to a certain extent, we need to be involved as humans because these children are very different from— We, humans, are very different from most ETs. We tend to have a lot of emotions and all of this influences, I'm sure, the children. If they don't have a lot of that, I think it's fine if the humans are not involved. But if they do, it's almost required that humans be involved because that needs to be nurtured, needs to be explained to the children. They need to understand how the emotions run and how to get a handle on them.

Sangi: Yes. Explain that to your species.

Sabrina: Yes.

Sangi: I can only do what is required at this time. I've taken over this program and I have to deal with it as it is. And I am tightening it up to make it a better program and a more integral program as it is. I see where in the past many things were inappropriate, but now things are different. Now, things are more understood. Events are coming to light, as it were. And we are getting to know your peoples as a beautiful population, whereas before they were not seen as such a respectful group. Do you understand?

Sabrina: Yes.

Sangi: Therefore, the things that happened in the past are in the past, and will remain there. Nothing to do to change that. But we will be working in the future and the present to make it worthwhile for people to have the hybridization program, for them to trust us again, want us to be helpful. We are trying our best to be a good example at this time of things that you would require of us. All the children do have good parents. And if the humans want to be involved—we cannot force them—we would very much hope they would want to be involved with their child in this realm because it would be very helpful to the child, of course, to learn their culture, emotions, the density.

Of course, they are taught that as well. How the cultures and things of Earth are. But if there are specifics that you want them to know about your culture other than generalities, then it is a great idea to get in touch with them to become a part of who they are, and be aware and loving of who they are. To share your love with your child is a beautiful and wonderful thing. At this point, we want to look at the future and not at the past. We are sorry for many of the things that have happened. Inappropriate. The abductions. Many, many things. But there are many apologies out there, and that doesn't change the facts: that it has happened in the past. We want to start and direct the future and make it a much more beautiful connection, a more loving and happy situation for all of those involved. Do you understand that?

Sabrina: Yes. I understand that. You know, the issue being now—it's how would you even be able to track the parents of all those children that don't know they have a child.

Sangi: Yes. That is a problem and we are working on it.

Sabrina: And you know, what was done with me, it was recent. It wasn't that far away.

Sangi: Yes, I know. And that's what I'm saying. We are tightening up. We're trying to fill in all the gaps that would not let anything like this happen again.

Sabrina: And we thank you for that because I think it's very important that we're treated as equal, that we are respected.

Sangi: We do not want to be appearing to be condescending in any way, because you are equal.

Sabrina: Okay. Thank you. I think Sarah has a question. Thank you for answering mine. I know you came into this in the middle of things, that you're taking over and new to this whole thing, but I do like the way you're doing things, tightening things, and the rules, and making sure that things are done properly. So, I do thank you for that.

Sangi: Thank you very much. I appreciate that vote of confidence because it is a very, very difficult job to fill in all those holes. There are a lot of people out there who are gatherers. But now, there's no more gathering being done until an official investigation has been done. I have called for that.

Sabrina: Okay. Thank you.

Sangi: You are welcome.

Sarah: Hello, Sangi. It's Sarah. How are you?

Sangi: Sarah, I am beautiful. How are you?

Sarah: I'm doing well. Thank you. I have a couple questions. One due to the many we've already expressed today. I was wondering whether, at some point, it'll be possible to have one of the hybrid children of Girk-Fitneer channeled through Jim, so they can tell us what's going on and maybe, you know, we can find out if there's anything necessary that we can speak up about or, you know, offer any suggestions.

Sangi: I think that would be a lovely idea. There are many children who are very well-spoken, who would love to speak to humanity as a whole. I do not know if they are prepared to do that today.

Sarah: That's okay.

Sangi: However, I can have that done in the future. In fact, we should schedule a time when the children speak to the human colony, and the world. Let them tell you what their lives with their parents actually are like, and the visitations of humans and so on. I find that when I do interact with any of the children, they have very positive things to say about both sides.

Sarah: Yes. The reason being, like Sabrina brought up, they have emotions that you guys may not be aware of simply because they are human.

Sangi: Pardon me?

Sarah: I said the reason being I wanted to speak with them, and I'm sure others would like to speak to those who are on Girk-Fitneer or even Erra because—

Sangi: Believe me, they are exhibiting—

Sarah: I think you're breaking up.

Sangi: Very interesting and very enlightening. Enlightening, because it appears that emotion in the fourth dimension that comes out stronger seems to be fueled also—the same thing that is happening.

Sarah: I'm sorry. You were breaking up. I didn't hear the last part.

Sangi: Ah. Is this microphone [malfunctioning]?

Sarah: No, I think it's the connection.

Max: The whole signal. It's the whole connection.

Sarah: It is the signal.

Max: Yeah.

Sarah: Can you repeat the last statement you made?

Max: I believe he froze again.

Sangi: What was the question?

Sarah: It was more of, I believe, addressing that we should speak to them to see what we can suggest because—

Sangi: Yes. You are breaking up very badly.

Sarah: Okay. Yes. So, what was the last statement you made about them speaking with us and, you know, their upbringing?

Sangi: Yes. You are breaking up very badly. I cannot understand.

Max: You were talking about the emotions, and what you have learned about them.

Sangi: Oh, yes. It appears they have stronger emotions, the hybrid children, even in fourth dimension because of the human hybridization. And it shows intellect and intuition. It comes usually when the emotions are strongest. It appears to come from a sense of intellect, spirituality, and intuition. It's very interesting, and a wonderful study at this time.

Max: Yes. And if there are any suggestions, maybe we can offer to the parents as well coming from, you know, our points of view.

Sangi: You have done so. Many of you have spoken to the parents and have given your opinions. Some have said, "Please hold my child more." Some have said, "Please bring them up in a religious background." And they had to learn a little bit about that religious background to let the child know, and give them a sense of what kind of background their human parents have. There have been many suggestions.

Max: Even to the idea of food as well, or—

Sangi: Oh yes.

Max: ...because we understand a lot of the alien species don't eat.

Sangi: Most of them do, but they don't eat like you do. They eat supplements and things that are created for them for the body to synthesize easier, and get better muscle tone and nourishment, but it is also flavored. They will have them try the flavors of Earth as well.

Max: Very good. So, it won't be such a shock.

Sangi: That is not easy for some of them, because finding those flavors on other planets is difficult. We will give them some, as we have synthesized many Earth flavors—about 300 or so common flavors across cultures that

109

earthlings usually eat.

Max: Yes. And I would like to ask, at any point, may I be able to meet with you specifically?

Sangi: Yes.

Max: To speak with you.

Sangi: I will be available.

Max: Thank you so much for that. I will pass the mic now.

Sangi: Have a wonderful day.

Max: You too. Much love.

Sangi: Much love.

Dan: Hello.

Sangi: Hello.

Dan: This is Dan. I have a question from Kris. She says she has a hybrid. Children that she never asked to have. She wants to know how many she has, their locations, and whether they're being properly cared for. I thought this question was relevant at the moment.

Sangi: All the hybrid children have regular alien parents: Two of them. We made sure there are always two, and that they come from loving families. We check these families out before they are put in the hybridization program. You see, they are part of the program. The parents. They have to understand what is happening, what may happen, how people will feel, how they must listen and be part of the instruction of the human parents. They are well cared for, well-nourished. Also, the education is well-done. The highest forms for these children. Now, yes, you may have—I do not know how many—there are 700 Krises. So, I would have to speak to you and know where you are from. I cannot do that right now through this means of communication, because I cannot connect, but I will let you know that if you have hybrid children, they are being well taken care of. They are being

110

well looked after and loved. These parents want children, and are very much interested in hybrids and in how beautiful will be the change they make to the galaxy.

Dan: That's wonderful. Yes. I'll have her contact Jim with more information, and her location, and all those things that are needed. Yes. Awesome. Thank you so much.

Sangi: That way I can connect more closely.

Max: Okay. If that's all that you have, Dan. Do you have any questions in the room with you there? Can we ask? I just wanna make sure that everyone is aware there should be a site or something specific just for these specific questions.

Sangi: Can you hear her?

Max: Not very clearly.

Sangi: Can you hear her talking?

Max: Not very clearly.

Sangi: I cannot hear her.

Max: She was saying that we need to have a specific place on Human Colony website, where all of this information could be amassed, or easily found. It could be addressed quite easily that way. It's what I was saying a little while ago.

Sangi: This has been suggested earlier, and that would be a responsibility. Someone on your side should take responsibility and actually do this if that is something that concerns your people.

Max: Yes. That way everybody could go to the human colony website at humancolony.org. I believe humancolongy.org would be the site that most people already have, and we'll try to get a hybrid-child-question section built, and everybody can put their information there so it can be addressed as it becomes available.

Sangi: I think it would be good if you share the information that you already know about your child on this site. The name, what their interests are if you know them, what species they are so that it could bring some community to the site.

Max: Yeah. That's a good idea. Thank you.

Sangi: Give some information. Give some communication. Share your love of your child with others. It would be like showing your baby pictures, only with the information.

Max: What a wonderful idea. Right. And now, if we don't have any more questions, Sangi, we would like to thank you so much for coming in today, introducing yourself, and giving us some ideas about what's going on with our hybrid children.

Sangi: Thank you.

Max: Your presence today is most appreciated.

Sangi: I appreciate you wanting to speak to me, and that you have such love and care for your children. Thank you very much. And I hope to meet many of you in the future and hear how you love your hybrid children, and how you are getting along with their families. This would be a lovely thing for me to put into the records.

Max: And do you know any blessings you might give us before you leave?

Sangi: Oh, I have a Fendorian blessing that I use for the children when I wake up in the morning. It is my hybrid children blessing to help all the children out there to have a more wonderful day. I will give it to you now. Just a moment. [Galactic Language] It says "Wake up and be wonderful. Wake up to the new light of day. Be happy and learn all the things that you need to know. And I send you blessing energy, healing, and love. Be well."

Max: It was beautiful. Thank you so much. It was wonderful to meet you today.

Sangi: It was wonderful to be here. Thank you so much. I don't know whether I will speak to you again.

Max: Can I say something here please?

Sangi: Yes.

Max: On that note, I'd like to say that I was with mine last night.

Sangi: Wonderful.

Max: And there was something I left him to do. He seemed apprehensive about it, and then he said...

Sangi: Your children are beautiful, and you will love them both I'm sure.

Max: So, I remember that from last night.

Sangi: Wonderful. I'm so glad. And it is recorded.

Max: So, yes. And I wanted to leave on a bright note.

Sangi: Wonderful. I am so happy for that. Thank you so much.

Max: Thank you. Namaste.

Sangi: Namaste. I will be going now.

Max: Oh, thank you for coming.

MEKESI: A YAHYEL HYBRID CHILD FROM MAYA

Channeled by Jim

Max: Hello.

Mekesi: Hello.

Max: Thank you for coming. Who are we speaking with?

Mekesi: Mekesi. I am one of the hybrid children on Maya.

Max: Oh, thank you for joining us. That's beautiful.

Mekesi: I heard stories that this place is fun.

Max: Yes. Fun is a great way of putting it.

Mekesi: Well, you visit me sometimes. Many people from your planet visited me and I am happy to see them. They are fun.

Max: Oh, thank you. I think I missed your name. Could you repeat that?

Mekesi: No.

Max: Okay. That's fine. Could we know how old you are?

Mekesi: In Earth years?

Max: I guess so.

Mekesi: Let me figure it out. I am two-point-one.

Max: Okay. Wow. You're very young, aren't you?

Mekesi: They allow me to come. They thought you should know what we are like when we are two-point-one.

Max: That's wonderful.

Mekesi: And we are appreciating you to come.

Max: Yes. That's very exciting.

Mekesi: You want to ask me about anything a two-point-one-year-old can answer?

Max: Yeah. What race are you from?

Mekesi: Race. Race. Oh, species. Yes, race. I thought of running. Animals running, people running like racing. Yes. Species—I am Yahyel and human.

Max: Oh, beautiful. You have very lovely energy.

Mekesi: Energy, yes. Lovely energy. I like lovely energies as well.

Max: Oh. Well, this is great. So, we did have some questions. Is there anything, first of all, you would like to tell us, the human collective, right now?

Mekesi: You are far away. You have lots of people just like we do, but you look different. I like all my friends. They all look different too. Some of them are kitty cats as you call them. Some of them are rough skins. Some of them are just like me. And some of them are different colors. Yes, I like the different colors. They're friendly. Friendly green, friendly blue. Friendly green, friendly blue.

Max: You are so much fun.

Mekesi: Pleiadians. That's what they're called. Pleiadians. It's a hard word for me. That's a hard word.

Max: I heard that Maya is a Pleiadian planet, but there's more than just Pleiadians there. Right?

Mekesi: There is now. Yes. Yes, there is. Now, there is. Pleiadian is a hard word. I can't spell it yet.

Max: Okay.

Mekesi: No. I can't spell it in your Earth words.

Max: No problem. Well, this is very exciting to have you come forth today. Wonderful. Have you been able to talk with any other earth humans about their experiences or—I'm curious what your take on our planet is.

Mekesi: Take? I'm not going to take your planet.

Max: Sorry. What I meant is, I'm curious what your thoughts on our planet are, what—

Mekesi: Thought.

Max: Yeah. What you think of us, or feel, or anything.

Mekesi: You are friendly. You talk a lot. You don't like to hold the babies that need changed 'cause you don't know how to change them on this planet. So, you hold the dry ones. You hold all the dry ones. Oh, you like to talk funny language. They are teaching me English, but I did not know what goo-goo meant for quite a while, and ga-ga, except that it was one of your artists on your planet. Gaga.

Max: Yes, Lady Gaga. That's very interesting that you're learning those words.

Mekesi: Yes. Well, there was—

Max: I don't think it's very helpful to learn goo-goo. I'll tell you that right now.

Mekesi: Well, I have learned that goo-goo is something that I do not want. And so, when they speak it to me, I say no. No goo-goo.

Max: Okay.

Mekesi: No goo-goo. Ga-ga okay, but no goo-goo.

Max: That is funny. This is very funny. What games do you play?

Mekesi: They taught us patty cake. Patty cake. It is a hand game. And we also do talking games. Repeat after me game. Repeat after me. Say mommy. Say daddy. Not sure why. Not sure why, but fun. I like saying those words. They are fun. My mommy and daddy, some of them—parts of me are from Earth. So, that is why they say that. And I understand.

Max: Do you have brothers and sisters?

Mekesi: Brothers. Oh, older. Yes. Older. Sister, older. Sister different than me. She is more like Mom and Dad, as you say. Less like me. I'm hybrid.

Max: Do you know other hybrid children?

Mekesi: Oh, yes. Many. Many friends. Yes. They are friends. I like my friends.

Max: Maybe you know my child.

Mekesi: What's your child's name?

Max: I believe it's Emuk, Amak.

Mekesi: No. No know that name.

Max: I see. Did you ever see me there in one of my visits?

Mekesi: Maybe. I don't know. Is that what you look like there? Black eyes, sun worshiper look like. Right. Very big like you, but the rest of face no.

Max: Maybe when—

Mekesi: Body, no. The body, no. No, I don't think I see you before. You're strange-looking.

Max: Okay.

Mekesi: Okay. But you come. I say hello. Yes.

Sarah: Hello.

Mekesi: I will say hello. I'm friends with everybody. Nobody I dislike yet.

Sarah: Are you able to feel other people's energies, to know whether or not you've met them?

Mekesi: Yes. I like other energies. Other energies good. Yes. Good fun.

Sarah: Can you connect to my energy and tell whether or not you've met me?

Mekesi: One moment. I do not see you.

Sarah: Yes, I understand. You can't connect to my energy.

Max: Connect to energy. I feel energy coming from you. So yes, that must be you.

Sarah: Yes, my name is Sarah.

Mekesi: Sarah.

Sarah: Yes.

Mekesi: That's been fun to say. Sarah. Fun to say. Yes, I feel your energy. Very nice. Very nice. Thank you.

Sarah: Very good. I believe I've gone to Maya a number of times.

Mekesi: Maybe we meet. I feel energy like yours before, human energy, but yours is a little bit stronger. Just a little.

Sarah: Yes.

Mekesi: Yes.

Sarah: Yes, I was told I take care of the babies there sometimes.

Mekesi: Ah! I'm no longer baby, but—

Sarah: Yes, I understand.

Mekesi: ...I'm still with the babies because I like to talk to the babies and we like to be around the babies. Me and my friends like the babies. The babies are—what is your word? Cute. Cute. I like that word. Cute.

Sarah: And you speak the Yahyel language right now?

Mekesi: Yes. I can speak Yahyel. My mother and father are Yahyel here. And part of my heredity—they're saying heredity—is human. Yes. Yes.

Sarah: Uh-huh. Very good. [Galactic Language]

Mekesi: You talk funny. But yes, I understand what you say. Thank you.

Sarah: Thank you.

Mekesi: But you have accent.

Sarah: Yes, I think so.

Mekesi: Human accent. That's all right. I still understand. I have to go.

They said I have to go.

Sarah: Well, much love to your whole family and everybody on Maya.

Mekesi: I have to go.

Max: Oh, that's too bad. Yeah, lovely energy. Thank you for coming.

Mekesi: It was fun. I don't wanna go.

Max: Oh. You are lovely. Thank you for coming.

Mekesi: No!

Max: Or maybe you can come visit again soon.

Mekesi: [Galactic Language] All right. They make me go.

Max: We are so happy we got to talk to you. Thank you. We love you.

Mekesi: Bye.

Max: Bye.

Illustration by Dahley Robertson-King

SENISHA OF THE ARCTURIAN COUNCIL

Channeled by Jim

Senisha: I am from Integrated Arcturian Space Council. That council which brings in portions of all Arcturian space.

Max: Wonderful, thank you. You know the questions, right? We're writing a book, with a chapter on Arcturians, like an article. There are some very basic questions we'd like answered.

Senisha: You realize that Arcturians are very private?

Max: Right.

Senisha: And that we as people and peoples—plural—have many different ways and cultures. But I will attempt to answer your questions as best as possible. If there is something we cannot tell you, we will be very blunt.

Max: Thank you. So, my first question: are other Arcturians from the star we call Arcturus?

Senisha: There are many peoples in these star systems—plural—of Arcturus. At least seven species. Meaning that we control seven species in Arcturus space.

Max: Okay. So there is a single star which we call Arcturus. It's not a galaxy, it's one big star.

Senisha: The star system is where I am from. Not all the peoples are from this star.

Max: Are there soul peoples from the same area in the sky?

Senisha: Yes. There are people within what you call light-years of us. We are familiar with one another. What do you need to know about this?

Max: Just want to make sure it's the same star we call Arcturus.

Senisha: We know which star you mean.

Max: Okay. Next question: what is the origin of the Arcturians?

Senisha: Arcturians are from the Milky Way system as you call it. We are from a star in Arcturus space. Now, other species that we are speaking about, that we can control space for, are not necessarily from this star system. But, they are also mostly from the Milky Way galaxy. What else do you need to know?

Max: Thank you. So, are you united; are a lot of Arcturians united? Are you speaking for the united Alliance?

Senisha: We. I am speaking for, yes. Integrated alliance, yes. Of Arcturians,

121

and those beings who choose to align with us in this area of space which is to be a peaceful unity for old times, so that we may be allies one with the other against any forces that may want to conquer this portion of space. We do not need to conquer large areas of the galaxy. But, in this portion of space, we maintain a peaceful alliance so that we may do our trading, commerce and any kind of business that we wish without any problems. Now, if someone wishes to join us in our alliance that is a possibility if they agree to be traders, merchants, and friendly peoples. We do have alloys, minerals, and compounds that are tradable with many different species and civilizations. We are amicable outside trade, even if they do not want to be part of the alliance. If they've things we need that are not common to our area.

Max: Okay. Thank you. What is the relationship between your council and Girk-Fitneer?

Senisha: Girk-Fitneer is a council or alliance, that is there for ascension purposes for the Earth. They also have peaceful alliances with many different species, seven, just like us. But, they've different missions and reasons for congregating. We are mostly commerce, and trade-agreement people. We do like the amicable trade of merchandise. We also share art, music, and cultural thought processes that make life more amicable, joyful and perhaps enriching. The Girk-Fitneer people, as they are called, are a group who come together for more political thoughts and processes, for also some trade; but mostly for prophecy and these kinds of certification, and for advancing other species.

Max: Thank you. So the Girk-Fitneer there considered Arcturian. And their leaders too?

Senisha: There are Arcturians within the Girk-Fitneer alliance. They are the leaders because they've the greater understanding of the space they built. Also, they are greater understanding of all galaxies in this proximity, they've a higher functionality and wisdom than the others in the alliance. They bear, however, greater responsibilities being with them because they've the final say on all decisions. Therefore, if a decision is wrong the Arcturians will be mostly to blame.

Max: Is your organisation the council, the Arcturian Council, which governs Girk-Fitneer?

Senisha: Our council is separate from Girk-Fitneer. We may have some trade agreements with them, but they are a separate entity.

Max: Okay. Can you tell me about the species, the main species we would be dealing with? Suppose, from the other Earth becoming part of the galaxy, we will be dealing with certain other Arcturians. Which would that be—which Arcturian races?

Senisha: That is an interesting question, because times change and thought processes do too. The importance of Earth is right now fairly high but it may lose interest in the future. So, those of us who would be interested in trading agreements with Earth would be the green and orange Arcturians. White Arcturians are from Agartha, as it's called. And, perhaps some of the other species that are considered Arcturian because they are close by but are actually separate species. Now, I do not think that Girk-Fitneer will always be interested in planet Earth as they are at the present. Once they reach their goals with the ascension and becoming friends with them, I do not believe they've much further interest. Perhaps some mild trade with your planet. The hybridisation program is their main function with your world.

Max: I'm interested mainly in the Arcturians who look human. Can you tell me about this?

Senisha: Yes. There are Arcturians who resemble Earth species.

Max: Tell me about the name, origins, and how they are related to us.

Senisha: They are from a farther portion away from Earth, and from the Arcturian area. But, still in the alliance with us. They are the Venszaza.

Max: Okay.

Senisha: They were early to be on the Earth's surface, one of the more ancient species.

Max: What color are they?

Senisha: They are various colors, but mostly fair-skinned like you.

Max: Venszaza, right?

Senisha: Venszaza.

Max: Are they currently involved with Earth?

Senisha: I believe they seeded the Earth long ago, but have a little interest at this time in returning. Right now they are going through some climatic changes in their portion of space. Their sun is unstable, therefore they are looking for other home lands rather than looking at scientific interests on your planet, or prophesies that may be spoken of this time. They are doing a scientific study of about thirteen planets where they may relocate.

Max: Okay, I understand. Venszazas have contributed to the human genome, so they must be genetically related to us, right?

Senisha: Yes.

Max: Was this during the time of Atlantis, or before?

Senisha: Before Atlantis, by one thousand two hundred years in your time specification.

Max: Our understanding that Atlantis lasted about a year makes no difference?

Senisha: Yes.

Max: Are they from your time?

Senisha: They did not stay around for Atlantis.

Max: So they were in the Lemurian times?

Senisha: They were nomadic.

Max: Did they see the Earth in the Lemurian times—assuming you understand me?

Senisha: They did. But did not interact that much with Atlanteans, Lemurians, Egyptians or any of the cultures that existed then.

Max: Okay. That helps. They are not the major contributor to the human genome?

Senisha: Venszaza were their own, they were more secretive about what they did on your planet, and the history goes back very far. But, they did not determine exactly what they did except for they did change history there. By speeding up evolution, so that a missing link will not be found.

Max: Oh, sure, okay. So some of the human-looking Arcturians are involved in the solar system character. What are those?

Senisha: Yeah. What are those?

Max: I am aware of the human-looking Arcturians working with other aliens in the solar system, and on the Earth project.

Senisha: Are you sure they are Arcturian and not Pleiadian?

Max: That's how they were characterised. Arcturians.

Senisha: I see. One moment while I check some information. There are some looking human Arcturians as you would put it. In the solar system that you occupy. They are interested in the wormholes slash black holes both behind Neptune and by Jupiter, and there is one by Saturn as well. These kinds of natural phenomena can be manipulated for space travel, and for other uses. Short of facts on transportation, but it must be precise calculations. They are also interested in observing some of the events on your planet. They will be more involved there in probably thirty or forty years, when things start to change in a more dramatic way.

Max: What is their species?

Senisha: What is the species that looks human? Is that the one you're asking about?

Max: Yeah, the ones you just mentioned. Human-appearing Arcturians in the solar system. What is this species? Sub-race of Arcturians—what is their race?

Senisha: Shork. The Shork Arcturians.

Max: Okay. Thank you. Wonderful. What color are they?

Senisha: They've a human look. Some of are dark. There are very few that are deep magenta or purplish, deep purple. Most of them look human.

Max: Thank you. Let's move to the orange Arcturians. They've been dealing with Earth.

Senisha: Yeah, orange and green species.

Max: Okay. Can you give their name?

Senisha: Let me see if it is appropriate for them to be given.

Max: Okay.

Senisha: They prefer to be called the Orange and Green Arcturians.

Max: Sounds good. What is their origin?

Senisha: Their origin is planet six. Arcturian sun space.

Max: Wonderful.

Senisha: I am from Planet three.

Max: What is your species?

Senisha: We're Venzu.

Max: Are you human-looking?

Senisha: Not particularly. We have a thinner body. Some may confuse us with the Grey species. We're not connected in any way. But we are not colored grey. We've a pastel color in our area, because our atmosphere shields us from the sun.

Max: Wow. Do you have a special shape of the head?

Senisha: The head is oval. Like some Greys. Some of your people have seen us and are familiar with who we are.

Max: Is your head divided into two parts, with a dip in the middle?

Senisha: It is slightly. It is not noticeable at first glance.

Max: It is not the species that I know.

Senisha: No.

Max: Did I meet you?

Senisha: Did you meet me?

Max: Personally, your species.

Senisha: You met my species, but not me.

Max: Okay. Interesting. So, what would be the way to identify you visually? What is a way to recognise you from the other species?

Senisha: We're five feet tall. We are thin and small. Our heads are slightly larger in proportion to our body than yours. Our colors are pastel.

Max: Okay.

Senisha: Pinks; light blue. Purplish, light purplish. Some are very pale, even a light pink.

Max: Have you got hair?

Senisha: No.

Max: Do you wear a dress?

Senisha: Sometimes a robe. A dress . . . I am not accustomed to the names of your clothing. Sorry.

Max: Okay. Sounds good. Are you guys presently in our solar system?

Senisha: We are presently not in your solar system. But we are visiting periodically.

Max: Wonderful. Do you have special ships, or do you use a genetic ship?

Senisha: We use orbs and egg-shaped ships for long shape-shifts.

Max: Wonderful.

Senisha: We do not use them for long-distance travelling. We usually fold space, or transport the ships to your area.

Max: I understand, thank you. Biologically, are you related to mammals, Reptilians, Nords, any of those?

Senisha: We would be considered humanoid more than any of the other things you mentioned.

Max: Do you give birth?

Senisha: Not any longer. Our children are grown in tubes or cloned.

Max: Okay. Do your children grow up in the family, or otherwise?

Senisha: It depends. There are some portions of the population whose traditions are to have family units. But in my portion of the planet, division and separation are fine, with reuniting of DNA species that are family units later in development.

Max: Are you making human hybrids, do you hybridise humans from Earth?

Senisha: It has been considered that we could do this, but has not been put into practice as of yet.

Max: So, are there any Arcturian species, our ancestors, other than Venszaza?

Senisha: Venszaza, we've been through your planet many times. It is hard to say who are all the ones that seeded your population. There is a little bit of many, many things that are DNA specific in your cultures, and so the answer could be yes by 87% possibility, probability.

Max: Which of the Arcturian species would be the closest to the humans by DNA sequence?

Senisha: Which, please repeat that question?

Max: Which of the Arcturian species would be closest to the humans by DNA?

Senisha: Venszaza.

Max: Venszaza. Okay, thank you. Can you tell me about the orange-green Arcturians?

Senisha: What would you like to know?

Max: Are they involved in the solar system?

Senisha: They are here in your solar system. Yes. They are involved in some very interesting practices on Mars. They are not mining the planet, but are making treaties with those people that are on Mars, and live within the Mars structure.

Max: Okay.

Senisha: They want to become apolitical for the sake of uniting the solar system after first contact on your planet. They are making inroads for political domination, even though they are not on your planet.

Max: Domination. You mean, they want to be good. Are they friendly toward Earth?

Senisha: They would consider themselves friendly, but they disagree on how Earth's being run, so would after first contact make several inroads politically to change how the planet works.

Max: Okay. Do they want to dominate politics, economy and social life?

Senisha: I'm not sure of the extent of their want for this. But they feel they will be a positive asset to your political realms.

Max: Okay. So how socially knowledgeable are they about human life?

Senisha: They are about 82.7% accomplished in understanding all of your worldwide government procedures.

Max: Interesting. So they are involved, interesting. So, they are passively involved without any active involvement?

Senisha: Correct. They are planning involvement. They are not at this time involved, but seek future involvement after first contact.

Max: Haven't they been involved in our politics and history?

Senisha: Some areas but not in this particular time.

Max: Okay.

Senisha: The galactic government does not allow them to interact in the way they would like, so they stay away.

Max: Are they in alliance with any of our enemies?

Senisha: It is possible they are making alliance with people that are of negative nature, but they are actively aligning themselves with as many species as possible. Not just one or two, but as many as they feel that will understand their place, and if they get enough people behind them as allies they may be able to sway the thought processes that are facing Earth in the future.

Max: I see. Right now we understand. Are they related to Mammals, Placentals, Reptilians, Nordics any of insects?

Senisha: I believe they proceeded from Amphibious backgrounds.

Max: So what height are they?

Senisha: Close to six feet tall. They've come from a larger water-type species, the oceans larger than the land masses similar to your planet.

Max: Okay. All right. Are they orange or green?

Senisha: They have orange, green, deep purple (very rare). But, there are those that are actually green and orange at the same time.

Max: Is there any difference?

Senisha: Like your Mulatto people, they are halfway in between colors.

Max: Okay. Are there any distinguishing features?

Senisha: The faces are wider than humans'; cheekbones are larger. The faces are longer.

Max: It cannot be wider and longer at the same time.

Senisha: Yes, it can.

Max: Okay.

Senisha: Their head is divided.

Max: Oh. On the top?

Senisha: Yes.

Max: Like the shape of the human heart?

Senisha: That is somewhat correct.

Max: Can you look?

Senisha: I cannot see.

Max: That's all right. Okay. I am aware of small orange Arcturians, like three-and-a-half feet tall, visiting Earth.

Senisha: Yes, they exist.

Max: What are they named?

Senisha: They are important to your solar system.

Max: What is the name of that species?

Senisha: Palakoshefendi Keta.

Max: Palakoshefendi Keta . . .

Senisha: Close enough.

Max: We need brevity. It's impossible to deal with such a name.

Senisha: The Fendi portion comes from Reptilian background. There is a bit of Reptilian in them.

Max: Are they actively involved now in the solar system?

Senisha: Yes.

Max: Are they friendly with Girk-Fitneer?

Senisha: Yes.

Max: Interesting. Are they mammals or placentals?

Senisha: They are also water creatures.

Max: Okay.

Senisha: I believe they are mammals and reptilian together.

Max: Okay. So you are familiar with the word Placentals? Placentals are the ones which give birth.

Senisha: They do.

Max: Oh, they do. Wow.

Senisha: Well, they do now.

Max: Okay.

Senisha: At one point they were an ailing society—about eight hundred and ninety years ago. But something happened. A natural mutation, where the eggs come out and immediately hatch. Eventually, this became childbirth.

Max: Do any of the species we've discussed have special powers, like natural teleportation?

Senisha: Mostly telepathy and mental communications. Psychic energy, not as strong as you might think, but does have some effect. They do have the ability to bi-locate, and do some things very efficiently with technology. Transporting, moving from one place to another, is easy for them. There are some in their species who have higher and greater psychic abilities. Telekinesis is rare, but is part of some of them. That is all I can think of at the moment for your language.

Max: Thank you. Which of the Arcturian subspecies are most involved with Girk Fitneer?

Senisha: Well, there is a combination of them. You see, there are many species within the Girk-Fitneer community, so there are all of these different Fendorians if you would like to call them that, or Arcturians. Arcturians and Fendorians of all different species, but who choose to be with the alliance.

Max: My questions was which one of the Arcturian species is most present in Girk-Fitneer?

Senisha: That's a good one. I am not sure.

Max: Okay. Which of the Arcturian species are known on Earth?

Senisha: All of those species have been catalogued by your scientific community.

Max: Okay. So, none of them stands out as most popular?

Senisha: No. But most visited are the small ones you mentioned.

Max: Arcturians involved in recent events we'd like to know about. Are any of the Arcturians famous people?

Senisha: No, they are not involved with the events on your planet. They are observers more than they are interactive. At least at this point, as far as I know. If there were any secret programs to become part of your infrastructure, MIC [Military-Industrial Complex], or your governmental areas, we are not aware of it at this time.

Max: Okay. Many now in our communities, lightworker communities, speak Arcturian language. Which would that be? Which of the species?

Senisha: Will be ours.

Max: That would be Venzu.

Senisha: Yes. Ours and the Zaza.

Max: Venzaza?

Senisha: Yes.

Max: Okay.

Senisha: Technically, the small Fendi ones.

Max: I see. Fendis.

Senisha: Fendis. The longer name, just call it Fendis.

Max: Okay. Fendis is good. So I understand these people are spiritually connected to Arcturians.

Senisha: Yes. Some of them are our star family.

Max: Have they been Arcturians in the past life, so now they reincarnate on Earth?

Senisha: This is very true, yes.

Max: So, that would be one of the three species you mentioned. Venzu.

Senisha: All of the species mentioned.

Max: All of the species. Are you incarnating interchangeably? From one species to another?

Senisha: Of course.

Max: I didn't know.

Senisha: Why not?

Max: I was under strong impression that soul has to match the genetics of the species. It's really hard to reincarnate from one species to another.

Senisha: No. Not true. The soul is a soul. It does not have to have a species to become life. It is life. Then it takes on a form after that.

Max: So the soul can incarnate into any species of compatible intelligence?

Senisha: Of course. The God puts the fire in you, but he doesn't make it into anything until you are born into that species.

Max: Do you have unified religion between Arcturian species?

Senisha: Yes.

Max: Are we aware of this religious teaching? Is it on Earth? Is it disclosed as one of the Earth's religions?

Senisha: No. It's similar but not the same.

Max: How would you identify it?

Senisha: It's universal. It is broad-minded, more faceted in spiritual realms than material.

Max: Is Jesus big in your religion?

Senisha: He is not spoken of as Jesus or Yeshua. But his presence is similar in many cultures.

Max: So his energy is present in your religion?

Senisha: The presence of that kind of identity, yes.

Max: Are you familiar with Law of One?

Senisha: Yes.

Max: It's not kind of Arcturian?

Senisha: No.

Max: Okay. Is the Council of Nine Arcturian, and are you connected to them?

Senisha: We know who they are, and are friendly with them. But they are not from the Arcturian space.

Max: What is your relationship with the Galactic Federation of Light?

Senisha: We are aware of them. But they choose not to communicate with everyone. It is not that they distrust us, but they've a mission, and the people that are within their ranks have chosen to maintain citizenship with one another more exclusive than inclusive of all people, all species. Now, this is not to say that they are not friendly or loving. They are secure one with the other, and they prefer this.

Max: Same question, this time covering your Counsel and the Ashtar Command.

Senisha: The Ashtar Command is broad. They speak to many species and civilisations about their cause, and how they want to move forward. They are part of the communication, yes. They are of a good group. We do not believe in all the things they stand for, but we know they are of positive field.

Max: Are Arcturians involved with Ashtar Command? Working on their ship?

Senisha: They've joined it. The people in my Counsel have not. There are many like those who joined Girk-Fitneer, and other alliances that are involved in Ashtar Command, because they see or have the same opinions and views of this particular group.

Max: Which Arcturian species would be involved with Ashtar Command?

Senisha: Once again, I do not know.

Max: Okay.

Senisha: We do not keep track of the individuals who go to different alliances, because that is their right.

Max: 50:52. Which of the Arcturian cultures are most involved with channelling messages to the Earth?

Senisha: Those from Girk-Fitneer—Arcturians who are in that alliance are the most communicative with Earth, although they do not communicate a lot.

Max: Many individuals have channelled generic Arcturian messages. Are those coming from Venzu, Venszaza or Fendi? Green-orange messages?

Senisha: There are different kinds of messages received by Earth through channelling, and it would be all different species of course. The most likely to channel through the Earth species would be Fendi.

Max: Fendi. Okay, thank you. The last question: what is your relationship to the Andromeda Council? What is the relationship between the Arcturian and Andromeda Council?

Senisha: The Andromeda Council is much less humanoid. They are many Reptilians and Insectoids.

Max: Okay.

Senisha: That would be the difference. The Mantis beings, Reptilians, the Draconians there are many of the less humanoids species in the Andromeda areas.

Max: Are you friendly with them?

Senisha: Yes, but they are sometimes negative, and sometimes not completely trusting.

Max: Okay.

Senisha: There are many kinds of communications, and we do trade with them, and do have some intergalactic meetings. This is all very positive.

Max: Wonderful. Can I ask one more question? Do you deal with Pleiadian cultures?

Senisha: Yes.

Max: The Pleiadians, Errans, Lyrans, Yahyel . . . what's your relationship with those?

Senisha: They are different species within these. We try to be friendly, and accept them for who they are. There are some in these groups who do not accept us exactly for who we are. Trade is limited, and communication as well but we try to be open to all cultures and species. Trade is amicable. But it is not always such as this.

Max: So right now we are very open to the Pleiadian cultures, especially Yahyel and Lyrans. Do we have to choose who we deal with as we develop our relationships? Or do we have to choose between Arcturians and Pleiadians?

Senisha: You will of course have to choose who you want to trade with, who among them might be amicable, and have things you need as well as items for them. So, yes, you will decide as a species in different governments who you will wish to trade with and be friends with, because there are different kinds of trade, and different kinds of wealth, if you will, with each species. Some of them will have more energy products, or technology, and some will have mineral products or rare earth or things of this nature. So, it will be interesting to see what your governments deem valuable. Some people have artifacts, art, music and things like that. But I think your governments will choose those species with technology.

Max: Are any Earth governments already actively involved with Arcturians?

Senisha: Yes. In a direct way the United States, China, Russia, Brazil and Egypt have had some contacts. Japan as well, Australia, there are many.

Max: Thank you. I guess I ran out of time. That was very helpful. Thank you very much for your information.

Senisha: Also England and Canada, you may add.

138

Max: Excellent. That is our understanding of Arcturians. Thank you—much appreciation.

Senisha: Much appreciation. We hope that one day we'll be trusted, and brought into your confidence as a good counsel to trade with, be friends, and share information; art, music, language and such.

Max: Thank you for your kind offering.

Senisha: That is why I have appeared today, to cement or at least extend a hand toward friendship and community. We are of good peoples, and our alliance or whatever you choose to call it is positive and enlightened.

Max: Thank you, we appreciate that. We are already friends with Girk-Fitneer, and we value your moment with us, and your help.

Senisha: We are more distant, but we understand where you are and what is happening. We extend to you our energies of success.

Max: Excellent, thank you very much.

Senisha: Farewell for now, perhaps we will speak again sometime.

Max: Yes, your openness is very valued, so I would invite you again to expand on what we've already achieved. Thank you.

Senisha: We understand that you believe Fendorians to be quite secretive, but you did not touch on any of the things that we could not share.

Max: Okay.

Senisha: Greetings and farewell for now.

Max: Greetings and farewell for now.

REINCARNATION

The body is temporary, but the soul is eternal. You are your consciousness.

Like your soul, you too are immortal. The soul connects to the body and makes it self-aware. Although the body can be alive, without soul and consciousness (akin to coma, or amnesia) there can be only a mechanical existence. Victims of Alzheimer's and dementia live still, perform basic functions, but their soul has gone. Communicating with them, you may notice this absence. The personality and occupying soul—life-force—can briefly return, then leave again, perhaps because life is not interesting, or the body has become damaged and only with utmost difficulty maintains this fragile link.

The soul is multidimensional, vaster far than the body in a way not easily accounted for by conventional physics—if acknowledging the soul at least as electromagnetic energy. Like a waterfall through a funnel, the body cannot contain the soul entire, but connects instead to a "collective," termed in metaphysics the *noösphere*. The soul uses its earthly life to gain experience, learn lessons and improve the world.

Although individual human existence is brief, the totality of events, intellect and sensory impressions are imprinted on the soul and remembered forever. When the body's vessel of flesh, bone and blood dies, personality remains with the soul and is immortal. Lives are short, but the timeless soul continually incarnates.

Each iteration is given character by the soul, which accounts for radically different temperaments even between identical twins—because their souls are unique. On the other hand, various incarnations of one soul share aspects of character, which nonetheless develop a new shape and singular personality.

Though largely similar, the vagaries of life's paths freshly affect each new personality. Every instance of incarnation occurs during a distinct historical period, accumulates wisdom, thus rises to a higher level. Likewise, each incarnation develops a new, and eternal, personality, and in turn these all join the oversoul. Yet, when desired, they can step out and independently act within the spirit world. In other words, different incarnations of the same soul can behave as one—or singly—at will.

The process of reincarnation begins with a soul choosing father, mother and genetics for the body.

From the perspective of human biology, recombination in a child of the parents' DNA is random. Distribution unerringly provides 50% of the mother's DNA and 50% of the father's. Yet, from the soul's perspective— able to pick and choose genes from both—these so-called random events are under its complete control.

LOVE

As a child's living presence strengthens the bond between its parents, the yet-unborn soul of this offspring commonly is responsible for actually cultivating that love. The soul desires incarnation; this yearning fires up love in the imminent parents. This is the soul-energy that powers familial adoration.

Sadly, when children mature and no longer require parental support, the love between mother and father often fades. Again, it can be realized that all along the child's soul-energy fueled this love. Children grow into young adults, and move away; the parents often experience a crisis in their relationship and must find new inspiration to stay together.

The soul chooses parents before conception and, when these meet, the new child's soul starts creating its future body.

CONCEPTION

Conception is fueled by trans-dimensional energies, and orgasm creates a charged vortex driving fertilization and attachment of the child's soul to the DNA of the zygote. The DNA works like a laser pumped with light.

To create the orgasmic charged vortex, electric oscillations in the parents' neurons synchronize, and pump the energy into the egg cell. This accumulated potential is focused by the uterus onto the zygote. The mother's brain and spine form a liquid crystal structure amplifying the oscillations—focusing energy into the uterus and creating a trans-dimensional vortex serving as a spark for new life, urging the child's soul into earthly reality.

As the egg cell divides and the embryo grows, for the soul there is more substance with which to connect; a process enabled primarily through the DNA and fetal neurons. As the body develops, the soul's link to physicality is strengthened.

ASTROLOGY

Birth is a significant moment in all life. Even before, the child is partially conscious, but the passage through the birth canal and the first breath are essential. With breath, a new part of the soul connects to the body. During birth, the child's brain is reprogrammed from passivity to active cognition. At this moment, the Earth's electromagnetic wave-forms are imprinted on the brain and body. At the time of birth, this pattern is defined by the relative position of the child, Earth, sun and eight other planets in the solar system. In astrological lore this is known as the birth chart.

The interaction of the wave imprint on the person's physical and energetic bodies at birth, with Earth's electromagnetic field during life, is the physical basis of astrology.

Interestingly, when delivery is not stimulated, the fetus defines the hour of birth—releases stimulants into the mother's bloodstream signaling the start of labor. Even more fascinating, the birth-hour is an inheritable trait written in the child's DNA.

DEPRESSION

Throughout life, we experience ups and downs in our soul development. Ups are happy times; downs manifest as depression (often conflated with "sadness," but far more serious). This happens to practically everyone, and in our explosive, increasingly fragmented world, can be considered "the new normal."

Cycles of development are synchronized with, and guided by, the planets. Biorhythms too play a role, and these cycles have varying durations—usually weeks and months.

In human development, not only the physical form grows, but so do a series of interconnected energetic bodies in spiritual dimensions. Our etheric body is responsible for health, the emotional for emotions, mental for thinking, astral for connection with the spirit world and atman body for connection with God.

After a person recovers from depression, usually they're connected to a new portion of the soul—a process of continuous, cyclical growth. The human soul also reconnects to the body in cycles akin to a tree's annual growth rings. Each circle signifies a period of expansion, during which the tree becomes stronger. Our soul similarly develops and strengthens. Moreover, each new stage envelops all previous cycles.

In the wake of recovery, it is not unusual for people to develop novel qualities. As the energy body progresses, attention focuses on fresh subjects sparking resonation at new frequencies and attracting unexplored connections in the spirit world. These in turn link to undiscovered past lives and their bounty of skills. Aim high in your spiritual vibrations and be amazed by the abundance of new energies.

As you move through the day, experiences accumulate. During sleep or meditation, these moments and insights are "uploaded" to the soul. In exchange, you receive answers to your questions and solutions to problems—some of which will resolve themselves in the external world. Indeed, sleep and meditation don't only solve problems internally, they do so actually by affecting the real world.

During sleep, the soul also helps regenerate your physical body. This is genuine symbiosis—mutually beneficial cooperation between flesh and soul.

The spiritual nature of life is most pronounced at conception, birth, sleep and death—points of entry to, and exit from, the earthly realm. From the material perspective death is pretty scary, but from the spiritual simply part of life's continuum.

DEATH

As the body dies, the soul gradually disconnects. Normal and peaceful death is helpful for the proper transfer to the soul of our life experiences. If the body perishes in a violent, damaging manner, the profound negative effect can be inherited in the next incarnation. This is a common source of past-life trauma.

Some people remember their past lives. Children especially are adept at such recall, but as maturity and its material necessities demand more and more, past-life memories lose their focus and become haunting fragments.

After bodily death, the soul and personality return home to another realm that sometimes is referred to as Discarnate World, located in the 7th—and higher—dimensions. There, your soul is healed from the life and death traumas; you will meet your already passed close friends and relatives, and those from previous lives.

You next proceed with a life-review, assisted by teachers and guides. This usually occurs in a classroom setting. Our universities and schools are modeled after a galactic archetype, and therefore the spirits use it to symbolize learning. As you review your life, you have an opportunity to see the totality of events not only from your perspective, but from involved others. There is also a chance to "replay" each scenario to see what might happen had you taken an alternate course. This way you learn the consequences (positive, negative, neutral) for decisions, and how they affect others. When now you make decisions, understand that from the spiritual perspective, ultimately it doesn't really matter *what* you decide, so much as you experience the process itself. In the afterlife, you'll be able to replay these matters any way you prefer.

144

The spirit world is a happy place, where the soul comes home. Bodily death is simply that: and end to the physical flesh, bone and blood. A farewell to the earthly realm. In the spirit world, death is homecoming and rebirth into essence. While your body's death might be mourned in the physical world, in the spiritual dimension your return and regeneration is celebrated.

When a friend dies, it is all right to remember them with love. But it is also wise to let them go, because too much grief and excessive attachment prevents a soul from returning home and following its afterlife path. You can always reconnect to a friend who is gone. Invite and talk to them in your meditations and dreams; offer prayers and love.

Time and space manifest differently in the discarnate world. Your friends there can always hear you, and communicate. If you don't hear them, or they don't appear, it is not due to unavailability, but to your unfocused state of receptivity. Reaching proper openness, where you can perceive them, will allow communion. It is only your vibration and openness that facilitate hearing and seeing—because they are present always.

While in the spirit world, you receive much assistance from teachers, friends and ancestors. Life there is very structured. Much of it is celebration and communication in groups. Some is classroom instruction, and other elements involve individual homework in an academic setting.

Some souls remain in the discarnate world for a long time, and jump back into a new incarnation quickly. Time spent in the afterlife is a choice of the soul, and depends on its level of development and preferences.

Also, there is an advisory committee that offers counsel in which direction to move. After you finish the healing process and life review, you can incarnate again, or become a teacher or spirit guide.

When you enter a new incarnation, you invite spirit friends to serve as your guides. Here, down below, each of us has several—some are human spirits, and others could be alien. As you go through life lessons, those tasked with your assistance must possess various expertise and strengths, hence spirit guides join you and depart when tasks are completed.

CHAKRAS

For the incarnation, you choose the general theme, lessons and topics to explore. For the first chakra, these are survival, health, procreation, basic physical labor and activities. The first chakra is also the entrance of fundamental energies of the universe and of Earth: the primary chakra responsible for grounding you to physical reality.

The development of the second chakra involves mastering basic communication and social skills, trade, labor, housekeeping and money.

Themes of the third chakra are willpower, ego, domination, hierarchy, management, duty, devotion, honor, war, fight, struggle and passionate creativity.

Fourth-chakra lessons are love, trust, intuition, kindness, healing, allowance, harmony, living in the flow, emotions and intuitive creativity.

Fifth-chakra themes are high-level communications, languages, music, prayers, poetry, clairaudience (audio telepathy) and discourse with the spirit realm. Sixth-chakra activity includes mind-work, creative writing, mental intuition, and communicating via visual imagery with the spirit world.

The seventh chakra covers direct, or intuitive, converse with God, prayer, understanding and fulfilling your life mission, finding and walking life's path and becoming one of God's earthly agents—a lightworker.

Spirit guides and their lessons exist to advise and navigate you through life, ensure assignments are presented appropriate to your level of development and to assist your journey to wisdom. Their essential power lies in the manipulation of seemingly random processes. What appears random to you is under the complete control of your spirit guides. They can arrange "coincidences" (also known as synchronicities), thus ascertain proper counsel aligns with your current phase.

Some humans can talk to their spirit guides, and reap valuable knowledge. You can converse, and display gratitude, during meditation; for the guides are close, powerful friends on your life path.

As earlier mentioned, during your lessons some spirit guides may leave and new ones join. Keep in mind that most guides, some of who are human souls, are traveling from the past. Lacking modern experience, their opinions might differ from yours, although they can access spirit knowledge, magic, know your life plan and glimpse (with limitation) into the future.

Usually, the lesson plan for your life is called a "contract." This is not binding and can be renegotiated. The primary principle of reincarnation is free will. Therefore, the result of your lessons is not predetermined. As you progress, a higher than anticipated level of spiritual development might be achieved—earning you the right to advanced instruction previously out of reach. Hence, your contract may be modified to include new levels. You may develop an unexpected passion and garner allowance to pursue a fresh path.

Similar to a computer game, you start at the lower levels and rise—from the first chakra (survival), second (basic communication), third (will power), to the fourth chakra—love and beyond.

DIRECTION BY SPIRIT GUIDES

Your spirit guides use special tools to propel you through the lessons. When you have completed certain assignments and need a push to the next stage, they send subtle messages. For example, if you've recently ended an intimate (or platonic) relationship, the guides will send thoughts and emotions urging you to move on.

Similarly, they may even send seemingly random emails or links to web pages. You might reach for a book, lose your grip, and have it fall open to a page with text reading "move on!" If you turn a deaf ear to these subtle messages, a complete stranger might—unknowingly—be employed to provoke action on your part. Failing that, temporary illness might be induced. Finally, the darkest scenario could involve accident or trauma to wake awareness and inspire you to move on.

The spirit side is not above using manipulation and/or deception to further its agenda, which might "explain" the role of so-called tricksters in parapsychological lore. I imagine the spirit side to be similar to the stock exchange market, where people make deals, trade opportunities and favors. Guides and angels help each other move their subjects in appropriate directions—a complicated network of mutual assistance.

MESSAGES

When you find yourself struggling with commonplace obstacles, feel the old ways no longer serve you and that you're swimming upstream, you must question yourself: *Am I on the right path?* Why have familiar methods of doing things become so difficult? Is it time to give up and move on? Maybe you've recently graduated from the previous spiritual lesson, and are pushed by your guides toward new disciplines.

Not all messages, of course, come from spirit guides; nor does every blockage or pain. Learning to discern friendly spirits' signals from external (and internal) others is crucial. A way to calibrate intuition is by experimenting. You are daily bombarded with subtle messages. When this happens, take note and see what happens if you follow them—or don't. Determine how the messages feel and smell to you. Pay attention to seemingly random events: glitching and/or crashing of electronic devices, anomalous text messages or phone calls, spontaneous knowledge acquired after a book or magazine falls open, or during unsolicited conversation with strangers, or introductions to new people. True, some of these messages are trivial, while others are jewels.

You'll recognize messages from spirit guides because, if you follow them, everything turns out nicely. If you don't, events can go sour. Whether making big or small decisions, learn to meditate on them, speak to your guides and listen to your feelings. The spiritual suggestions can be subtle, so it takes practice to perceive them. For example, you may ask your guides whether a trip on a specific date is advisable, and sense their answer. Some people sense better with their mind; others favor the heart, or hands, and even stomach—the "gut instinct." These sensibilities are determined by habits and active chakras. Sensations can be interpreted as answers: Absolutely, Yes, All right, Doesn't matter, Better not, No, Absolutely not. As you practice intuitive communication with your spirit guides, you will learn to pose precise questions and receive answers.

Among your friends might be several graced with strong intuition. Ask them how they receive answers from spirit guides. A very good way to do this is through tarot cards—specially designed to prompt life advice. Purchase a deck and read the accompanying booklet; all you need to start. I recommend the Tarot Mucha [after art nouveau pioneer Alphonse Mucha—ed.], which is very light, optimistic and of high vibration. It is under USD $20 on Amazon.

As you develop your intuitive communication with spirit guides, you will learn to recognize subtle suggestions, avoid blockages and repetition compulsions on your path, and to move with the flow.

Along with elusive suggestions, apparently random messages, synchronicities, blockages, traumas and accidents, spirit guides may use pains to guide you along your path. These usually are reversible: as soon as you stop being stubborn and move in the right direction, the pain disappears.

To avoid extremes such as pain and accidents, I recommend listening to your guides in concert with professional or amateur psychics. Some individuals can talk to spirit guides and directly ask which path to pursue. I suggest regularly consulting psychics and channelers. This aids not only navigating your life but, even more, with your psychic guides and healers you can magically influence external circumstances and raise the level of your lessons.

While communicating with spirit guides, keep in mind they can give only general advice. Akin to school teachers, they're prohibited from providing complete solutions to your problems, because in order to effectively learn and retain knowledge, you personally must search for, find, and "live" the resolution. Guides can only urge you toward planned lessons and explain any specific problem you must face. They can show you a door, but self-discipline must be exercised to open it—on your own. So, the key to solving a problem begins with confronting it—seizing the opportunity to master the lesson.

As previously mentioned, what most matters isn't any specific decision, but that you recognized—and faced—the problem. Experienced the challenge of *having to decide*.

LESSONS

The difference between lessons in school and real-life challenges is that, in school, the problems have clear solutions: you can discern whether you've "correctly" solved a problem because the answer is pretty. In life, you are often placed in a Catch-22 situation, where seeming solutions cancel each other out, and you must not simply choose either good or bad, but between one bad and another—the proverbial "lesser of two evils."

Yet, as a rule, we are given lessons which serve our learning, even though the problems may remain unsolved. Even more, among possible problems, we, as physical individuals, usually choose those equivalent to our level. Problems too difficult to figure usually are beyond our comprehension. This is an example of the law of attraction: our vibration, through resonance, attracts us to challenges which correspond to our vibration.

TEKKRR (LYRAN) ON SPIRIT GUIDES

Channeled by Jim

Max: Can you speak more about spirit guides? How much are they involved in general? What's the ratio between things which are . . . events which are under their control and desire and random happenings?

Tekkrr: Your spirit guides are there to help you when you have needs. They help you when you call upon them. They do not necessarily help you with every situation, because they do not hear what you need necessarily. They know some things you need, and they will help you as much as possible. However, it is interesting that a lot of people do not even know they have spirit guides, and so they cannot help them as much. But the more you can speak to your spirit guides, the more you get to know them, the better they can help you.

Max: I have the opposite, very mystical perception for the whole life. Anything that happened to me I perceived as a message of God, spirit guides and angels.

Tekkrr: Yes, there are those outside your spirit guides that will help you as well . . . because you call upon them, pray to them, ask for their help. They are there when you need them. You call on your daughter, your son. There are those who help you. But when you get to know those people better, the better they can help.

Max: But my recent understanding was that many things are happening at random, and there is no one responsible for those in the spirit world, in higher worlds.

Tekkrr: But you can ask for help with those random things, as well. "Help me with the random daily life," and they can help with that.

Max: Yes, I got it. The question is, was I wrong interpreting everything that happens to me as positive or negative? Any event where the randomness was expressed, I was interpreting as a message. And now I kind of realize maybe it wasn't a message—maybe it was just random.

Tekkrr: Not everything is a message, not everything. You are correct.

Max: So what percent of the middle-sized events of my life are in the control of higher forces?

Tekkrr: The day you spoke of many broken things, your spirit guides had nothing to do with that; however, aliens did. But it had nothing to do with your spirit guides, and so that's what they told you. "It was not us."

151

Max: So my world view was very egocentric. Everything was around me, to guide me somewhere, and now I realise that maybe I'm creating those events and nobody else is guiding me. That it is kind of a random creation of my own outlook. Is it right?

Tekkrr: To some extent, not completely. There is spiritual activity all around. Everyone and yes, it is for you... but to be egocentric about it is not the purpose. You are in a community, a world and so some of these things that happen to you are not to be seen as just for you, but you are learning so you can help the world. You see, it goes out from you—not into you.

Max: Yes. Thank you. Negative events, like repetitive negative events . . . I go offer my help, it was turned down. I go to another place, offer my help, it was turned down. For the purpose, is there a higher guidance there? Or I just failed several times?

Tekkrr: There is higher guidance as well, because you'll find your perfect spot when you are ready for it and then that will be where you blossom and grow. They are holding you back for a reason which I cannot tell you at this moment, but there is a reason.

Max: I understand. So the ratio, at least in meaningful events, between random failures and higher guidance is what? One-to-one? Or is it always higher guidance?

Tekkrr: You have such a scientific mind. It does not make sense to think of it that way.

Max: Oh, where am I wrong?

Tekkrr: They help you when they need to, and when they have to; and you will fall into mind whenever this happens. Not in one-to-one ratio. It's not a ratio of any sort that we know of, because it happens as it happens. You see, the synchronicity of your world and the synchronicity of our world come together, but it's not in an algorithm that your mind can understand or any human mind actually. There is a mathematics to it, but not what you think.

Max: What is the best way to ask the guides to help us?

Tekkrr: Simply by being honest and open . . . truly yourself, your perfect self. And, in love, ask.

Max: But do we do it mentally, or do we speak it aloud?

Tekkrr: You can do it . . . there are some of you who must speak aloud because the density of your thoughts is too close, and they cannot be depicted separately from one another. So saying it aloud is the safest.

Max: What is the power of spirit guides? What can they do? For example, I'm driving and I feel . . . yesterday I was driving and I felt my tire kind of go flat and I prayed . . . can you kind of watch over me? Is it in their power to watch over us?

Tekkrr: Yes, they probably are the ones that gave you the inkling that it was something to pray about. They got a hold of your attention, and you got a hold of theirs, so in that case it was one on one, but not always.

Max: So it is in their capacity [yes] to control . . . But they can't see me, right?

Tekkrr: They can; they don't see you until you look in the mirror, but they see your inner parts. They can see as spirits would see.

Max: Chakras?

Tekkrr: Yes, they can see that.

Max: Now, they discovered very recently that I had chronic, a small chronic illness and apparently they didn't know about it until another friend, alien, told them. How is it possible that they see all the chakras? How can they not know about the illness?

Tekkrr: They do not look at that sometimes. They are more spiritually oriented, so they do see some things, but they are not understanding if they are not human. Some of them are not human, so they would not understand it as a flaw in your body; and some of them are human and would see it as just something that they've seen many times before and would not be concerned about . . . they are more concerned about your spiritual well-being; and they're more concerned about preserving you in the sense that you don't have major accidents or things of that nature. They can suggest things to you if they feel that your body is that far unable to function. They can suggest to you what to do about it.

Max: When I'm writing poetry, are they involved?

Tekkrr: If you involve them they are.

Max: Ohh . . . so I can write poetry without their help.

Tekkrr: You can write poetry without their help. And grant duplications. Yes, but they do help you.

Max: What about near-death experience . . .?

Tekkrr: Yes, they are those that will let you see things in your near-death experience. As you are heading for death, your spirit guides will help you along that channel, that path . . . till you are inside the gates of the spirit realm.

Max: Here is a much-related question: when I meditate I . . . for the last few months I kind of lost consciousness. I'm unconscious, and then at some point there is a click and I see the light coming. Where is that coming from? The light in my mind, is it my higher self? Are these spirit guides?

Tekkrr: It is probably your higher self, but for each individual can be someone else. For you, I believe it is your higher self and your subconscious.

Max: Wonderful. So when somebody enters or exits . . . there is a jolt . . . he kind of shifts and sometimes it's multiple jolts. Recently I discovered when I meditate I also get a jolt, and after that . . . usually is like a handle there, and then there is somebody . . . the light is entering.

Tekkrr: Yes, this is definitely a new channel opening. You are bringing in that particular light, higher self or perhaps a spiritual entity coming with higher self.

Max: Oh, wow! So when I exit, I'm happy there somewhere in another side, and then usually I'm in a hurry, so there's a time event, like somebody

154

is coming or buses are arriving and things like that. So somebody brings me, like pulls me down and I arrive to my body before the alarm rings, or the bus arrives, or somebody enters the room. Who is doing that?

Tekkrr: I cannot answer that. I do not know. What it may be—is part of your third-eye perception at this time.

Max: Oh, thank you very much. I really appreciate your assistance and insights.

LESSONS CORRESPOND TO CHAKRAS

As a rule, we are given lessons which serve our learning, even though the problems may remain unsolved. Even more, among possible problems, we as physical individuals usually choose those near our level of intelligence. The problems beyond our reach commonly are outside our comprehension. This is an example of the law of attraction: our vibration, through resonance, attracts us to challenges which correspond to our individual vibration.

This principle can often be seen in how our strong chakras correspond to the level of problems on which we choose to work. Your most active chakra determines how you see life. Put simply, if your first chakra is active you see life as a lesson in survival; second = communication; third = fight; fourth = love; fifth = poetry; sixth = research; seventh = service to God. There are, of course, more complex variations but the main idea is that your vibration/level of development defines your lessons simply because that's how you interpret external circumstances.

To better understand this principle, ask yourself what is your favorite color? The chakras generally correspond to colors: first = red; second = orange; third = yellow; fourth = green; fifth = blue; sixth = purple; seventh = violet. This is one of the clues to your most active chakra.

Another derives from your highest enthusiasm. What excites you? Common themes for first-chakra lessons are basic survival, food and reproduction,

155

health, physical labor, nature, nurture and workout.

Second chakra: communication, money, sales, Facebook, movies, TV, sex and hugging.

Third chakra: relationships, domination, subordination, hierarchy, management, fight, fight for freedom, competition, competitive sports, war, government service, duty and honor.

Fourth chakra: love, trust, compassion, kindness, feelings, intuition, energy healing, unity with people and nature, improvisation and expression of feelings in various arts.

Fifth chakra: work with sound, poetry, singing, channeling, communication with spirits, arts related to taste and smell, kissing, psychic work and healing via sound.

Sixth chakra: inspired research, science, engineering, mental work, psychic work via vision and understanding, psychoanalysis and inspired creative visual arts.

Seventh chakra: service and direct communication with God, embodiment of God's love on Earth via selfless service.

Not all people have a single dominant chakra. You may have two, three, or any number of active chakras and variable interests.

Exploring your highest excitement at this stage of life helps you identify what kind of lessons you're currently learning and—importantly—recognise where you're headed. You can easily see that present-day humanity is still stuck in the lessons of the lowest 3 chakras—survival, sales and war. You can now better understand the sacred meaning behind the idea that humanity is awakening to love and compassion, the guiding screed in the New Testament. The shift from third chakra—domination, war, fear, subordination and tribulations of the Old Testament—to the fourth—love, trust, compassion, kindness and unity of the New Testament.

You may reflect on your past, determine lessons completed, those you are presently learning and which are beckoning in the future.

Interestingly, when you are working on a certain level of lessons, the next usually seems like magic. The physical worker of the first chakra is fascinated by the sales profession. The second's art of communication strikes him/her as magic. This same person is fascinated too by the apparent glamour of competitive sports, heroism of war and honor of third-chakra soldiers. The manager of third-level chakra is inspired by ideas of unity, magic of intuition and miracles of healing under the fourth. The compassionate service people of fourth-level chakra—nurses, massage therapists, caregivers—are fascinated by sound-healing, music and prayers of the fifth. Further, fifth-level singers are fascinated by the sixth's inspired science, whose scientists are in turn awestruck by the seventh-level's direct connection to God.

Intriguingly the circle closes, and seventh chakra loops back to connect with first. Seventh's purple transitions to the red of first chakra. Correspondingly people of God usually are very close to nature, and live simple lives rich with sacred activities related to the earthly. Similarly, physical workers of the first chakra have a direct, unsophisticated connection to God.

Another thing to consider is that chakras are interacting with each other.

Their wave-like nature is similar to music's sonic signatures: chakras harmonize as notes in a chord. The trio 1-4-7 harmonises the idea of unity: first chakra is about unity with nature; fourth—unity with all sentient beings; seventh—with God. The colors of chakras 1-4-7 are red, green, violet. Resonance present in these allow for easy shifting from activities and lessons of one chakra, to another in this triad: from physical labor (1) to love and kindness (3), and to unity with God (7). And vice versa. In general, there is good resonance and agreement between chakras separated by 2: the above-mentioned trio 1-4-7, and duos: 2-5 (communication) and 3-6 (mind, structure, logic and rules).

Let me explain. There are several traditions by which chakras are translated to musical notes:

1. Root: C = red

2. Sacral: D = orange

3. Solar plexus: E = yellow

4. Heart: F = green

5. Throat: G = blue

6. Third eye: A = indigo

7. Crown: B = violet

From the musical analogy, you can deduce very interesting observations. Nearby notes and chakras, when activated simultaneously, cause dissonance: the focus on nature and survival (1, root) somewhat conflicts with the focus on communication, sales, TV and sex (2, sacral). The latter (2) conflicts with fight, domination and hierarchy (3, solar plexus). The latter (3) clashes with the focus on love, kindness, unity with humanity and intuition (4, heart). Less discordance is found in higher chakras: heart (4) and music/poetry: (5, throat) are in harmony. The latter (5) often can cooperate with mind (6). There is considerable dissonance between mind (6) and divine bliss (7)—a big challenge in meditation to silence the ever-chattering mind (6) and to shift into the vibration of divine light (7).

Notice that among the pairs of nearby musical notes (the seven primaries—white keys on the piano) is E and F, because they are not separated by a black key. The other pairs make a two-tone interval, but E-F a one-tone. That translates to the major disagreement between the fight theme of solar plexus (3) and peace theme of the heart (4). This is the major transition that humanity makes at this age: from fight to peace. Anatomically, the solar plexus (3) is separated from the heart (4) by a diaphragm, which corresponds to the veil between our reality and higher dimensions of the spirit world.

The old humanity struggles with the vibrations and lessons of the lower three chakras: survival, disease (1); TV, sales, uninspired communications, mass media, social networks (2); war, hierarchy, anger, fight, fear, suffering (3). Higher dimensions, aliens, spirits and God are invisible to old humanity because of the veil. To awaken to the higher dimensions, humans need to raise their (our) vibrations one by one, transcend the veil symbolized by the anatomical diaphragm and move into the heart (4) which is beyond the veil, and to the other higher chakras 5-6-7. This will transform war (3) into peace (4), competition (3) into cooperation (4), hate (3) into love (4), fight (3) into service (4), uninspired chat (2) into poetry (5), fear-based thinking (3) into inspirational creativity and visionary insight (6), fear-based religion (3) into sacred divine spirituality (7).

Too, you may notice that odd-numbered chakras—1-3-5-7—have a more masculine quality with aspects of labor and giving.

Even-numbered chakras 2-4-6 lean toward the feminine: receiving, accepting, analyzing and watching. These chakras also cover sex, love and provocative beauty.

There also exists vital resonance between pairs separated by one or more chakras.

Chakras 1 and 3 have a common trait of active labor and physicality. Both are about force. In first-chakra activity this is simple labor, but these workers lack courage, sense of duty and self-sacrifice. When they earn that, they rise to third-chakra vibration.

Progressing to elevated vibration is not easy. It takes time, effort and learning strengthening the spirit to handle higher vibration. If the spirit has not grown, the individual is excessively strained by higher vibrational activities. A physical worker of first-level chakra cannot be simply appointed as a manager, ruler, soldier or officer (3rd chakra). He must cultivate skills and spiritual qualities for the strength, wisdom and protection commensurate with such challenging jobs.

Another interesting resonation and synergy is 4-6: heart-mind connection, green-indigo, F-A musical notes. Presently many people have a blocked heart chakra, due to trauma induced by contemporary upbringing and life. Intellect dominates the heart-mind balance. It is very important to have symmetry of heart and mind. Heart intelligence is beyond the veil, and very wise. Bereft of heart, mind flattens life into an arid chaos driven by ego, fear and anger. Reconnecting to heart intelligence restores the mind, balanced by spiritual guidance and healthy ego.

The main work toward retrieving heart intelligence includes receiving and giving Reiki energy-healing, development of empathy, positive attitude, meditation, prayer, dance, yoga, healing childhood and adult traumas via reminiscence, retrospective forgiveness and emotional work. Very helpful for reconnecting with the heart is creative writing and autobiography, emotional painting and dancing—all busy the hands, in turn driven by the heart chakra and inspirational element of the mind.

Next important resonance is 5-7 between throat and crown, sound and divine, blue and purple, musical notes G and B. This resonance is best expressed via chanting, affirmations, prayer and poetry using sound to reach divinity.

There is also resonation between 2 and 5, sacral (2) and throat (5) chakras, orange and blue, notes D and G. This covers communication involving both chakras. Unfortunately, the greater part of humanity remains in the early stages of spiritual development, chooses not to advance, and still is learning lessons associated with the first two chakras. Physical laborers (1) are beginning to learn communication (2). Television and Twitter are of great assistance to them. The meaningless chat of television, conversations and commercials belongs to second-chakra vibration.

Yet, it is possible to shift to a spiritually meaningful communication of the fifth chakra. These higher-level exchanges include spiritually inspired music, movies, art and person-to-person dialogue. Many are able to determine high spiritual vibration from low. Each individual chooses the sound corresponding to their vibration, thus some might nullify poetry and classical music—switch to something easy with low-grade humor or vapid soap opera drama. Incidentally, cursing is usually of low vibration: first, second, and even lesser chakras.

Observe the language and vibration of your communication with others and yourself. Be attentive while shifting up and down, making a deliberate effort of upping your communications while staying true to yourself. Of course, it doesn't make sense to sing opera instead of cursing, but boosting moods is usually a great idea. Cursing can even be healing, since first chakra is also responsible for health. More often, though, the tone of true kindness is most uplifting. Be harmonious; bring harmony to others.

If you find that draining, keep in mind that you are not responsible for the happiness and emotional shades of others. Only they can choose which vibration to occupy; you can offer examples of your high vibration, sharing light and commitment to selfless service.

Pay special attention to the art of equanimity—keeping your composure no matter what. It requires vigilance and restraint to keep your cool at all times, but serves you and others in maintaining a high general vibration. Learn to heal, if you can, your negative emotions without spilling them onto others. Equanimity is one of the most exact measures of spiritual development. If you are nice to strangers but explosive with your mother or child—even a parking officer—that is not good enough.

Another resonance exists between chakras 3 and 6, solar plexus, will power, hierarchy (3) and mind (6). Understand that, for many, graduation into the third chakra is an achievement. Humankind's primary historical triumph was development of will, responsibility and duty. Third chakra is that of a manager and warrior. People with this chakra think fast, are grounded, and make fewer routine mistakes—required of warriors and managers alike. Their talent is to submit others to their will. They can be decent leaders, but to become true champions must cultivate visionary qualities, which are in the sixth chakra. This demands up-shifting vibration by three levels. Warriors attempt this with will-power, but the sixth chakra is not about heat—but cool, inspirational thought and vision. Hence art and spiritual growth are demanded in order to develop sixth-chakra vision.

It is inarguably challenging to shift from anger, fear and a competitive mindset (3) to motivational thinking, harmony, vision and unity. This can be achieved through consistent development and harmonization of all higher chakras: heart (4), throat (5), third eye (6) and crown (7).

BUDDHA ON CHAKRAS

Channeled by Jim

161

Rowie: Buddha, it is a great honor to have an Ascended Master with us. I would like to ask a question: As humans, we look at the sometimes linear aspects of our chakras. Can we connect chakra to chakra, or does it have to be in a linear fashion?

Buddha: No, the chakras are not linear in any way really, they are orbs, circular. They are not flat and linear. You can connect your chakras in any way you like in many senses, and you can connect them to others, but you are not at that point yet, you are not advanced enough to know how to do that. But it is the heart chakra that I want you to connect first. But yes, you have a linear thought pattern about many things, and many things are not linear. Time is not linear. I do not know how to explain it any better than that. Do you understand?

Rowie: Yes, I understand. Would colors help with the linking of the chakras? This is what occurs to me.

Buddha: Yes. Each chakra has its own color for a reason. And that reason is to show you how healthy that chakra is. So, if you have pink instead of red in your root chakra, you need to bring more color into it. And how do you do that?

You can look at colors. You can bring colors into you. It is amazing how easy it is to energize a chakra by looking at colors and thinking positive thoughts.

Rowie: Namaste, Buddha. Thank you!

Buddha: You are welcome. I wish I could have explained it a little better. There is more depth to it than that, but the colors come to you in nuances, and that's what I was trying to explain. The deeper the red, the greater the strength, the deeper the blue, the greater the strength. And if you are green, this would be mild.

BUDDHA ON HEART CHAKRA

Channeled by Jim

This was one of many Hucolo group sessions, streamed live and open to the public. Usual Hucolo members were present. Buddha, channeled by Jim, gave us a series of talks covering chakras. This session—from the series' mid-point—explores the heart chakra.

Buddha: Today I want to speak about the heart, which is the most powerful and important of the chakras in third dimension. You realize that many things come from the heart. Telepathy starts from the heart. When I was just a child and learning about the chakras, when we got to the heart I had not a problem, because I was born of the heart and that was what I had chosen to become. That was my destiny of the heart, and behind every chakra is the answer to all your questions, because you bring your lives with you behind each of your chakras, and the heart is the recorder of them all. Not every chakra contains information about every life, but the heart does. It has a presence in every life, and accompanies you always. That is why you are able to come back with love. Even as an amoeba started millions and millions, even billions of years ago, there was a central location within, and that was the heart. The memory of that amoeba comes with you a billion years and changes you. Every life gives you a slight change, but it is still the original life.

Max: Yes, thank you, yes.

Buddha: All right. Also the heart pulls the chakras together. It is like the magnet, pulls down from the sky, up from the earth. It is so strong, it pulls, it is the magnet that pulls things up and pulls things down to keep you balanced so you can move forward. Without that balance of the heart in the center, there would be no balance within the chakras at all, and you would be gone from one thought to the other without wholly connecting. If you would realize that every thought is connected to the heart, in the sense that it comes from a central location in your being, not entirely the mind, there to intellectualize, yes, but the heart is there to bring it all together in an emotional pattern that equalizes through body and mind. Is this making you aware of something?

163

Max: Yes, thank you, yes.

Buddha: Yes, so the heart connected centrally through the body in its energy patterns is actually the control area for the body, even for the mind, because without the heart then we have just the darkness.

Do you understand this?

Because the other—the spirit—the third eye, the communication, the solar plexus, the sacral, the root are all connected so that they can be energized by the heart, or else take a dark turn.

And you do not want a dark turn. It is not that you would not be alive without the energy of the heart or the chakras; there would be some soul. But they are put there for reasons: of balance, understanding, connection within the community of the universe and the world you live in.

Are there any questions before I go on? I sense there is a little confusion out there.

John: When I meditate, I feel warm at heart. Why do I have this feeling?

Buddha: Yes, there is warmth and heat in truth, in the center of the heart. When you are feeling this during meditation it is much about healing yourself, your emotions, those things within you that need balance or understanding. And so, when you do a meditation and you feel heat in your heart, let it burn out those things, things that are not supposed to be there.

As human beings we have many emotions, and subconsciously we have many emotions as well. If we let the heat of the spirit of meditation burn out those things that are not supposed to be there, it purifies all the processes of connection within the chakras and without, within the mind, soul, spirit, and body. And that is why the heart is central, it is the love station. The center of those things that are spirit. This is how you were born, spirit within flesh and the heart is the secret reaching to that spirit.

John: Yes, thank you so much.

Max: I wanted to ask about the blockage of the heart chakra. It looks like our Western education intentionally blocks our heart chakra towards

164

disbalance, head over heart. So, how about restoring the balance of head and heart, synchrony and communication between them?

Buddha: Yes, when you intend your meditation, what happens? Does it go to your head? No, it expands out from the heart. When you meditate, it may not feel that way, but it always starts in the heart. It does not start in the brain, because you are letting the brain go. Do you understand? You are letting the brain feel free of itself, you are letting the body go, you are letting the emotions go. But the love, the meditation is intended always starts in love and therefore to get through the blockage, you have to intend it to break through, because, yes, modern society as I see it does like to partition the heart. They would feel vulnerable. But vulnerability is the only way to get through everything in the heart. You must be vulnerable and accept that it is going to maybe even hurt a little to find those things that are in the heart, and purify it

Now, so many things in the heart . . . there are so many things about the heart chakra that you must know. I know that you know it is the center; I know that you know it now controls things, but did you know that you could change the control in your bodies through the heart chakra to help energize the other chakras? And I do not just mean saying that the heart chakra can be energized or energize others. No, if there is a problem, if there is an imbalance and you are aware of your body part that needs healing, there is a chakra for that and the heart can help heal your body. The heart chakra is amazing, because it can heal, be telepathic, and actually a controller of the intellect. So, your heart chakra, centralized as it is and with all the information that you have and read about the heart chakra, you do not even realize how strong the energy here is, because if you let the heart chakra die you have no control over your experiences. No control over your future. Let the heart chakra beam for you, intend that it be the strongest element, so that your eyes, third eye, and spirit are opened to a third, fourth, and fifth-chakra event.

Now, I think I am speaking over your heads.

Max: I think it sounds great.

Buddha: Are there any more questions, before I go further? Please ask. If you do, it is not a foolish question if it helps you to learn.

Max: The beat of the heart and the magical blood. The beat of the heart energizes all the organs, all other chakras, and kind of gives the beat to the body. And the chakra—is it connected to the heart somehow? Is the heart chakra center of the heart, or is it shifted a little bit? Does it also give the beat to all other chakras through non-physical things, non-physical means?

Buddha: Yes, that is a good question, because I can tell you this: if you are having heart problems, physical heart problems, you must go to your heart chakra; there may be a problem there. There may be a problem in your generations of hearts. Find out what has happened in those past chakras of hearts, and you may strengthen this human physical heart, you may strengthen your physical areas by going to the right chakra and then concentrating on the heart.

Does this make sense to you? The solar plexus and the sacral, if there is . . . and the root even . . . if there is problems in the organs, if there is problems in sexuality or creativity, you can concentrate on those chakras that are connected to those parts of the body and also your reflexology. If someone does reflexology: Concentrate on the heart, and they are doing this with you, so that all is brought together in a central way and the power is suppressed in the right area of the body. The heart is strong, the heart is vital, you may see it as the beginning of telepathy, oh yes, and that moves to different places as telepathy becomes stronger and your chakras will be able to connect with another.

The heart will be the first connection, of course, and it will become part of your sexuality, your love, part of who you are as an advanced being, because you will be able to connect in a way that you never connected in the heart. Know the emotions, thoughts and understandings of what the heart really means in a personal relationship. At this time you are not connected by the heart in many ways, but you are in some ways, as you begin your telepathic rise. Your hearts will start to connect. That web around the world of light and understanding will grow stronger, when the heart is the strongest within you, the heart chakra is also strongest. This will mean less illness. When you discover that the heart can control many of the facets of your health, you understand that it is also helping others. When you connect

166

heart to heart you help each other's hearts as well as the physiology.

So this is part of your enlightenment, part of your move forward. This has not been revealed to you yet, and it is advanced thought, but you are the first to hear it, that this can be where healing begins in your lives and in the lives of others. Do not doubt it, do not doubt it, do not doubt it, because it is essential that the energy of the heart be released as you have been taught. The spirit rises up and becomes at the end of the flesh, and you have peace. When it moves out that is enlightenment. But it will be more than that in the future as your telepathy grows. As your telepathy expands it will also be enlightenment and healing for others. You will carry the healing of yourself, and with that heal others.

Now, there are times when we must let go of our spirit, because it must go to the next dimension. This world is done, this heart is finished with its purpose in this world. So you must know, when this happens, that the chakras will unwind. They may unwind from the top or they may unwind from the bottom, but you can help yourself pass to the next world more gently by unwinding them yourself, when the time comes. You will know when the time is and it will be a time of peace and great thought and great recollection of this past world. All the thoughts of remembrance that will come to you will bring through your chakras, and be there for the next life. I am only telling you this because it happens anyway without your attention. But, to be aware of it is something great.

Max: Does unwinding create strings? Are chakras made of strings which record the life experience?

Buddha: They are made of waves of energy. You can unwind them by going counterclockwise in your world, but do not do that now. Wind up clockwise and make it even more powerful, as powerful as you need it to be, to be totally balanced in a good frame of mind. Now, surely as human beings, there will be times, when you are discouraged or feel other things, other than joy and positivity and enlightenment, but to acknowledge that, that is a learning time. Acknowledging it as a positive thing brings you to a new phase of understanding. You must understand that everything negative that happens to you has a positive outcome, if you would let it. So, let it be positive, then whenever you have that negativity within you stirring up, you

167

thank spirit or whoever you feel deserves thanks.

That is important, to be true to yourself in the thinking of your higher guides, your spirit guides, Mother Earth, Gaia, Universe, God, the golden strings. It's awareness that these are the lessons life has brought to you, and thank God for them and that will energize the heart chakra automatically. You can hold your heart chakra and give thanks for those things that are negative, what you see as negative. And turn them positive, because they are learning experiences, even if you were to stub your toe, you can learn from it. You understand?

Max: Yes, Yes!

Buddha: This is a great knowledge. Please be aware of it. The next time I come, I will speak to you about communication and the throat chakra. But heart chakra, I could speak many, many hours about, because there are many things that are undiscovered within yourselves that are all connected to the center, the heart. Most of you know already that this information will help you. It will help you, it will help you. Do not let it pass lightly, for I will not speak it again, although this is being recorded, I believe. You may hear it again, but not directly from me.

Max: I have another question. Is it an appropriate time to ask?

Buddha: Ask!

Max: I am analyzing my anger. It's connected to pain in my heart.

Buddha: Yes.

Max: I feel vulnerable and it causes pain in the heart. I feel vulnerable because I am striving to achieve something, and then I get pain and it stops me, and I'm trying to protect myself by disconnecting from things. What would be your advice?

Buddha: Let go of the pride, accept everything as it is. There are many things in you and in everybody, that we want to keep in ourselves, that we want to say: this is how I am, that is what I am—therefore, that these are things I do not want to give up, because if I give this up, it will show weakness, it will show that I am vulnerable. It will show that I therefore keep the pain there, because there is something that you do not want to give up. There are parts that you hold on to because it would be embarrassing, or a negative emotion, for you to experience. However, you find when you release those negative and proud emotions, they will lighten you. You will be filled with something that wants you to express to others to do the same, because you will have a freedom beyond that which you have now. Freedom to understand others the way you do not now, because you are holding on, you are keeping partition, you are hiding these feelings and thoughts and emotions.

The heart does not want to hide; the heart wants to express. It is hard for some people to express, and that will come with the throat chakra as well, but first the heart has to be open, has to be cleared and understood as pure. Now you may say: How can a heart be pure in this world? But it can be. The heart can be purified, surely you have to do that more than once in your life, because things attach, things happen, you gather things into your heart, into your different chakras, into your body, into your mind. Surely you understand that every now and then you change the filter, because it collects things that don't need to be there. And those emotions, pride and jealousy and things of that nature need to go. They have no room in the growth. You may still grow and have them, but you are not growing as fast as you could. They hold you back, and those lives that you held many years ago and continue to hold on to, because they have never been righted. You must say them out loud, you must burn them in your heart with that truth, burn them in the heart, because the lives that you have told, that have consequences, have consequences for you.

And I do not want to leave on a sad note, because those things that you have burned out already which I have seen much purification among you, much love being generated among you, many tears shed, because of love and because of guidance by each other and the heart reaching out and touching each other.

You felt it already, but it can be even stronger, when you release these darknesses, these things that don't belong, and many humans cannot do it. It is too strong, too embarrassing, too hard, but let me tell you: Call on

169

spirit to help, call anyone by name that you know can help to burn this away, for with that in there it causes disease, anger; causes you to be imbalanced, not necessarily in the heart, but it causes imbalances in the body, in the actual physiology, in the chemical resonances. How it all works together it hurts in some way, unconditionally hurts in some way.

Therefore let love burn in your heart. Feel that burn. Feel your excitement. Your highest excitement as it is labeled comes from the heart as well.

Are there any questions now?

Rowie: Buddha, it is a great honor to have an ascended master with us. I would like to ask a question: As humans we look at the sometimes linear aspects of our chakras. Can we connect any chakra to any chakra, or does it have to be in a linear fashion?

Buddha: No, the chakras are not linear in any way really. They are orbs; they are circular, not flat and linear. You can connect your chakras in any way you like in many senses and you can connect them to others, but you are not at that point yet, you are not advanced enough to know how to do that. But it is the heart chakra that I want you to connect first. But yes, you have a linear thought pattern about many things, and many things are not linear—time is not. I do not know how to explain it any better than that. Do you understand?

Rowie: Yes, I understand. Would colors help with the linking of the chakras? This is what occurs to me.

Buddha: Yes. Each chakra has its own color for a reason. And that reason is to show you how healthy that chakra is. So, if you have pink instead of red in your root chakra, you need to bring more color into it. How do you do that?

You can look at colors. You can bring colors into you. It is amazing how easy it is to energize a chakra by looking at colors and thinking positive thoughts. Do you understand that?

Rowie: Perfectly! Namaste, Buddha, thank you!

Buddha: You are welcome. I wish I could have explained it a little better, there is more depth to it than that, but the colors come to you in depths of nuance, and that's what I was trying to explain. The deeper the red, the greater the strength, the deeper the blue, the greater the strength and if you are green this would be mild.

Sara: I have a question: How can we connect to our heart? It is a little challenging to meditate. Is there another way of doing it?

Buddha: Yes, there are many ways to get through the heart chakra. When you cannot meditate, you give thanks—thanks to all the things that have been good to you, for all those things that have been harsh. You thank for the fact that you cannot meditate, because there is a lesson there: there will come a time, after a while, when you will find yourself moving into your heart in a different way, and perhaps you are trying to intellectualize your heart. Let your heart be as it is. Grasp it, hold it and love it and feel energy coming from it. Now, you don't feel any energy. That's fine, because there is energy coming from it still.

Do you understand? The way to get to the heart is through the spirit, and the way to get to the spirit is through thankfulness and understanding that joy comes with learning lessons. Joy comes with giving thanks to all things.

Sara: Thank you.

Buddha: You are welcome. And if this does not work at first, do not give up.

Sara: Is it necessary to be able to meditate?

Buddha: It is not necessary to be able to meditate; it is helpful, however, to be able to. Some people cannot meditate. They do not understand the concept of it, nor what it does, and therefore they can bring in that information in other ways through the heart. The heart understands the reason for meditation, and the heart understands why you do not comprehend its presence. Therefore, just go about your business, thanking and loving, and then when it hits you, when that mind thought hits you that it is time to meditate, because meditation will come to your mind, this will be your time, because you will then understand the meaning of it and how to move your heart with meditation, how to expand, I should say, with meditation.

Sara: All right, thank you.

Buddha: You are welcome.

Sabrina: What is the best way to help someone whose heart is in emotional pain? Can you answer that?

Buddha: You are helping them get through their pain by feeling their pain with them. Do you understand this? You are pulling that pain out of their heart, and sharing it with yourself, and you, having a healthier heart can get rid of that pain and therefore your connection with their heart will help them. Now: I understand that it takes time to pull all that pain out, because they believe the mind controls it. They are not thinking that the heart controls the pain. So you must control their pain with your heart.

Sabrina: Yes. So what is the way to get the pain out of the heart, whatever its cause?

Buddha: When you have the pain in your heart from someone else, then that is when you meditate and intend the pain to go away, and intend for this meditation—those of you who meditate—intend for the pain to go and for them to understand how to let go of the pain, because we give these messages to each other through prayer and through telepathy, and we do not even know. We are so attached to the feeling of individuality, we are so attached to the very thought of being just who we are, that we do not realize all selves can help others simply with the intent itself.

This is part of your telepathy, of your understanding of what a higher being can be, because you all will come to be higher beings at some time. But try it in your earthly body. You may not be successful; you may not be able to do it yet, but it will happen with the human race that you will be able to do the things only you dream possible. If you dream it to be possible, it is possible, because you cannot dream something that cannot be.

Max: Yes, yes, thank you!

Mary: Hello, Master Buddha. This is Mary.

Buddha: Hello, Mary!

Mary: Do you meditate, and if you do, do you meditate by yourself or with groups of people? And what is your intention when you meditate?

Buddha: My most high intention is the healing of Mother Earth, and the healing of those that live upon her, because there is much, much darkness there. Even with the rising of many spirits and many vibrations there is so much darkness, and I pray for the rising and darkness to be overcome. But yes, I do meditate alone and I do meditate in groups, because when you meditate alone you are bringing the energy to yourself and sending the energy out to those who need it, and when you meditate in a group you connect with them and become a community of meditation, and that is very strong. Very strong indeed, especially with spiritual beings becoming a great light for those [missing end of sentence, distortion] . . . Did you get that?

Mary: Yes, I got it. Thank you. Thank you so much, Buddha, much love to you!

Buddha: Much love to you as well. I must go now, unless there are more questions.

Max: There is a belief that the heart has its own mind and its own consciousness. So I wonder, what is this mind, how is it connected to our subconscious, how is it connected to our higher self, what is the mind of the heart?

Buddha: The mind of the heart is to give the individual those things that it wants, that it is most helpful to accept. The mind of the heart knows the body, knows the mind and knows the spirit, and therefore works to filter, connect and purify the body, mind and spirit.

Max: Yes, yes, basically yes. That's its function and does it in a smart way.

Buddha: Yes, and it is to give you the power to understand the mind, body and spirit. Not only does it help to control it and make it feel better or worse, as some people intend themselves to be, but it also creates its own

173

reality with the mind, body and spirit.

Max: Yes, thank you very much. It is so much joy, so much learning to be with you and learn from you.

Buddha: Thank you. I could speak about the heart for many time-zones [or whatever . . . but I don't think that is correct]. But it's good to speak to you. I hope that you understood.

Max: Yes, yes, it was very enlightening and very clear. Thank you very much. Much appreciation.

Buddha: Namaste, and much love, and I feel your hearts, I do feel that your hearts are good and that your hearts are wanting to express what I was speaking of. But make sure you purify them so that you can connect even better to those things that are you, and to come to you. The law of attraction, as you call it, comes with a pure heart. Do you understand that? It does come even when the heart is not pure, but it is limited by those blemishes, those things in the heart that are held there, that are not supposed to be, and if you get rid of them the law of attraction will be everything you wanted to be. It is very hard to keep the heart pure continuously, and it cannot be done on Earth. It cannot be done, but you can revisit it every week, every day, every time you want. And if you can't purify yet, you will be able to.

I must go now.

Max: Thank you.

Buddha: Namaste. And much love!

The group: Namaste, much love.

HIGHER SELF

In addition to spirit guides, you may receive advice from your Higher Self. Your Higher Self is quite different from the spirit guides, who essentially are your friends, although sometimes give you a lot of trouble. The Higher Self is *you*. It can be defined as the future, wiser you or an aspect personality.

While you are playing the field and unwitting of the future, your Higher Self knows the game plan. Often, the Higher Self is your future incarnation, the finest version who shares much of your personality. Yet, since each incarnation has a unique experience, you are subtly different from your other "instances." Your Higher Self includes "you" and all other iterations, past and future.

Infrequently you might be connected to more than a single Higher Self— one after another. In this case, your first Higher Self serves through the early years, when another Higher Self moves in and takes charge. That may happen if you have reached a certain level of spiritual development, earned new lessons and work assignments which require additional expertise. However, both of your Higher Selves comprise part of your identity, vibration, and unique branch-length in the Tree of Life. These two would be related.

It is instructive to visualize the Tree of Life—Yggdrasil in Norse mythology—as hewn from light, souls shiny berries adorning branches. Your past, present and future life would be perched on the same little limb. The image for past and future periods would be "beads on a string," or spheres with a common core. Like concentric circles, past incarnations are embedded in future ones. The largest sphere would represent the Higher Self.

Some people are in constant communication with their Higher Self. It is beneficial to speak to it as frequently as you would speak to God: it is the personality most vested in your progress, and intimately related to you. It *is* you—a kinder, brighter, stronger and wiser version.

When you are creative and feel inspired, energy and happiness surge, peaking at the vibrational level of your Higher Self—you receive expansive bliss. In converse, when you feel disconnected and lost, it is likely your connection to the Higher Self has been severed. A universal tool for reconnecting is meditation.

TIME

You have likely heard many times: Time is now, time is an illusion, time doesn't exist. But what does this mean? As an imaginary exercise, visualize arriving late to an airplane, job interview or date. You would quickly realize time, although illusionary, is very powerful. Time is an illusion because reality is too.

The physical reality in which you live, where you read this book, is a collective dream. Realize also that time and duration are the very basis of this illusion. Physicists—correction, quantum physicists—refer to "our" reality as the space-time continuum, because time, space and energy can be converted to each other, at least on the level of elementary particles under extreme conditions. Quantum physics, at least on the primitive level, reached an understanding that this reality is essentially an illusion; that matter is made of energy. One hundred years ago, while pondering the speed of light, Einstein realized that time—seeming so stable on Earth—would under extreme conditions flow differently. In his visionary experiments, he concluded that a spacecraft traveling near light-speed (186,000 miles per second) would experience time dilation: the crews' clocks would slow down. From their perspective, time on Earth would quicken.

For about a hundred years we've known time is an illusion, but a very persistent illusion absolutely necessary for life on Earth. Time is one of the fundaments of existence. You already know the conventional understanding that life is based on several fundamental elements: earth, water, air, and fire—greatly respected in alchemical, metaphysical and shamanic traditions.

Time is as important, or even more so, than these elements. Essential for the biological father, heartbeat, blood flow, respiration, brain processes . . . all movement unfolds through time. The illusion of time comprises all others: birth, life, childhood, growth, maturation, love, marriage, work, health, decline, aging and death. The whole illusion of physical life experience is based on the illusion of time. Imagine yourself a creator designing a planet, a human race, wild green nature. Imagine too trying to invest the life on this planet with beauty and intelligence. You would utilize time and desire, because this is the totality of what you know.

You might improve the society; make the life more beautiful, see less of suffering. You might even build a paradise allowing the people to live forever, but you would require time to construct this grand illusion.

Time on earth flows in one direction. You wake in the morning, go through the day, and sleep. God forbid, if you didn't sleep you'll feel pretty bad next morning, next day. In the fourth density, time seems to be less solid, less deterministic and more fluid. It looks like the aliens exist under less pressure of time. They can stretch, squeeze it even without technology. Some of them are able to naturally shift from day to evening or to morning; exist in several zones simultaneously. some can speed growth, or delay and create pockets in time. So, the surround of life progresses, and they have as much time as they need.

It is even possible that in the fourth entity, time could be multidimensional. Time travel, not only back and forth, but right, left, up and down. It is hard to understand but the experience might be comparable to reading several books at once, or monitoring several tabs on an internet browser, or watching multiple movies in one sitting. This could prove distracting, but it seems that, in the fourth entity, the beings are talented multitaskers enjoying richer experiences by working simultaneous timelines.

Presently, humanity already started experiencing several qualities of the fourth entity. Many people develop psychic ability; some the beginnings of telepathy, and people started noticing that the time flow is not as smooth and constant anymore. Recently, a Mandela effect was discovered: we meet people who remember that past very radically, or very different. It looks like several timelines converging, and people with various histories came to the same reality and play now on the same field.

The name of this effect was coined when people attending the same conference discovered that some of them remembered—were absolutely sure—that Nelson Mandela was alive. Some were absolutely sure he'd died long ago. So it was hypothesized that those who came to this gathering did so from differing timelines, and affected external events. It has also been noticed that as we live, our past is changing. Sometimes this change is subtle; others radical. For example, Russia has many times rewritten its history.

Before 1970, Russia believed in one history. After the communist revolution, history was rewritten. Old books removed, and new history created. Everyone read, and studied this. So, after 70 years of Soviet regime, the whole country was pretty much believing the altered history. Then the Soviet Union fell, and yet another new history has been discovered. Now there exist groups who believe in various historical scenarios. Once you accept that we live in a collective dream, it's easy to realize that the past in this collective dream is also an illusion. A very elaborate ruse, but since it is a collective dream it is subject to change. As you live your life, realize that you create your past from your present. In your journey, learn that you change a little in time, and sometimes you change a lot because of new awakenings, ambitions, and fresh perspectives. Exploring your new past from a novel angle, it starts to change.

Maybe if you can remember your past, the past of abuse and suffering, you wake and choose a positive outlook—comprehend your past as a turmoiled period of learning. You'll develop a new tool added to your past, and gratitude for the lessons you received. Your choice, the choice of your soul to come into this life and choose the plan for these lessons, was beautiful. As beautiful as the present. You can choose too a beautiful future.

Some people are very talented in handling time. Others are often late, miss appointments, and their relationship with time is completely troublesome. Learning skills on working with time might be helpful to you. Remember: although time is an illusion, it's a very powerful illusion . . . basis of this collective dream.

Once I worked in a small company, and my sole qualification was being very good with handling time. I assisted management with planning. Worked with a calendar and kept track. My presence helped others in the company to synergize, so their efforts didn't go against each other—which is very rare not only for a small company, but for *any* company.

Look at your own life. You might have conflicting interests and activities; constantly running out of time, sacrificing certain events in favor of others.

Imagine how wonderful it would be if everything you have done, everything you would be doing would be synergized, all your activities would help each other. So, this is the art of working with time. Same relates to your health. Remember that most illness results from poor timing. Basically, the illness is when your body has trouble, when some systems have trouble synchronizing to physical reality.

The very word *disorder* means that the processes get out of order, lose proper sequence, they're *not orderly*. Something is too much or too little. Say most of the disorders result from improper timing. Different by-chemical processes in the body become too weak or too strong and that causes the disorder: problems with the heart, mind, thyroid, hormones, immune system and so on. In essence, what energy healers do is harmonize these processes and reorder timing. Disorder is a loss of coherence between the proper processes where the waves do not cohere, do not coordinate. Health is harmony when the waves are coordinated, synergized. Waves exist in time, so it all comes to harmonizing their behavior.

The first step in time-work is to acknowledge the existence of time. Be thankful, for this is the basis of life and beauty. Offer your respect and love to the timekeeping elementals—wise and powerful spiritual beings who take charge of time and duration. They help you to endure the experience of life's illusion. Next, realize that time is a collective creation. We are in a collective dream and each of us creates time as we go along. Offer your love and respect to the illusion of life and to the beauty of the planet. Realize that you are a co-creator of this beauty, of this life.

Your soul, with the help of billions of others, the elementals, angels, planet, sun, stars and galaxy, all collectively run a sophisticated program called life in the universe, but your soul is running your own program and co-creating, recreating the universe and the physical life within. This is the nature of the matrix. Choose to appreciate the matrix, offer it your respect and love. It is the ultimate choice.

If you want to live a good life, it is only logical, makes a lot of sense and is necessary to respect and love the fabric of the matrix. Reality has a quantum nature; we are shifting through static pictures at a rate exceeding one billion frames per second, and your soul has created the movie of your life within

179

itself. It is your soul which creates time in your own reality simulation, in your own matrix.

Your physical focus of attention plays a very significant role in the creation of this time. Your primary creation is that of the Now; the current moment; the past and future are created from Now. For most of you, it would be a very unusual way to look at reality, and it takes time to figure how time works, pun intended. So, take your time with experimenting with time creation . . . and to observe closely how you create your own reality.

Notice how the focus of your attention affects the time flow in your reality. That the focus of your attention is very rarely in the present and very often either in the future or in the past. Experiment with shifting the focus of your attention back and forth, future to past, past to present, and from the future to the present. See how your reality is affected by shifting your attention. Realize that time flows differently, depending where you focus your intentionality.

Notice also that somehow you often lose track of time, sometimes minutes, tens of minutes, even hours. When you hurry, it helps to be present and in the moment. Time slows. Focused on the unknown future, time speeds up.

So, here is a practical meaning of the idea: time is now. That means that if you focus your attention on the present, it helps you to harmonize the creation of your reality in your soul and it helps you to manifest things. Notice that when you lose something, or things go right. It is usually because you lost the connection with reality. You get tired, you disconnect from time, disconnect from events and fail to create a good reality. Take heed that you create a much better reality, manifest things much easier, when rested and in harmony and health.

So, play with the shifted focus of your attention; harmonize your relationship with time. Notice wonderful, peak moments. Be vigilant in attending to your health, state and the symmetry of your mind's processes. Remembering this harmony assists you in its retrieval.

NEEM KAROLI BABA (MAHARAJ-JI)

Channeled by Jim

Neem Karoli Baba: When you start this journey, you are a blank page. The world writes a story on you. And the words sink into your body, mind and spirit. Part of you understands this story is true, but your truth or someone else's? That is what you must decide moving through the energies surging among this level of consciousness.

You will find truth and shadow combine to make something very different than what the truth should be. So now, as you enter this place through many, many of these contortions of thought, understandings and teachings, learnings from society, parents, peers and many others, you must decipher genuine truth that must fill the spaces of your being. For this is your temple, as you've been told before. And the temple holds the greatest of information, is where the spirit resides, where you go to worship and comprehend the things of atman. Therefore, cleanse the temple and fill it only with those elements you know to be absolutely true and steadfast in your existence. Truth about who you are may be slightly different than truths of others. Their journeys are not the same; there can be but one truth, one sincerity, one purity for you. And that is where you must reside.

The temple will be filled with this purity, this understanding, and push out those things that do not resonate as completely pure. Your heart fights with the third dimension, and the dimensions of the negative, of those who live around you, for they are enforcing their own energies for good, or bad, or indifferent; pure or impure. They are there to be part of your deciding of what is you. Peer into them deep, and see the myriad aspects that may or may not resonate with you. And you may not understand why they feel the way they do, but take this intervention. It is not who you are. You must understand; your purity must filter out exactly who they are, and be true to your singular understanding of them because God has created you just as well. He is the one who applies the filter within that you must use. Sometimes this filter can be too strong, accepting only miniscule grains of understanding.

181

Thus, be vigilant in remembering to use a filter meshed with purest love, and through it perceive the world. You may not grasp right now what I'm saying, but I can tell that your filter is very pure in some ways. When it comes to your family, you want to bring out the truth in the greatest possible way, but you have problems because their filters are not pure, despite that you tried to purify yours. Infrequently that angers you—and rightly so. You desire for them to be pure filters. Do not let this anger you. Let your full compassion fall on them, your authentic unconditional love teach you who they are through the eyes of their own words, the soul of their own understanding. They can be easily understood. The motion of love in its purest form does not anger. It does not represent anything but God. Sees only the God-portion of the being and accepts it entirely. Yet there is part of the experience that must be taught to those upon whom you gaze.

Be of love in this teaching; you are in many ways a great teacher. Your wisdom is full of understanding, but do not limit yourself or others. Let love's freedom express itself—the truest integrity. Even if it seems unlikely others will understand, it is the greatest form of expression, is purity. Your sexuality also is surfacing much in the deep pool of your thoughts. You are wondering what is right and what is wrong. Do not look at it that way, but instead how to express, and determine what is inexpressible. Figure the accepted from the unacceptable; what is paining others, and what brings joy to yourself. Do not tangle yourself in the net of right-and-wrong expression. That is not the question. Is it love, purity, or something else? Truly you, or something else?

These are the questions, not the right and the wrong. What can you give that someone may be able to accept in order to unite empathy and understanding of humanity—who you are as an individual. Learn from all things. Prepare your thoughts for all things. Do not dissuade any thought process until you know it is not for you. Do not indulge in judgment unless you know the bringer of words is impure.

This is the word from Baba. Understanding of purity, and a filter in your heart through the love of God. All things are in the temple, but do all belong there? Your heart is full of greatness; your mind sees, comprehends what the normal person may see. Be wise, for wisdom overshadows intellect and sometimes seems foolish, but is the deciphering of humanity in a way they can apprehend beyond introspection.

Be of good health and great understanding one to another, for wisdom sometimes comes through the words of a child and not from the highest realms. I love thee with all my being and resonate with your joy when you find it—that comes from your inner purity. Your wisdom is growing, blossoming. Do not stop; but feed it. Remember that your innocence, what is left from childhood, is the strongest part you. Why? Innocence is pure and purity is power. Are you with me?

Max: Yes. Absolutely.

Neem Karoli Baba: I love you. I love you. I bring you this because it is time for the world to wake to greater understanding of God. Purity, wisdom, enlightenment. There are too few holding the power of love, a power that can move the greatest of hearts, the darkest of mountains. The most negative things can be destroyed with love and reshaped into positivity. They are never destroyed for long, until reborn in some other way. I do not like the word "destroy." But in this case, it is the truth. There are some things that need to be moved out, changed. For these things would be destruction and rebirth. I am full of joy that the heavens are with you right now. You have much angelic support. Thank you.

ROOT RACES AND THEIR MISSIONS

The first root race was Polarian. It was ethereal, composed of etheric matter. The second root race was Hyperborean (Kimpurushan). Hyperboreans were colored golden yellow. Hyperborea was on Plaksha continent covering Northern Canada, Greenland, Iceland, Scandinavia, Northern Asia and Kamchatka.

The third root race was Lemurians. Their main mission was the development of the human heart (4th chakra). They were somewhat ethereal, focused neither on material progress nor technology, and existed in a higher dimensional level. Since they were not meant for this density, it is hard to tell when they lived, but likely over 500,000 years ago.

The main mission of Atlanteans (the 4th human race on Earth) was development of the material body (1st and 2nd chakra). They greatly advanced exploration of sex and genetic engineering, but their civilization fell after they ventured into war and exploitation of masses (3rd chakra). The destruction of Atlantis also ended the Lemurians. Those who escaped Earth before the Catastrophe settled elsewhere in the universe, and are called Lumerians. (Lemurians: from Mu, their location on Earth. Lumerians from Lum—light.)

Elongated skulls of Atlanteans.

Although Atlanteans often incarnate as modern humans, the Atlantean race was distinctly different from modern humans, the Atlanteans were not Homo Sapiens. They were taller, and had elongated skulls.

The mission of Homo sapiens' civilization (the 5th human race) is the development of will power (the 3rd chakra, the chakra of warriors). You can see this in the nature of many humans. Luckily, not all are focused on 3rd-chakra activities, and even those who are do not always express this chakra via war.

Since the final fall of Atlantis around 23,000 years ago, the Earth was in a dark period called the Age of Pisces. Now the planet transitions into the Age of Aquarius. This shift is about 40 years in duration, with the focal point at 2012. The Age of Pisces was characterized by the fall of vibrational levels accompanied by high polarity. Humanity was in a state of confusion, and under a great deal of mind control and manipulation by forces of darkness. Now these forces have receded, and humans are beginning to re-awaken their psychic and telepathic abilities.

Our religions also have divine missions: Judaism develops mind; Christianity, soul; and Islam, will-power. All of these traits contribute to collective soul.

Among nations the divine assignment for Americans is the development of self-respect.

At the time of Lemuria and Atlantis, the planet was openly visited by extraterrestrials. The history of Earth was intertwined with and influenced by wars and events on nearby stars. Many of the large stars in the sky are nearby, and are part of our cluster. Here is a list of bright stars which can be considered members:

Arcturus, Alpha Centauri (A and B), Proxima Centauri, Altair, Antares, Betelgeuse, Canopus, Fomalhaut, Orion, Polaris, Procyon (A and B), Rigel, Sirius (A and B), Tau Ceti and Vega. I included in this list primarily the stars which are known in our culture, visible from the Northern hemisphere. As we research aliens, we should check out southern hemisphere stars as well.

CONSCIOUS EVOLUTION

Archeology clearly shows that complex biological species on Earth appeared in the following order: insects, amphibians, reptiles and mammals. Yet it is unclear which of the technological civilizations were here first: insectoids, reptilians or humans. The Solar System was seeded by the Lyran feline humanoid race about half a billion years ago. The Lyrans were peaceful and of high spiritual vibration. They colonized and seeded intelligent life on multiple planets within the solar system, as well as other stars within the local cluster. At a later time, there were giant bipedal Reptilians from the planet Maldek, whose orbit was located between Mars and Jupiter. While the Lyrans were peaceful, the reptilians were militant. They were large in size because their planet was big, but after it was destroyed their descendants became smaller. They remain few in the 4th

185

density, and are still involved in the negative manipulation of humans on Earth.

Although the visitation by aliens was commonplace in ancient cultures, more recently it moved underground and became secret. The negative elite on Earth (The Cabal) was governed by higher-dimensional negative aliens which included Reptilians, Nephilim, Orions, Nordics. Not all parts of these races are negative; there are factions within each that are friendly towards humanity.

Prior to World War II, certain negative aliens shared their technology with the German fascists, and this initiated the Secret Space Program (SSP) by the negative human elite. In the 1930s and 1940s the Germans were able to build space stations on the Moon and Mars, and this launched the runaway civilization. After the end of World War II and the defeat of the Germans, the SSP continued, and surviving factions of German military secretly joined with Americans in the development of the SSP.

By now, the runaway civilization recruited or abducted humans from many races on Earth as workers, and developed their manufacturing facilities in the solar system and other stars in our cluster. Presently, this runaway civilization has many thousands of workers. It developed manufacture of technological goods which it uses to trade with hundreds of civilizations all over the galaxy, while control of the SSP remains in hands of negative aliens.

This runway civilization continues to extract material resources and people from the Earth, and is responsible for the ongoing economic and social crisis. It possesses many alien technologies including mind control, free energy, teleportation, star and dimensional travel, the use of stargates, portals and wormholes, time travel, time manipulation, transfer of souls, human cloning and hybridization of humans with other species.

Although technically advanced, this runaway civilization is still located in 3rd dimension and can travel to the 4th for only short periods of time (under two weeks). There are many crimes committed by the runaway civilization, the worst of which are slave trade, ecological crimes on Earth, genocide of humanity, economic exploitation, mind control and lowering of

186

humanity's spiritual vibration via technological means. Many of the crimes against humanity are restricted or limited by positive ETs from higher dimensions, angelic beings and the consciousnesses of the Creator level.

Much negativity is still permitted on Earth because of the collective free will of humanity. The laws of creation make free-will a priority, so if the human collective wants war and drama, then it is permitted. Yet there are powerful forces that ascertain that humanity perpetuates and the damage is only partial. The total nuclear annihilation of humanity has been prevented many times by higher-dimensional positive ETs.

In recent years (2012-2014), there was the return of the positive Blue Sphere Alliance, comprised of three types of intelligent beings: Blue Spheres, Blue Avians and Golden Radiants (triangles). This alliance has powerful technologies and has established a quarantine around the solar system by way of a surrounding blue sphere that allows only positive and neutral beings to pass through the barrier. The negative aliens and negative humans are not permitted to leave or enter the solar system.

Assistance from positive aliens and neutral trade are still permitted. This recent change improved the situation. The next positive steps towards the recovery of humanity are expected to be Disclosure, Open Contact and Awakening.

We advocate for Disclosure during which the governments shall disclose their contacts with the aliens. We advocate for the Open Contact in which humans and the friendly aliens start meeting openly. We call for the Awakening of humanity to the reality of the ascension, so humans can make a choice about ascension individually and collectively.

The time frame for these events is not yet defined. It will be determined by the readiness of humanity. However, the first event—Disclosure—can happen at any time because there is already plenty of information about the aliens publicly available. Some of the public is ready, and pressure is building on governments to release the info. Every year, public awareness of alien presence grows; alien information enters into mainstream understanding. Also, there are positive factions within SSP who want to assist the Earth rid itself of the exploitation and crimes of the SSP. So there are good people within the Program who intend to help. Solar Warden is a positive group among them, popularized by David Wilcock and Corey Goode.

BLUE SPHERE ALLIANCE: ORIGINS AND ASCENSION

Channeled by Jim

Max: I have questions about the distant past, the fall of humanity, like how and when it happened. I would like to speak about the future, the dimensions, planets, and ascension. I have studied information by Ashayana Deane, and would like comments on this information—it's too much for me, and I need more clarification.

Central Information: Thank you. You've connected with Central Information.

Max: Hi, yes.

Central Information: What is the question?

Max: Let's start with the first. I'm writing a book, and the information from blue sphere alliance changes the perspective a lot. Is the story about the fall of humanity, and return to the higher dimension, and when did this fall happen in our time? Some numbers say it's half a million years ago, and others twenty-three thousand. What's the factual answer?

Central Information: Original fall of your peoples?

Max: Yes.

Central Information: There was more than one fall in your humanity. There were times when the population was removed from your planet, returned, removed again, and then returned.

188

Max: Right.

Central Information: Why are there discrepancies in your information?

Max: The downfall from the higher dimension to the lower dimension, when did it happen?

Central Information: That was very long ago. The estimated time is 416 million years.

Max: Thank you. So the Atlantis on this Earth was already in the lower dimension?

Central Information: Yes.

Max: Because that was one of the critical question to understand. And what was the role of the Blue Sphere Alliance in that?

Central Information: Blue Sphere/Blue Alliance was not considered blue alliance at that time. It was called something else. Various species visited Atlantis, but were not an alliance. At least the ones you know today. Those that visited Atlantis were individual species who have come to be known as the Blue Sphere Alliance. They were traitors, communicators. There is not a word that will describe exactly what their function was on the Atlantean culture. Their connection to the Atlantean culture included many different things, very diverse. So, they cannot have an actual title but they did work with agriculture, minerals, supplies, radiation, weaponry, crystals and intelligence information.

Max: What is Blue Avians and the Golden Radiant?

Central Information: Golden Radiants first, then Blue Avians. Blue Avians were very attached to Atlantis at one time and to the Egyptian culture. They so much liked it that they became part of it in some ways. Others did not like it as much and moved on, after trade, or whatever business they had with Atlantis.

Max: Previously I spoke to Ores, ah, a Blue Avian. Is that the same as Horus from ancient Egypt, an Egyptian God?

Central Information: Yes.

Max: Thank you. Uhm, who am I speaking to now?

Central Information: You're talking to the information center.

Max: Excellent. Thank you. When did the fall from the higher dimension happen? Is it correct that the previous planet was called Terra? The higher-dimensional Terra?

Central Information: Terra Ha.

Max: I was thinking Terra Ha would be the future, and the past would be Terra?

Central Information: What would be the difference between the next section and the past? Similarities are occurring, they will take the same name.

Max: Oh, so it was Terra Ha.

Central Information: Correct.

Max: Thank you. And is it right that Terra Ha, when it fell, divided into Earth and other planets? Of different locations?

Central Information: No. It divided itself from the third dimension, but did not create the other worlds.

Max: Is it divided from the third dimension? I think it fell from the fourth . . . did it?

Central Information: Correct. It divided itself from the third dimension. As it fell the third dimension was what it left.

Max: Thank you. So is it right that all planets of the solar system are descended from Terra Ha?

Central Information: Correct.

Max: And also the planets in Pleiades and Andromeda?

190

Central Information: Third dimension as it is, was. The default, the falling of another dimension. So now, third dimension appears and multiplies in its own way. But it was born of fourth dimension as fifth dimension was the father or mother of fourth dimension.

Max: So the Earth is not the descendent of Terra Ha. There were other copies—like sister planets of Earth?

Central Information: Correct.

Max: Also had humans—

Central Information: Correct.

Max: Is Erra in Pleiades also sister of Earth, and fell from ahh, of Terra Ha?

Central Information: Erra is unique, because it is still fourth-dimensional. It did not fall, but was a falling portion from another dimension. It is not fallen from Terra Ha.

Max: Okay. My next question is about the humans. From which dimension did we originate? Were we created in fourth dimension, or third?

Central Information: It would appear that, according to your histories, you did not fall in from dimensions but worked up from lower dimensions. However, since there is no beginning, and no end, it's just part of the circle.

Max: So you think we started from third, went to the fourth, then fell from the fourth, third, then we are raising back to fourth. Is that right?

Central Information: Yes. These things happen all the time. Kalar, Kalar reyz, stars collapse upon themselves, creating black holes. Black holes build so much energy and density, they eventually cannot hold their own weight and become something else.

Max: Thank you. What was the connection between ahh, Atlantean civilisation on Earth, and the civilisation on Terra Ha? Was it also called Atlantis, or something else?

Central Information: Terra Ha and Atlantis are different. They did not exist at the same time. Ahh, as material one with the other. Terra Ha was far previous.

Max: So there was no Atlantis civilisation on Terra Ha?

Central Information: No. Only in the reflection of—of Atlantis you will find Terra Ha. Terra Ha was there when Atlantis was there. However, they were not interacting.

Max: Ahh. Was Lemurian civilisation present on Terra Ha?

Central Information: No. Lemurians were also third-dimensional at that time.

Max: Was origin of the word Lemurian, is it somehow related to Mu?

Central Information: Its relation to distant civilisations is removed. The Mu, the Lemurians, were ancestries of Cashyan Yieta. The ancients.

Max: And what was Mu?

Central Information: Mu, in your history, is the letter M in the Greek alphabet.

Max: Were the Blue Avians created as guardians of our dimensional transfer?

Central Information: The Blue Avians existed before you needed guardians. They assumed that position eventually when they saw that you were going to be attacked.

Max: Oh, did they attack?

Central Information: No one attacked. They assumed guardianship before this event. Reptilians, Greys, Insectoids were all planning different strategies of how to exploit the minerals and properties from your planet. They were not working together but in separate thought processes. However, when they realised they all were thinking similar thoughts at similar times, some of them united.

192

Max: So, we are talking about the modern Earth?

Central Information: Yes.

Max: The guardians of, ah, Terra Ha?

Central Information: The guardians of Terra Ha were in that particular dimension. They're not of our dimension.

Max: What's yours?

Central Information: Ours is between dimensional ships. Therefore, we can exist in more than one dimension. Therefore, it is not considered our dimension.

Max: What's the difference between Blue Avians and Angels? Angels are also interdimensionals.

Central Information: Alien species is the Blue Avians, Angels were created in realms. And that is the difference. There is a different energy source for each. If you want to consider Angels a species.

Max: Are Blue Avians evolving like other species?

Central Information: Like other species? Evolving. Yes.

Max: Golden Radiants as well?

Central Information: Yes, evolving. All things exist outside of spiritual realms, evolve.

Max: And same relate to Blue Spheres? Right?

Central Information: Blue Spheres are technologically not evolving.

Max: Oh, Blue Spheres are not ascension?

Central Information: They have ascensions, but they do not have all the qualities of life.

Max: So, do they have DNA?

Central Information: There is evidence that they have DNA, but it is not evolved.

Max: I see.

Central Information: It was interlaced.

Max: Who created and developed Blue Spheres?

Central Information: The Blue Avians have developed these spheres, along with the help of the Golden Triangle realms, golden realms, whatever you want to speak of. In that, they can be called many things.

Max: Thank you.

Central Information: They do these things together because they are of light mind.

Max: The ascension—are they coming back to the fourth dimension?

Central Information: You will return to Terra Ha eventually. But your ascension is not about changing of dimensions, it is about evolution.

Max: Right. So at this point we're evolving, and, some point in the future we will evolve to—shift dimension, is that correct?

Central Information: Yes. But you're not quite there yet.

Max: What is the range of estimated times? Because some people think this will happen in our lifetime. What do you think is the probability of that?

Central Information: Zero percent.

Max: Thank you. What are necessary steps for the ascension?

Central Information: There are many steps; your people are not ready for ascension.

Max: Which key element is missing?

Central Information: Inclusion.

Max: What kind of inclusion?

Central Information: Too many people are self-sufficient, and not including anything else. All people must be included in the step forward.

Max: Oh, so it's global unity and desire, global desire for ascension?

Central Information: It is not necessarily a desire but it is a unity. To understand that people are to be fair with one another, and equal. This revelation is spoken about but it is not practised.

Max: Thank you. In Ashayana Deane's writings, Dian speaks about the dimensions as much as the universe. She says that the ascension will bring us to universe number two, where Terra Ha is. Is that correct?

Central Information: That is correct. She is correct. Let me explain. The universe is filled with all dimensions. Therefore, when this, when you are one with the universe you realise that you are part of all these dimensions, and will move forward into the next one. Until you're able to understand . . . the—criteria for movement to the next dimension. You will stay in that particular one.

Max: So the second universe does also have dimensions from one, two, three, four and up?

Central Information: Of course, Max: the third-dimensional beings— would they be invisible to us, or in a different universe? If you knew how to see them you could. But, you would have to be aware of where you are, and what you are looking at.

Max: Okay. Thank you very much.

GRINDAL (ZESPOD, FRIENDLY REPTILIAN)

Channeled by Jim

Grindal: Hello.

Max: Hey, Grindal. How are you? What's new?

Grindal: I'm working in Israel right now, and a lot of things are going on there. So, I have to stay put for the most part in that area.

Max: I see. What are you doing there, what are you negotiating about?

Grindal: Ah . . . the political, political stuff. I have to get moving there because of the way things are looking with your new guy. The president. They're all up in arms about him, you know, 'cause he's not really very supportive of them. Most other presidents were. This one is not. They're a little worried.

Max: So what are you doing, what's your purpose?

Grindal: I can't tell you all I do. But I can tell you that I am helping things come together a little better.

Max: Excellent. Someone has asked me to invite you to—invite your comments on things happening now. A lot of things are happening. We've really changed a lot of things. How should we deal with them, what's the expectation?

Grindal: Yeah, well, what are you gonna do? You have to live with it, that's what you're gonna have to do. Ah, yeah, he's gonna change a lot of things. You're gonna—everybody is gonna see it differently.

Max: The question is, how much time have you got? Should we drop everything and rush somewhere or can we wait?

Grindal: Where are you gonna go? They're gonna find you no matter where you get to.

Max: [laughs]

Grindal: But, um, yeah. You know you don't need to rush off right away. But, there may be a year or so. Umm, depending on if some of the things he wants to do will actually come to pass, which I don't think so. But, if they do, there will be a real possibility of war on your shores. Let's hope not.

Max: Is trust a new development?

Grindal: You have to understand that aliens don't care about your politics, except for Girk-Fitneer mostly. In this case they don't care who your president is. They just care about what the world consensus is. That's all the aliens care about. Not just one country. Of course yours is a big country. So, they do care, but, they don't think it's gonna make that much difference.

Max: So, the first contact is not coming, right? Open contact with the nation?

Grindal: Nah, not this second.

Max: How about the disclosure? Is disclosure coming?

Grindal: Disclosure will be coming soon, yeah. I agree with that. And, it needs to come . . . for many reasons. But we can't go into that right now.

Max: Blue Sphere Alliance. How serious are they?

Grindal: As a heart attack.

Max: [laughs] Is it positive or what?

Grindal: Yeah, they are a serious group. Yeah, don't mess with them. They have their criteria. They have their thought processes. And they are very positive, but they do things their way. You can't tell them what to do.

Max: That I understand. Are we ascending or what?

Grindal: They are not. But they are protecting the ascension from attacks outside. They are trying to let it happen more quickly. So that you guys can be more useful. How's that?

Max: So, they say there is zero chance that in our lifetime we ascend, right?

Grindal: That is probably correct. I mean, I don't know. But—if they said that, that's probably right.

Max: Our civilisation just—our secret program stepped out of Earth, and there are millions of people now there, is it right?

Grindal: Not millions. No. Are you kidding? You'd miss millions of people from the Earth if they were out there. But, yeah, they are starting to create out there, that's true. But there's not millions yet.

Max: How many then?

Grindal: Probably tens of thousands.

Max: All right.

Grindal: You would miss some people if they left the Earth. Especially the ones they are talking about. The scientist, and the space people, and all that. If they were to disappear, you would know about it. But what would they do, put clones in their place or something? You don't know, they might've. But there are about ten thousand now because they've been up there quite a while.

Max: How important are they? The runaway civilization?

Grindal: Well, they could be important but they are not important yet.

Max: And ah, Agarthan's people on the Earth are inside, in other dimensions. The story goes that they are eager to help us, is that right?

Grindal: Yeah, there is a lot of different species they're willing and wanting to help. Some of them are doing better than others. But, yeah, they want to help.

Max: I'm talking about humans. Humans from down there. From inside the Earth.

Grindal: Yeah, there's not that many humans inside the earth—there are some. But yes, everybody inside wants to help the planet, but for their own selfish reasons. Yes, they do wanna help; because they don't wanna be wiped out, and they think that they will be if they don't help. But, anyway, they are wanting to help everybody on Earth for their own reasons, you know. They don't want the Earth to disappear, so if they just want to help

198

for their own selfish reasons that's okay as long as they are helping.

Max: What should we expect from the release of new technologies? Free energy, and telepathic . . .?

Grindal: There is one coming. Tesla's brain is gonna return. So . . . when that happens. When Tesla is reincarnated, or whatever it's gonna be like. He's gonna be able to let them know . . . how to do all these things again because he has all that knowledge already.

Max: Nothing yet?

Grindal: It's—it's coming soon.

Max: How about Russia? Anything new?

Grindal: Oh yes. There's lots of news about Russia. They are working to try to be the world's biggest power, that's why they want Trump in their back pocket. They want the two of those countries to work together to dominate the world.

Max: [laughs]

Grindal: That ain't gonna happen.

Max: Of course.

Grindal: It's not gonna work, but that's what they want. Then there will be more in their favor. [laughs]

Max: Ah, finances too. Should we expect the collapse? Or is it delayed now?

Grindal: It's delayed. That's funny, because your new president . . . a lot of other nations are gearing up their alliances, so to speak. To um, tighten everything up, because they are afraid he's gonna, ahhh, try to get to them somehow. So, 'cause they know he's a financier and he's into business. That's why they are not sure how good he is in that, 'cause they don't really know who he is yet. They are gonna be very protective of their money. Finances right now will be a little tighter, and a little more stable.

199

Max: All right. Thank you much.

KOORFALIEN (BLUE AVIAN)

Channeled by Jim

Koorfalien: My name is Koorfalien. I am in direct contact with, and a portion of, the Blue Avian culture.

Max: Thank you. Welcome. You are on record. I intend to publish this piece.

Koorfalien: If it brings no problems to any individuals, I will accept that.

Max: Thank you. I recently learned about the spheres and your mission, so any explanation, any insight into your mission would be wonderful.

Koorfalien: We've always been close with humanity's many cultures: Egyptian, Atlantean, sometimes in the Greek culture and many times in mythology. We may have changed our appearance for some of these visitations and interventions, but we are always here to help and to guide. We are here to protect as well, but not on a hands-on basis. We are here to protect in a more doctrinal way, have those around us controlled so they are not interfering with your particular space. Therefore, we are in charge of allowing exit to those beings and cultures presently visiting you.

Max: Wonderful. Are you working with other species on your ships?

Koorfalien: "Working with" is not the correct term. We are serving as managerial staff to many of them.

Max: Are you physical in nature?

Koorfalien: That is an interesting question. In some ways we are. In others—to you—we would not appear physical. In our own realm, though, [we are] physical.

Max: What percentage of time, in your realm, is spent manifested in solid form? Do your bodies appear and disappear, or are you like ninety-nine percent in your body, and present?

Koorfalien: We occupy bodies to maintain them, but can assume various forms. We are in it at all times.

Max: Excellent. Thank you. How closely are you related to Reptilians and Dracos?

Koorfalien: We are not of a humanoid species. However, we are not like the Dracos, Reptilians, Insectoids or Mantis beings. We have a different physiology. We are more bird-like, and follow an avian trend. Whereas Reptilians and Insectoids will follow their own trends, as far as what life consists of for them. Our tendency is more in the sensibilities of the air. Theirs are earthbound.

Max: I see. Genetically, are you closer to Reptilians or Earth humans?

Koorfalien: We are closer to Earth humans than to Reptilians. That's not to say we are *that* close, but as far as how we interact socially in our thought processes, are much closer to human than they are to Reptilian, Mantis or Insectoid. Also, physiologically, we are not that close to any of these.

Max: What is your genome? If we compare those of yours and ours, what percentage of the genome would be similar?

Koorfalien: Sixty-one percent.

Max: Thank you. Are there hybrids between Earth humans and your species?

Koorfalien: Not at this time. There was once a hybridization program thousands of years ago. They created the pterodactyl species.

Max: Right. On Earth I think of the birds as very close to reptilians and [indecipherable] which can fly and have feathers. Otherwise there are a lot of genetic similarities, but pretty far from mammalian.

Koorfalien: Yes. Their bones are hollow. Ours, in some places, are hollow too but not completely.

Max: So, are you related to our birds?

Koorfalien: We had something to do with them being created as they are, but at this time we are far removed from that scenario.

Max: Are you genetically related to all birds?

Koorfalien: In a small way, yes.

Max: What percentage, say, of your genome is similar to birds from Earth?

Koorfalien: Well, it depends on *which* birds. The genome percentages go from 52 to 76.

Max: Thank you. Are you an egg-laying species?

Koorfalien: We did at one time lay eggs. That is no longer part of our reproductive system.

Max: How do you reproduce?

Koorfalien: We reproduce differently than we would want to speak about. This is something personal for us.

Max: Ah. Do you bring up children in families, or outside of them?

Koorfalien: It depends on the culture of where you were born in our relationship to your status.

Max: So, are you individuals all connected to a hive mind? If so, how strong is hive mind?

Koorfalien: Higher mind being God, as you call him.

Max: So, you have a hive mind which you call God? I was thinking about the collective mind of the Blue Avians.

Koorfalien: The collective mind of the Blue Avians does attach to all things. Minds in the collective, in the God and spirit areas. We do not see things exactly as you do, everything is a collective; every species. Although there are individuals within these, they are nonetheless connected and, therefore to us, our collectives. God has several personalities—collective intelligences, energy, and we see in him these many things. One facet of him does not define the totality of the God-mind and its profound energies.

Max: Right. So, you are constantly communicating with a certain aspect of God, and perform his will?

Koorfalien: He allows us free will, although there are those who claim only humans have that—this is incorrect. God creates all individuals and creatures with free will, therefore we are able to act upon that. He does give us specific missions if we choose to further his business. There are portions of our society who will act upon his desires, and others who won't.

Max: Are you in the same dimension as our friends the Pleiadians, Yahyel and Arcturians?

Koorfalien: No. Their dimensions are slightly different from ours.

Max: Are you comfortable visiting in bodily form, and staying on, their worlds?

Koorfalien: It is not necessary at this time to visit their world, but they may interact with us as they please, and we with them.

Max: Will they be able to visit your spheres, and feel physically comfortable?

Koorfalien: With some help.

Max: So, it's not usual.

Koorfalien: No.

Max: What's your relationship with Girk-Fitneer and Galactic Federation?

Koorfalien: We realize they exist, but do not have any interaction with them, and are considered a casual ally. We do not agree with all the things they are doing, nor do they necessarily approve of all our activities.

Max: How do you resolve disagreements?

Koorfalien: We do not resolve, but discuss our contentions. If they do not resolve we let them stand, and maintain mutual respect. That is how the universe survives.

Max: Is there a meeting, or council, where you discuss things?

Koorfalien: If necessary, we send representatives to address councils, alliances, formations of councils and foundations or federations. We have people engaged at all times with their inquiries. We try to help as much as possible, if they want that.

Max: There is constant communication. You have a direct phone to Girk-Fitneer, Galactic Federation and so on. Right?

Koorfalien: I wouldn't call it constant.

Max: There is no appointed person who is always . . . [unclear]

Koorfalien: In our group, there are some dedicated to the particular alliances, foundations and councils. They speak for us. If there are questions or problems, these are brought before higher levels of government.

Max: Oh, you're talking to Corey Goode, the human, right? That is, you as a species.

Koorfalien: Corey Goode speaks our voice, yes. I am not the one who always or usually speaks to him. He has someone that is an ambassador to he alone.

Max: Excellent. Many of our Girk community members would be happy to telepathically—or by other means—connect with you. I extend an invitation: speak to us, and through us.

Koorfalien: Yes.

Max: Did you consider expanding the idea of human colony to your areas of control? If so, our volunteers will be happy to visit if you're interested.

Koorfalien: We are not here to take control, but to inform and give counsel. Also to protect against those who may interfere with your culture. We are present to provide information perhaps vital to your survival, or to the continuation of Ascension. But beyond that, we are here to help maintain status quo.

Max: Excellent. Were you the ones who dictated Ra Material through Carla Rueckert?

Koorfalien: I did not hear the question.

Max: I might be pronouncing her name wrong—but Ra Material, the voice behind The Law of One books.

Koorfalien: And what about Ra?

Max: Did you dictate the book, from Ra Material?

Koorfalien: We are in charge of Ra Material.

Max: There's a book series on Earth titled The Law of One. The first volume is RA MATERIAL: BOOK ONE.

Koorfalien: It is part of what we are.

Max: Excellent. So, in the Ra Material, it was said that Carla Rueckert and Don Elkins were the creators. Carla was the first channeler. An essential book in our culture, channeled between 1981 and 1984. My point being, in the book you acknowledge, understand humanity is limited because you were too much separated from us.

Koorfalien: Yes. The separation has been great because we were with you at some periods, but now the divide has expanded. You—as a people— have changed. Our understanding, hence, is not as great as it once was. But our current understanding is sufficient. You understand?

Max: Yes. Thank you for explaining that. If at any point you want more information, we would be happy to provide in any way, which is friendly.

Koorfalien: Yes. If it is necessary. If it is ready for your people to hear.

Max: Thank you. Are you talking to human governments directly?

Koorfalien: Your governments cannot be reckoned or reasoned with in any way useful to us. We stay out of that particular situation.

Max: Thank you.

Koorfalien: Besides, we are not here to interfere that way. Our process is merely educational and preventative.

Max: Are you aware of the Human Colony Community?

Koorfalien: We are aware of all things around your planet, and all its cultures.

Max: Okay. All right. I think I ran out of time. I would like to thank you for the contact—do you have any questions for me?

Koorfalien: No.

Max: Would you mind, in your language, giving us a blessing?

Koorfalien: A blessing for humanity, or for you personally?

Max: For humanity.

Koorfalien: In our language?

Max: If possible.

Koorfalien: I do not know if you will be able to come through, but one moment. The blessing will be given, but not heard by your ears.

Max: Okay.

Koorfalien: It is a download to humanity, as we always share our thought process with your people in many ways. I interpret that your people are moving forward and need our help, but we will give it only when they ask. There will be times when that is inappropriate, but we do help as much as possible. As for blessings, God is the One—as you call him by many different words and titles—who gives the blessings. We ourselves are but speakers of words.

Max: Thank you. I invited your telepathic communications directly to me.

Koorfalien: You shall receive a thought process. It may not be at this moment, but when it is appropriate to download and connect with you.

Max: Thank you. I appreciate your visit. I appreciate the contact and thank you much for the protection you provide for the solar system. Thank you much for your good intentions and for allowing us to express our free will.

Koorfalien: You are welcome. We are more scientifically than morally involved with you in many ways.

Max: Thank you. That is all from my side. If you have any questions, I'm open.

Koorfalien: I am finished.

Max: Thank you.

Jim: Hello. How are you doing?

Max: Good. Thank you. Nice session.

Jim: Good. I'm glad.

HEALING

Energy healing has existed since time immemorial. In the old days, healing was done by shamans, priests, medicine women and medicine men. For thousands of years, there stood a barrier between official, sanctioned practice and so-called alternative treatments. Even in ancient kingdoms, doctors were approved by the state and shamans were widely persecuted.

For thousands of years, alternative medicine was a secret art practiced by initiates and hidden from the public. This changed when the arts of Yoga and Reiki were released to the West in the 20th century.

Modern medicine utilizes imaging technologies to find tumors and visualize fractures; employs surgeons to excise tumors and reassemble broken bones. Cutting-edge biochemical diagnostics detect disorders, and pharmaceuticals are prescribed to fix the problems. While modern medicine has thrived in certain areas, it still fails in many others. One major dilemma is that pharmaceuticals help in the short-term, but prolonged use leads to toxicity—particularly in the liver. Nowadays too many die from side effects of overly-prescribed medications.

Another problematic field is psychiatry. Psychological and/or emotional problems are ailments of the soul, and cannot be entirely managed with drugs. Many of these are addictive, offering only short-term solutions based on treating symptomatology. Perhaps for similar reasons, medicine fails to adequately address the lacerating effects of chronic inflammation: effectively treated in the short term, but lacking enduring resolution.

Alternative medicine approaches these problems very differently, with a worldview espousing the soul as primary, the body simply its manifestation. We therefore believe that many chronic illnesses and disorders stem from soul maladies that later afflict the body.

For example, tumors and inflammation begin with psychological trauma, and transform into psychosomatic pain. If the problem of the soul is not solved, only then do the pains manifest as swelling or tumors—malignant or not. Energy medicine fixes the soul on a quantum level, preventing and healing recurring problems.

Some illness is better treated with energy medicine; others more appropriately by conventional means. For example, the majority of modern energy healers still go to the dentist because—in this case—material medicine is more effective. Also most bacterial infections are difficult to treat with energy medicine, so antibiotics sometimes are used even by energy healers.

Discernment is required to determine disorders optimally treated with energy medicine from those best handled by traditional means—heretical thinking according to the official viewpoint. Take it with caution.

Energy healing is best known as Yoga and Reiki. The art of Yoga uses disciplined exercise and postures to normalize energy flow and prevent illness. You learn from an instructor, and heal yourself. Reiki applies healing techniques to both self and others.

Although Yoga originates with India, and Reiki with Japan, these arts share roots and employ similar concepts. Both were secret until released to the West. Reiki is based on Qigong, known in China and related to Yoga's understanding of bodily energies.

In Yoga, this healing energy is called "Prana"; in Qigong "Chi"; and in Reiki "Ki." Reiki means "Healing Energy." Until recently, these disciplines were hidden. With today's explosion of internet and printed resources these philosophies, doctrines, and techniques can be easily accessed. In addition to Reiki, Yoga, and Qigong there are Tai Chi, healing touch, emotional freedom technique (EFT), hypnotherapy, Thai Bodywork, shamanic healing and others. Sharing various methods (EFT, healing touch, and hypnotherapy are westernized; while Reiki, Qigong and Yoga retain—respectively—styles from Japan, China and India), the fundamental conceit is that optimal health requires flows of spiritual energy. In addition to the material energy of the body, there is a known physical flow of spiritual energy. Physical problems result from blockage and/or distortion in this vital current, coursing along many nerve paths and through multiple dimensions.

There exist trans-dimensional vortexes of life energy, called chakras. The central is the heart chakra: a vortex ranging from the heart forward—and behind—via the back. Three major chakras function below the heart, the lowest of which is the root chakra, corresponding with the spinal base.

Above the heart are three more major chakras. Atop the head is the crown chakra, characterized by the highest frequency and color violet. The root chakra is symbolized as red, with the lowest frequency. Each chakra is identified with a color and frequency, connects the individual to certain dimensions, and governs specific bodily processes along with influencing spiritual and social functions.

Chakra frequencies hold also a physiological meaning. The brain and spine are embedded with nerve networks that carry repetitive electrical oscillations. Since the longest pathway runs between the brain and spinal base, signals traveling there require the most time—that's why the root-chakra frequency is lowest. Those of each chakra roughly correspond to the distance between the head and coincident vertebrae. Although the electrical oscillations are physical phenomena, they resonate with spiritual channels that cannot be measured by conventional instrumentation. Yet humans, as conscious beings, can connect to these wavering cycles on the soul level in order to perform healing work.

Energy healing cannot be separated from the idea of spirituality and, by nature, life energy itself is non-material: essentially a miracle utilizing the healer's spiritual work to remove blockages and restore vital flows. Pain fades, inflammation shrinks and health returns.

In Reiki, the healer uses their hands to move energy and normalize flow. In yoga, exercises, various focused postures, and breathwork combine to improve and maintain the stream. EFT comprises repetitive movements and healing affirmations.

In addition to gradual energy healing, which is easy to rationalize, there is the instantaneous type—anomalous and likened to a miracle. In gradual healing, we work on rebalancing, clearing negative energies and removing blockages. With instantaneous recovery we simply wake up feeling the crisis is over. Nonetheless, prayer and wishes for healing with no limitation remain worthwhile "rituals."

Miracles *do* happen. Although reality often seems grim and dark, there is always hope. Many people have been very close to death but were mysteriously saved. In some cases, near-death experiences (NDEs) have ruptured mundane reality, opening awareness of the spirit's seemingly miraculous power. Spirits and angels often intervene, sparing people from imminent doom. Sometimes the body actually dies, but angels restore the life-force. Infrequently the decedent even remembers dying, and coming back. Numerous accounts (many in open, medical literature) exist of near-death experiences.

These miraculous healings and NDEs illustrate that so-called mundane physical reality is not wholly "real," and might very well be a radically sophisticated simulation, or "matrix" reality.

Why do some people survive accidents and illnesses, while others prematurely die? Much depends on the soul's desire and its life contract.

A soul may sometimes choose an unexpected exit from life, some of which are harrowingly dramatic and even provide a learning opportunity for those left behind. Spirits and angels, from an overview of system development, decide who stays and who goes. That's why, for example, wars are permitted—so long as they don't lead to complete species annihilation.

An instance of truly unexpected exit can be found in the death of John F. Kennedy. Even a cursory biographical review reveals that, by the time of his death, JFK's body was worn out. He had considerable difficulty performing his presidential duties (which would exhaust even a healthy, much younger man or woman). Chronic back pain from a war injury had him using strong narcotics and psychoactive drugs. His death actually didn't stop the democratic reforms, many of which were sanctioned posthumously. So, from a certain perspective, his assassination was one of the most efficient ways of soul-exit, offering high drama, conspiratorial intrigue, and urging humanity to wake up.

A similar point can be made about the premature deaths of famous celebrities such as John Lennon and Marilyn Monroe. Consider this from the point of view of the eternal soul. It might be sometimes beneficial for the soul to exit, and incarnate in a new body. The soul chooses when best to step away from life, integrate experiences, and manifest into fresh life better serving spiritual growth and—better still—serving humanity: harmonization of the collective dream.

Tragedies are acceptable from the higher perspective. Death, sickness, pain and suffering are a natural part of life—an illusion supported by a powerful structure comprised of a multitude of interdimensional beings: wise spirits, elementals and angels. Some kindly serve the process of dying, recovering human souls and life experiences. Others exist to keep us sick and shorten our lives, parameters partly defined by creator beings, partly by the collective of human spirits. It is an artificial simulation, unique in the galaxy

211

and valued therein because it allows for quick spiritual progress.

Spirits from other stars come to experience life on Earth and incarnate as humans. Hence, if the spirit comes from another planet and of course lacks experience here, their first incarnations could be short due to the demands of mere survival. Life on Earth demands special skills, requiring several incarnations to master—the high price paid for the experience.

Ascended Masters such as Jesus, Buddha and Confucius are souls who achieved a high level of spiritual development, earned the right to escape the incarnational cycle yet chose to remain to help us in our collective spiritual evolution. Many lightworkers have special relationships with Ascended Masters. Praying, and inviting them for healing is wonderful, because these consciousnesses combine deep understanding of humanity with spiritual wisdom.

MEDITATION

Meditation is absolutely essential both for self-healing and spirit growth. The modern society offers us many artificial goals: money, fame, career, possessions and sensual pleasures. You are supposed to look a certain way, behave a certain way, be interested in certain things and enjoy certain things. Yet, you have already awakened to realize the vanity of these attractions. From the spiritual perspective, the main value of life is the opportunity for spiritual growth. It is growing the purity, power, and integrity of the spirit that matters. All material goals are temporary and illusionary. They can be nice tools and prompts for the spiritual growth but their value is temporary.

As you get experience and mature, you discover that the main answers are not to be sought outside of your consciousness, but inside. You discover that your inner life is of primary importance.

Modern people are trapped in their daily routine and external pleasures. They look for external approval of other people, are so busy working and having fun after work that they forget about their inner life. But sometimes, maybe after a big shakeup, people awaken to the realization that inner life is underdeveloped.

It is very important to pay attention in your inner life - and meditation is one of the best ways to face your own consciousness and engage in your inner life.

In meditation, you disconnect from the outer world and focus inside. For some people, it is difficult to look into their own soul because they find much of hidden fear, anger, grief and pain. Processing and resolving these negative energies is one of the goals of meditation. Another goal is to connect to your spirit and through your spirit, to connect to God directly. In essence, meditation is a phone line to God. During meditation, you upload to the Creation all your problems and download the answers.

Keep in mind that your physical health and the health of your soul are tightly linked. The physical illnesses which results from psychological trauma are called psychosomatic. In chronic illnesses, the psychological trauma, pain and inflammation often go together. It is the cause of frailties, allergies, heart problems and many neurological, digestive and skin problems.

The biological system responsible for inflammation is called the immune system. One of its functions is to hunt infections. Another function is to keep the seeds of cancer under control and to constantly eliminate any cells that convert to the cancerous state. When the immune system becomes too weak, it allows cancer and infections. When immune system becomes overly active and non-discriminate, it causes chronic inflammation, such as in arthritis, psoriasis, allergies, chronic pains, sickness behavior and depression. Many brain disorders such as Alzheimer's and other neurodegenerative disorders are caused by inflammation.

In almost all chronic pain diseases, there is a combination of pain which results from over-excitation of nerves and inflammation. This is a self-activated and self-reinforced cycle where overly active neurons activates the inflammatory response and the inflammatory response in turn closes the cycle by overly activating nerves. So inflammation and nerves activate each other creating a self-enforcing circuit.

213

Even mainstream science recognizes the connection between psychological trauma, the activation of neuroinflammation. Mainstream science recognizes that stress contributes to arthritis, allergies, psoriasis and cancer. Stress is a psychological disbalance and is the disbalance of the soul. 'Psyche' is the soul in Greek and psychology is the knowledge about the soul.

What is not understood by mainstream science is the spiritual energy. The traumas of the soul could lead to disease not only chemically but also through spiritual energy mechanisms. The traumas of the soul produce negative selfish programs which feed of on the energies of the body.

This negative energy blocks the flow and amplifies itself. These negative excesses of energy are connected to cells through the cellular and magnetic vibrations, largely, through the vibrations of DNA. These negative energies reprogram the genome in the cells to behave selfishly and without harmony with the rest of the body. There selfish cells can induce cancer, inflammation and pain. Energy healing and meditation are among the best tools which help with removing these negative energies, blockages and vortexes.

One of the main goals of meditation is reconnecting the mind and the soul. It is inner work which integrates different parts of the mind together and to the subconscious. In meditation, the traumatic experience is uploaded to the spirit and becomes part of the accumulated collective knowledge. In return, healing is sent down from the spirit to the body. It is similar to healing that takes place during sleep, but in meditation it can be more profound and guided by your intention. Meditation is very efficient in reducing stress, pain and inflammation, and this is statistically confirmed by the mainstream science.

The nature of modern human life is very unnatural, pun intended. The stress of modern life is very artificial. The majority of living beings in nature are not stressed out. Look at the cats and dogs, they are constant reminders that life is possible without stress. Yet, modern civilization has developed many ways to stress out a human.

For many, being constantly stressed-out becomes a habit. People become workaholics and continuously are worrying. Even when these worriers have free time and could take time to rest, they still find ways to become stressed out. Many watch stressful movies, read stressful news and continue to be immersed in the stressful information flow.

Yet, a meditative state is very natural. It brings you back to the natural balance. Many traditional human occupations are balanced and non-stressful. Gardening, cooking and washing dishes are among those occupations which bring you back to the balance if you allow yourself to relax. These kinds of work are among the easiest ways to do a meditation practice.

Of course, there are many ways to meditate. They might look different but the purpose and the results are very similar. All these ways bring you back to balance, they bring you back to yourself and reconnect you with the spirit.

Here, I will describe a very basic meditation available to anyone.

First, you need to find a time to meditate. Some people have plenty of free time and some people have no time left for meditation. Those who have no time are usually the ones who are stressed out the most. In this case, the shortest meditation could be only 15 minutes once a day. But the most optimal for busy life would be 3 times a day, 40 minutes each.

The times for meditation can be subtracted from your sleeping time. This way, you would still have time to work but you will become healthier, more balanced and less stressed. If you are working usual working hours, you can fit one meditation period during lunch, one after you come from work and one when you go to sleep.

There are many people who meditate much longer. It's not unusual to meditate 10-15 hours a day.

Next, it is important to find a quiet protected place for meditation. In an ideal situation, you would go to your room, put a sign on your door "Don't Disturb" and lay on your bed. Many people use their car for meditation during their lunch break. Meditation in nature is wonderful. If you are a beginner, it's important to avoid distractions, but as you become used to meditating, the distractions won't bother you anymore. You would be either able to stay in meditation by ignoring the distractions or pause the meditation, deal with urgent problems and come back to meditation again.

Find a position for meditation which is best for you, and can produce the best results. Lying down has advantages because you can completely and easily get disconnected without being worried about your body. It is better to lie straight on your back in the most comfortable position with a pillow and a blanket if needed so you can have as few distractions as possible. The straight symmetrical position has the advantage that your body becomes a better antenna and is more symmetrical in resonating so it connects to the spirit in a better way. However, lying on your stomach or your side is also acceptable, whatever is easier for you.

Some people don't like to meditate in the horizontal position because they easily fall asleep. But merging your meditation with a nap is a rather good idea. In sleep, you also upload experiences to the spirit and download health, harmony, coherence and orderliness from the spirit. The difference between sleep and meditation is that in meditation, you use your intention to connect to the spirit. You guide yourself in the process, and you bring back the specific results. Meditation often is sleep with intention.

Many people practice meditation by sitting in lotus position or in a chair. The advantage is that your spine is straight and vertical and this way your body is balanced and connected to the Earth energies in a different way.

Meditation in a sitting position prevents you from falling asleep. Sitting position is classical for meditation, traditionally in Hinduism and Buddhism people meditate in lotus position. The position you choose for meditation is important because the bone structure creates a resonating antenna to uphold a spiritual vibration.

Meditation while standing or walking, doing repetitive work is also a good idea. Although it doesn't allow you as deep penetration to the spirit, and to disconnect from the body completely but the repetitive motion has its own virtues and benefits, it creates a wave which is used to connect to the spirit. Among best moving meditations are meditations in the shower and while washing dishes.

It is helpful to find a quiet place to meditate. Some people are very sensitive to sound, and some people can disconnect very easily. As you become more balanced and more guided by the spirit, you will find yourself more protected in this way, and you won't have to be on guard all the time. It can be easier to disconnect from the body when you know you are safe.

There are a few tools that help blocking incoming information. Some meditators find helpful using earmuffs. Earmuffs specially designed for woodworkers have best sound protection ratings. Avoid electronic active noise blocking headphones since they bombard you with ultrasound and electromagnetic waves. On other hand, using \meditation music is \a good idea. Very often, the music will prevent you from falling asleep, while helping to create harmonic vibration and disconnect you noises and distractions. A sleeping mask for your eyes would also help you with the meditation.

Many guided meditations are available on YouTube. A guided meditation is a good for beginners. It hypnotises you into a meditative mood. As you select a meditation on YouTube, preview different ones and see which one resonates with you and gives you a feeling of trust and protection. As you practice more and more, you might find that meditating in silence allows you to get into a meditative state faster and be more connected to your own experience and your own soul.

It is very healthy to meditate in a place with good energies and fresh air. As you become sensitive to energies, you can feel which energies are best for you. Such places could be the top of a hill, or seashore, on a river, or a place near a little creek - any place with a natural water.

A forest is a great place. Artificial places like churches, domes and houses with pyramidal roofs are great. Yet some other places are pretty negative. When places are charged with negative energy and connected to past or present suffering, you would need put a special effort to adjust to this negative energy. One way is to separate yourself from it. Another is to transform it into a positive energy. Remember that you are a healer and take on yourself a mission to heal the past and present trauma using your meditation. Intend to make the energies positive and work on that in your meditation.

217

You begin the meditation by finding a comfortable position and adjusting your pillow, blanket and earmuffs. Relax the palms and put them on your stomach in the most comfortable position. You can put your relaxed right palm on the solar plexus and the left palm just above your on your navel. Adjust your positions to feel more comfortable. Focus on your breathing and intend to breathe slower and deeper than usual. Use your belly to breathe.

Choose an intention for today's meditation. A typical intention would be to upload your problems to the spirit and get back the healing and the answers. If you have any questions for spirit, pronounce them for yourself and expect to have at least some resolution by the end of the meditation. That resolution doesn't have to come in words. It could just be a better understanding, a better acceptance of the situation.

It is a good idea to say a short prayer. In each meditation, you might address a specific aspect of God or Spirit. You can address your prayer to the one God, the Creator, Divine Mother, the Universe, the Source, Yeshua, Jesus, the archangels or a specific angel or archangel, a specific friendly alien, a specific ancestor of yours, or to a spirit of your favorite celebrity.

On a different day, you may be attracted to a different aspect of God. So, do it as you feel better. Keep in mind that from a certain perspective, they all become one, they are all united in the spirit, and they all are aspects of God and you are as well. A typical prayer starts with gratitude, continues with the invitation of help and ends with gratitude. Here is an example of a typical short prayer:

Thank you, the Universe, for this experience.

I invite your healing energy.

I thank you for sending me the healing.

Time, from the spiritual perspective, is much more fluid. It is therefore okay to give thanks for the healing which may come later in your time. Gratitude is also one of the best remedies for stress. Gratitude not only heals trauma, it also helps you on your life path in mysterious ways.

218

Once you found the time and space for meditation, and once you're comfortable and have silences visual and audible distractions and once you have begun your conscious breathing, are you actually meditating? How do you know you're doing the right thing? What do you actually do during meditation?

All that has been said until now was physical. These are easy steps to accomplish, but the next step is not physical - it is spiritual. You can program a robot, to lie down, close eyes and to breathe deeply, but only a spiritual being like you can meditate. So what is the secret?

The secret is to make a transdimensional jump. Until now, all actions are physical and can actually be described in words but as you do such a trans-dimensional jump, what you will feel and see there often cannot be described with words and can not be perceived with physical mind. You will need to shift from the physicality, and from physical sensations to the area where you don't feel, dont think and where your consciousness exists beyond physicality.

So, we are asking for a miracle and this miracle is actually accessible to anyone. Some people disconnect from the physical world with ease. For others, it is a skill which can be developed. What makes this much easier is that you are not alone in this journey, you are being helped by spirit guides from the other side.

A desire to meditate, a desire to shift to a higher reality is sufficient. If you get in a quiet place, and quiet your mind, you will be helped to shift. Another understanding that helps to meditate is to understand that meditation is essentially a form of a sleep. It is a sleep with intention.

The Dalai Lama said sleep is the best meditation. What makes meditation much easier is that you go to the other side every night when you sleep anyway. All you need to do now is to go to another side with intention to connect to spirit, to upload your worries, to download your health and to assist your spiritual growth.

Brain imaging studies and brain wave measurements show that in meditation, you reach the same frequency of brain waves as you do when

219

sleeping and dreaming. Only because you do it with intention and consciously, you can achieve a higher harmony, higher coherence and a better connection to the Spirit.

When people meditate, they usually go to a higher vibration, a happier place, a better balance and to state of self-healing. Yet there are a few people who drift to darkness. There are some people that are so stressed out and are so prone to depression that when they meditate, they habitually go into sadness and connect to lower vibrations. Meditation for them can become a sour trip.

If you meet this kind of experience, look for help from someone who can guide you to a higher vibration. It can be a guidance in person or through a YouTube video. A great help in such situation is Reiki energy healing.

One of the ways of using Reiki is to guide meditation and a Reiki session can become in essence an assisted meditation. Getting the high vibrations of high-connectedness through Reiki, could be of great help when you are depressed and stressed out even during meditation. Even if you are not stressed, Reiki could be a great path to uplift your meditations to a higher level.

During a Reiki session, the healer places hands on your head and then on your heart and sends a spiritual energetic vibration to your head and heart, which brings you up to a healing state of mind. As you receive Reiki, remember the vibration, so later, when you meditate on your own, you could reproduce this vibration and induce these brain waves which allow you to connect to the spirit at will.

As you shift in your meditation to another dimension, you shift through the veil to another side of the existence, there are certain signs which can help you to understand that you are moving in the right direction. As you invite communication with your favorite Aspect of God, use your intention, it matters! Intend the Aspect of Got to come to you and it will come. It may appear as a sound, a vibration, as silence or frequently as a light which you will see inside your head and not through your eyes.

It is a spiritual vibration which creates a physical electric wave in the visual cortex area of your brain. DNA and neurons in your brain work as a portal from higher vibrations of the spirit to lower vibrations of the mind. As you see that light, move towards it. Embrace it and discover for yourself that you can make it stronger. It is in your power to go in that light and make it stronger. The same relates to other sensations which you might get, like the warmness in your heart, a healing light in your heart - it is in your power to move towards them and amplify them.

As you feel them and you feel they're good, embrace them and make them stronger, moving in that direction. In a good meditation, your soul becomes disconnected from your body. As you shift into a higher dimension, you lose the control over your body. This often feels as numbness: you may feel that you cannot move your hands and legs. Welcome this state because it is a sign of a good meditation.

Usually, you would still be in control of your breathing. Enjoy breathing deeply and slowly in a comfortable manner, and just welcome the numbness and heaviness in the rest of your body. When you come back, don't worry if the control of your body is coming back too slow. Give your soul some time to reconnect to the body and to take control of the body. It may take 15 minutes to come back and it is healthier to come back slowly.

Begin to move your fingers and toes and give yourself time to reconnect. As you become reconnected, it happens automatically and subconsciously. You might feel an urge to wake up and move. If you do, move slowly and don't rush. As you often have leftovers after waking from a sleeping dream, coming back to physical life after a deep meditation usually takes a little bit of time and practice.

In these moments, before fully coming back, you can use that time to ask questions and get answers. Prepare your questions for the spirit in advance and this time of coming back is a wonderful time when you're partly still connected to the spirit and are partly in control of your mind. You can ask questions and get some intuitive answers. Expect to feel the answers, and have a good feeling on what spirit is recommending to you.

There are many good visualizations which help you to get in a meditation state. Many guided meditations can give you these visualizations. I would recommend to visualize as you breathe the air in, that you're breathing in the healing energy of the universe. And as you breathe out, pump it into your heart and visualize a ball of glowing energy in your heart-a golden flame in your heart.

And this is about it. There's not much more to it. It is going to the point where you are quiet and still, when you are disconnected from your worries in your body and trust that spirit will come and your focus of attention will shift to the area of higher vibration where it can dwell in the spirit. Release your worries there and bring back the answers, the healings and the spiritual upgrades.

There is not much instruction what to do when you are in the spirit, since words fail to describe the spirit world. The instructions can only help you to achieve the meditation state and beyond that you can trust your spirit guides to guide you. Remember you are visiting this place in your sleep anyway, so the meditation is only different in that you add your intention to it.

CLEARING YOUR MIND AND DISCONNECTING

Many people have hard time disconnecting from their thoughts and quieting down worries. Realize, it is only for the time of meditation that you have to quiet them down.

In meditation, if the worry or a thought becomes excited in your mind, don't push it away. Be kind to it. Just talk to it and ask it to wait until you get out of meditation. Basically, put it on the side burner. Put it on the shelf and say to it that you will think about it later so you don't have to think about it during the meditation. You can delay the thought and clean your mind.

Among many visualizations for clearing up your mind take the one which is good for you at the moment. You can visualize washing dishes or washing windows. I recommend visualizing a windshield wiper which swings in front of your vision and removes all the thoughts, all the images, and concerns which pop-up in your mind. Just wipe them out and have your mind clean and empty.

It takes a lot of integration and purification work to be able to disconnect from the physical reality and shift into the stillness. In your physical body, there are several points where you can put your focus of attention for the meditation. One of them is the heart. You can focus the mind on your heart and intend it to stay there. As you notice your attention to wander away, bring it back to the heart and intend it to remain there focused on love and peace.

Another good focusing point is in the middle of the forehead called the third eye. You can focus your presence and attention on this spot on your forehead. Third place which you can use to focus is pineal gland, located in the center of your brain just a bit above your ears.

It doesn't matter that much where you focus your attention. What matters is that your mind gets to the point of stillness and balance, so it can stop thinking. If your meditation works well, then after the meditation you should get more energy and more health. And amazingly, the world will be better and friendlier to you. Your problems will gradually resolve to your favor. Meditation is a miracle work and the main miracle is that while you quiet your mind, there is something done in the background without your conscious intervention. Something is done subconsciously to help your physical life and help with your problems. As you come out of meditation, repeat your prayers and thank your spiritual helpers for their help. If some of your meditations are not as deep as others, don't worry because the depth of meditation depends on many factors and one of them is planetary alignments. As you meditate, you may notice that meditations come out very different depending on the moon phase. Take it easy, there is a natural cycle which we can not change but we can surf the waves created by the planets: new moon favors new beginnings, waxing moon favors growth, full moon favors transformation, waning moon favors harvesting and completion.

Sometimes, meditating is easy and sometimes meditating is almost impossible and you remain awake during the whole meditation, don't shift to the other side and don't feel the numbness. All the attributes might be wrong, yet it does still help to meditate even if you don't go fully to the other side. Even partial meditation still has lots of benefits for your health, your spirit and your practical life.

In addition to typical meditations which require to be still and involve full disconnection from reality, there are meditations on the move that happen even without all above attributes. These are useful when you are active., can not find a quiet place to lay down or sit in a comfortable position.

Sometimes, a good meditation might take a second. Good meditators are meditating non-stop while continuing their daily routines. Ideally, we should be in non-stop meditation, a hundred percent of our time, connected to spirit and not losing the balance.

Consider dolphins. Dolphins are unique in a way that they are always awake and they are always asleep. Their brain is divided into two halves, each one is awake while another is asleep and these two halves take turns. Thus, a dolphin is always conscious and always connected to the other side.

Dolphin is an ideal perpetual, continuous meditater. In your meditations and awake life strive to achieve this balance. Strive to be always conscious in physicality and on the other side. This idea is very similar to the idea of lucid dream, except lucid dream is about dreaming, but here this idea is expanded to awake life as well. Let's call it lucid awareness - be always aware either in physical or in dream.

Although this continuous meditation can be achieved only by special ultra-pure, ultra-advanced spiritual people, if it doesn't come easy, consider an alternative path.

Instead of striving to constantly being aware, strive to frequently alternate between the meditation state and the awakening state. Strive to be like a pendulum. Shift to and be in a meditative state, and then shift out and be in physicality. This serves your practical need and also it serves the spirit. In physicality, you can go in any vibration you like. You can be earthly, practical, and grounded. This also helps you to connect to the majority of people which are tuned to the physical side of the world. So shifting down helps you to connect with other people on their level of understanding.

And then you go back to a higher level, and there, upload all your experience to spirit and receive back the answers and the healing.

Going back and forth is natural. You can do it at any time and get results. It takes practice, and commitment and it also takes connecting to spiritual teachers and helpers with meditation.

Being in the presence of a teacher and a group of meditators helps very much to rise to a higher level. Even most experienced of the meditators still learn more when they connect to other people. Unexpectedly, you often will find that everyone can be your teacher, even from people of lower developments can help you in your meditations and help you raise in a new level.

LOOKING INSIDE

Since the main work of meditation happens on the non-physical and spiritual planes, it doesn't really matter what physical actions you utilize to achieve the effect. This is why there is no single formula for meditation, although it is very helpful to start the meditation in the standard way with the help of guides, teachers or teaching materials.

Once you learn to shift in a spiritual area and achieve spiritual results, it is possible to start doing the meditations anywhere and not necessarily in a quiet protected place, nor in any special position, but anywhere, at any time, during any activity. For some people, it might be even easier to do meditation during repetitive activities, rather than in complete stillness.

Keep in mind however, that it is really helpful to be in a protected environment and in a sitting or lying position to fully shift out of the body, to avoid falling and getting physically hurt. Also, if you are a beginner you might get spiritually hurt by negative influences, traumas, or negativity in the environment.

So it's better to begin in a protected environment when you're sure there are no disturbances. It's important to turn off the phone and once you finish the meditation, if you're not fully protected, don't open your emails and text messages until you really get back to physical reality and are protected again. Many people when they start to meditate, have trouble facing themselves and become restless and distracted. It often happens that if you have a lot of hidden trauma, anger and pain, meditation could bring these to the surface.

Many beginners when they face themselves and look inside, they find pain and for a modern human, it is painful to look inside. It takes some conscious purification and integration work during the meditations and in conscious awakened time to face these pains – to discover the pains and hidden traumas, resolve and to disconnect from them. One common practice that help to resolve past traumas, is the understanding that the past is in the past and it doesn't help you to hold on to past trauma. It slows you down and blocks the energy flows and hurts your health.

So the secret is to separate the lesson from the trauma, the pain and the trauma itself. Many practices include the Buddhist practices of meditation, psychoanalysis, and past life regressions. You look at the past trauma, understand what happened, separate the lesson from the trauma, keep the memory of the experience, forgive yourself and others involved in the trauma and release the pain. You know that you have resolved the trauma when you have healed the pain, and can think about and remember the past experience clearly without feeling the pain as before. Instead, you feel forgiveness, compassion, and love for yourself. You don't feel ashamed anymore, and can separate your current state from the past.

You'll shift to the new form of yourself and realize that the past experience is in the past and it is separate from you now. You understand that all experiences are stored in Akashic records and become the possession of the universe. All experiences and lessons belong to the universal consciousness, and all experiences are equally valid. You can let go of the pain, heal the trauma and move on. You can heal many of your past traumas by yourself, but it often helps to also get help from a friend, a teacher and a healer. So it is very helpful to connect to other healers and become a healer yourself. Finding friends of high spiritual vibration is a really good help in spiritual growth.

A POEM ABOUT GOD

Received viaLakesh (Blue Pleiadian)

Channeled by Jim

I bring myself down into meditation, up through meditation

And the air around me, the atmosphere charged

With that unlike the body, and unlike the soul.

You bring life into me, bring me up from my down,

Bring me through when I cannot make it.

And you are the light killing my darkness;

You are the light bringing no shadow for me.

I run toward you in my spirit mind,

And catch only the shining element that you leave behind.

WALKING THE PATH

From the spiritual perspective, the purpose of life is to go through lessons and earn experience. It's not that the body has a soul, but that the soul employs the body to obtain physical experience and thought/interiority to cultivate spiritual growth. The purpose of your life on Earth is not predetermined: you are tasked with charging your life with purpose—free choice. And you may choose to serve the Spirit in its desire to obtain experience; to help your soul grow.

What do spirits and aliens want from us? Surprisingly, from many channelings, a consistent answer arises: spirits and aliens have a predominant concern: they desire our metaphysical growth. This is the main measure of our progress. It is therefore one of the major options in your choice of purpose.

As you work on your meditation and spiritual growth, you may invite your Higher Self into your body and submit to guidance of the Spirit. This doesn't relieve you from solving practical questions in physical life, but takes the weight of responsibility for your life's direction. The burden gradually is offloaded from your mind, and taken by your Higher Self. As the responsibility falls from your shoulders, back pain vanishes.

As an agent of the Spirit on Earth, you become a messenger, a worker, and may choose to call yourself a *lightworker*.

Hindi words related to this choice are avatar and bodhisattva. An avatar is a manifestation of God on Earth. Bodhisattva is a spirit that has achieved liberation, but chooses to remain on Earth to help people. Also there are Ascended Masters, who moved to the Spirit, but serve Earth denizens from the Spirit side.

As you begin committing to and working for the cosmic intelligence on Earth, you will be given more energy, assignments and assistance with completing these tasks. You'll still learn your lessons, but will be also plugged into the matrix of lightworkers who labor on behalf of the Spirit, and walk the path assigned by the higher Spiritual intelligence.

The choice is yours. Meditation is one of the greatest tools toward that path.

TEKKRR: ON DOLPHINS AND WHALES

Channeled by Jim

Tekkrr: You will see, in the near future, that the dolphins and whales will become more active and more communicative. Scientists will be dazzled by

228

what they learn, because these creatures are collectors of light who hold positivity onto the planet, and spread light communication across the oceans. As you are connected one to another, the dolphins and whales will bring that connection to other lands. They bring in light too from other areas of the universe: from the andromenant to the alien whale and dolphin alliance. They have a ship within your space, and it is working.

As you know, the vessel is tremendous in size, and filled with water. But these entities comprise various colors and wear clothing, to meet with other delegates. So, if you have a dream or vision of a dolphin or whale bearing colors, know that that is their clothing. They paint themselves with different colors, as to be socially accepted by other species, to not appear naked, and be intelligent and provide an acceptable protocol. They are of profound intelligence.

Their language is trinary; with every sound comes different layers of tonality. Embedded in these layers you'll find sentences, not merely one word. That is why they were never to be understood until now. The knowledge will emerge that, with a single sound, they are speaking many words. That sound mutates, and brings in precisely the words they most need, because they know their speech potentially will mutate in the water, and expand into the sentence, or paragraph, they need to verbalize. Hence, one emittance of sound is not simply any single word, but many.

EZRA (DOLPHIN)

Channeled by Jim

Ezra: Hi?

Max: Hi.

Ezra: It's difficult to connect, a moment please.

Max: Welcome.

Ezra: That's better, who am I speaking to?

Max: I'm Max, I'm in the San Diego area and I saw some beautiful dolphins today.

Ezra: Thank you; it is difficult speaking through humans since we have a trinary language but we will adapt, thank you for appreciation.

Max: Do you have any questions for me?

Ezra: We always question about human behavior, it is illogical, therefore we do not expect answers that are making too much sense to us.

Max: I wrote the book on irrational human behavior. It's called WELCOME TO EARTH! A GUIDE FOR ALIENS.

Ezra: Yes, understood.

Max: Do you have access to books?

Ezra: Not in the same way you have. We have information coming through light beams, so that we can read partial information if necessary.

Max: I invite the light beams to translate my book to you.

Ezra: Very well. Have you ever tried communications with us?

Max: Yes, every time I see you I sing you my songs.

Ezra: Do you feel our energies?

Max: Yes, of course. I need to be in a special state for you to manifest.

Ezra: You are an ocean-goer, as I understand.

Max: Yeah, I go on a kayak and when I see dolphins I chant to them, and to sea lions.

Ezra: What is their reaction?

Max: Sometimes none. Sometimes a lot of nice communication, and they dance around.

Ezra: It is depending on their destination at the moment.

Max: Yeah, I know, and the other times I'm too excited, so they just go away. They don't like too much excitement.

Ezra: They would rather see you be at ease. Over-excitement can be dangerous to us. We have learned that when there is a great deal of excitement it can either be very positive or very negative. Either way, it can be dangerous.

Max: My first question: are you communicating with other human-looking cultures, such as the alien humanoids, people from far away?

Ezra: Yes, allow me to explain that. We hold light for this planet, we extend it and are sending energies to the planet as a whole. Even though we are water creatures we can connect energies with humanity.

Max: What are these energies, and how can we identify them?

Ezra: They are heart energies, fire-soul energies. We have souls like you, and fire in the heart. We connect in that similar way that you connect to each other.

Max: Do you relate to our gods?

Ezra: Your gods?

Max: Are you praying to Jesus, or any other?

Ezra: There is one creator being whom we find worthy of our praise.

Max: Can you share their name?

Ezra: We call him Derah.

Max: Is this related to our Ra from Egypt?

Ezra: No.

Max: I see. Derah. Would you know Ram, Indian God Ram?

231

Ezra: I know of him through human information.

Max: How about Kali?

Ezra: Kali, yes, these are ancient names.

Max: Krishna?

Ezra: This is more modern.

Max: Yahweh?

Ezra: Yes, we say Yahweh.

Max: One of your deities?

Ezra: He can be called this; it is an ancient form of his name from the beginning of the Earth.

Max: Are you in telepathic contact with our cats?

Ezra: With some animals, yes. Cats, yes, but not all cats; not all dogs. Dogs are harder to communicate with. Cats listen better.

Max: How about elephants?

Ezra: They can understand us to a point, but are not good communicators.

Max: Okay, are you in communication with Ganesh?

Ezra: Ganesh is an elephant head. He is not the same as elephant species, and yes we can connect to his energy. However, we do not call him Ganesh.

Max: The dogs and cats. You are from Sirius, aren't you?

Ezra: Sirius area. There are other dolphin and whale species in Andromeda. We have travelled many trillions of miles.

Max: Are you traveling now?

Ezra: There are portions of our species that travel constantly.

Max: Nice. So are the dolphins travelling in outer space?

Ezra: We are not into galactic travels at this time. We choose to remain here for this period and for the future.

Max: Do the members of galactic community have ambassadors with your people?

Ezra: Yeah. They come and they go. They come underwater in their ships and we have meetings. I am the ambassador of this planet to other places. That is why I speak now.

Max: And you personally live on Earth, right?

Ezra: I live here, yes.

Max: Are you now on Earth?

Ezra: Yes.

Max: I see.

Ezra: I am not to leave again for another several months. Our calendars, our time resolutions are slightly differently calibrated.

Max: Wait a second, are you going to say . . .

Ezra: Yes, but we do not have to use your time sense.

Max: This is a lunar calendar?

Ezra: Yes.

Max: By the way, there was a strange phenomenon last week. The ocean receded, and I think there were three of four trees down and they stayed down for almost a week. Do you know the reason for that?

Ezra: Yes. A great chasm opened at the bottom of the ocean, but that is not all. There was some water taken from the planet. That is all I can tell you.

Max: Is it related to the swallow of lashes?

Ezra: There is some relation, but not as you probably imagine.

Max: Is it related to the hurricanes?

Ezra: Hurricanes right now are man-made.

Max: So they are not responsible for taking the water out?

Ezra: No.

Max: I see. Another question. What's your relationship with whales?

Ezra: We keep along very well. We both speak the same kind of language. Not exactly, but it's similar.

Max: Do you cross incarnate whales to dolphins and vice versa?

Ezra: There are all kinds of cross incarnations within the galaxies and universe, so you yourself would be a cross section of other species as well.

Max: Do you often incarnate in Earth humans?

Ezra: There have been instances where we can learn from that incarnation.

Max: So it's not frequent?

Ezra: It is not frequent because it is not necessary for us to know some of the things that you know and deal with some of the things that you deal with, and thus we are headed for a higher understanding and a higher position in leadership in the galaxies, eventually in the way of prophecy.

Max: Do humans reincarnate as dolphins?

Ezra: Yes.

Max: Really?

Ezra: Not often in the past, but more often recently because they are discovering how advanced we are and they want to learn more about us.

Max: Do dolphins incarnate as lions and tigers?

Ezra: Yes.

Max: Is it fun?

Ezra: Not usually.

Max: Are you related to cats?

Ezra: It is more dangerous to be a land animal than to be a sea dolphin.

Max: Yes, absolutely, so are you related to cats?

Ezra: Distantly, in some strange way, I would say we are.

Max: And who are you closer to genetically, cats or dogs?

Ezra: Cats.

Max: Are you in a relationship with Girk-Fitneer?

Ezra: We are not aligned with them, but we do speak as friends, so that is a relationship we do have.

Max: Do you have a favorite human-looking alien species with which you communicate a lot?

Ezra: Human-looking species are much the same.

Max: So you don't have any favorites?

Ezra: This one is not our favorite since you are too violent.

Max: Of course.

Ezra: The Kior perhaps is better.

Max: Can you say again the name?

Ezra: Kior.

Max: Kior, I see.

Ezra: They look very similar to humans, but are very much advanced.

Max: How about elephants and tureens?

Ezra: There are other human looking species that are more violent than you, but there also are others that are better.

Max: When you go to the ships, air-breathing ships, air-filled ships, is it easy for you to be there? I think with modern technology you can surround yourself with water and have some sort of propulsion system right?

Ezra: There is water where we go for our convenience and for our comfort.

Max: So you have to surround yourself with water, you can't just get air in some sort of a space suit, can you?

Ezra: Not usually. We do have the ability to stay in the air for a while, but it is not always comfortable after a certain period of time.

Max: Would it be possible to surround yourself with a thin layer of water so you're buffered, but there is air?

Ezra: There are some species that give us water suits like you have mentioned.

Max: Can you transfigure yourself into human? Is it easy for you?

Ezra: No, we cannot change our shape.

Max: Like shape-shifters?

Ezra: No, not shape-shifters.

Max: Are you visited by aquatic aliens in rough oceans?

Ezra: There are some that do visits; you would be surprised how busy the ocean is with alien ships, they are not detectable in the water from radar. They are also able to stay away from any ships that are human, or hide from them easily in the fourth dimension.

Max: Right, my question was does anybody come out like aquatic species which could swim in the ocean, and they would communicate with you?

Ezra: Of course.

Max: Are there any species you would like to introduce us to, so we would know who is living on our planet?

Ezra: That would be up to them.

Max: Can you pass our invitation to friendly species to introduce themselves?

Ezra: Yes.

Max: Because I just realized there might be a lot of friendly aliens right here in the waters.

Ezra: The waters hold more aliens than the soil does because they are less detectable there.

Max: Who is in charge of keeping peace in the ocean?

Ezra: It is how it is in nature. Nature has its way of governing the situation, but we have let ourselves know, let ourselves be known as peaceful species and we are not often hunted as we were in the past.

Max: In the water down below there is no police, correct?

Ezra: No, there is an unspoken code followed which must stay for the sea to survive. It is a command of the food chain. We are in that chain, but not as much as we used to be. It's not necessary.

Max: I think there are other intelligent species, let's call them conscious and intelligent, in the water other than mammals. Maybe even a few are known mammal species?

Ezra: There are, yes.

Max: Are you in communication with them?

Ezra: They are in the lower depths, and we are in the higher. There are more shallow depths.

Max: So you are not in Martian communication?

Ezra: We do communicate, but it's not something that is often necessary. There are great animals at the base of the ocean hidden in the depths.

Max: How do we say "ascension"?

Ezra: Ascension.

Max: How do you see the planet ascension?

Ezra: We are aware that it is going through this kind of a change, and we are here to move the lights as much as possible and therefore see it only from our perspective. As going fairly well, there are places however that do not hold lights well. Japan, China and Korea. These places hold light, but only because there are so many of them. They do not hold bright lights and there are not many of them.

Max: Do you see a jump coming, like when they finally have a reason for threshold and there will be a jump into another density?

Ezra: It will be a gradual movement.

Max: And what do you think will make it, or how long will it take? How many years?

Ezra: We are not that good at predicting what is to happen on the whole planet. We know that in the waters, things happen more quickly in some regards, but on your planet happen radically. It could be a radical change for you, but we see more of a gradual movement in the process. The portions will be wake-up calls for those who need to understand they have to start doing something or begin their missions.

Max: So how do you think we will proceed when the jump happens? Will you stay in the Earth or will you move to the next . . .

Ezra: Of course we are here to stay.

Max: There is that understanding that some of the humans will move to another terra high planet.

Ezra: The next dimension up from this one is terra high, not being moved there.

Max: You are not moving there, right?

Ezra: We are not moving there. There are some of us there already.

Max: Are you in telepathic contact with them?

Ezra: They must contact us as we cannot contact them.

Max: But you are talking, right?

Ezra: Yes.

Max: Interesting. Is your society also structured? Do you have anyone similar to priests?

Ezra: There are different occupations. Yes, there are those of us that are higher in understanding. So they may be called priests.

Max: Do you have teleconnect abilities?

Ezra: No.

Max: Can you tell other fish to come closer using your mind, so that you can eat them?

Ezra: We can communicate what our needs are to others.

Max: Can you protect yourself using your mind?

Ezra: At times mental abilities help. Communications also help. We speak much like humans in the sense that as children we have to learn the language just as you do, but it is helpful to teach the children how to get out of the others' way as quickly as possible.

Max: Are you in control of magic? If you hear four-dimensional energy can you use it to move things around?

Ezra: Interesting question. We are not in charge of four-dimensional energy. Those in the fourth dimension have charge.

Max: I see. Can you teleport naturally?

Ezra: There are times when teleportation is necessary, but those are rare.

Max: Can you talk to the planet?

Ezra: Mother Gaia as you call her is in constant contact with us.

Max: What is the news from Mother Gaia?

Ezra: There is much news. She is going through great turmoil now, but there are many [of us] helping her to stabilize.

Max: Do you do this collectively, like all dolphins?

Ezra: We do have daily routines that will help us.

Max: So do you synchronize by the ocean or by the tribe? Is there a global synchronization between all of you?

Ezra: Yes. In some respects. We can communicate over long distances, and do know what is happening because our thoughts are sometimes connected. The vibration of our speech is trinary, and the heart of that is a higher frequency that can reach into greater areas of the mind. The long distances.

Max: Do you have a hive mind?

Ezra: I would hope that it is high.

Max: No, I mean hive.

Ezra: No.

Max: Do you talk to the ocean?

Ezra: The ocean is our home. We can talk to it and it can speak to us in some ways.

Max: What is the character of the ocean when it speaks? I just wonder.

Ezra: The character is strong. The ocean has its reasons and they are never-changing. They are consistent and constant.

Max: I'm on the ocean frequently, and depending on the day it feels very different. It does change, right?

Ezra: You might be aware that the ocean has its rules as well, but its reasoning is always the same.

Max: How intelligent is it? Is it very wise, or doesn't actually think in human terms? Is it more like a part of nature . . .?

Ezra: It is part of nature. It does things as part of nature, and how it is within that, and does what it must to maintain life.

Max: I'm just thinking that we all consist of water, so might be all synchronized with the ocean.

Ezra: Some ways you are. The ocean is synchronized with space and gravity and light.

Max: Thank you. Is there anything else you would like to speak about?

Ezra: I cannot think of anything. I was surprised that you called us.

Max: Thank you. Do you keep poetry?

Ezra: Poetry is in trinary language.

Max: Is there anything translatable to us?

Ezra: We think it is more abstract than you might wish. But here is a sample of something small. The energy flows through us, giving us the ways of nature yet higher-bounding thoughts are in the energy as well.

We race with it, but yet it is always ahead and we are always reasoning that we can capture part of it, and yet when we do capture energy, it is only for our own use and not for the purpose of extraordinary effects.

Max: Do you have more?

Ezra: Did you like that?

Max: It was great to connect to your way of making poetry. It was very new for me. Wonderful.

Ezra: There are others, but we are not considered great poets. Here is one other that I found interesting from below the surface. The sun ripples upon the tops of the sea like a different place, a different existence but when you are there looking down at the ripples and the sparkles, under the oceans seem to be a better place. So it is true that you can be fooled by a beam of light. A piece of thought that does not connect to other things in your world. You are therefore curious about all the things you cannot know.

Max: Can you get us more?

Ezra: Are you enjoying this?

Max: Yes. Thank you. It is a very new thing and very enjoyable.

Ezra: The elegance of motion that we portray exists within DNA. We are that, that move is graceful and yet powers that water away as we cut through and then all the entities around us are smaller and greater in their small motion within the density of the sea. Not thinking but taking for granted that it exists for them. You cut through and splash on surface and it is like breaking into another round but yet the sunshine feels warmer and it is comfort when you return to your place of beginning.

Max: Thank you. If I hear more it will be great. If it is over it is fine, but more will be wonderful.

Ezra: I would like not to spend too much time giving you trivial things. They are trivial, but in some senses when we pass them down, they are relatable to children. So they may be able to sleep or gather that they are of a greater essence. Do you understand?

Max: Yes.

Ezra: A child's story is always one of eye-opening thoughts. You wanted more?

Max: Yes.

Ezra: I will give you one more. This is for the children and there you are. Where you were not before open your eyes and let the sea cleanse your vision. Let the sea show you who it is. Let the sea be also a parent but let me be with you in all the things occasions that are nurturing. And let the sea teach you of its other wisdom. The water that flows around you, you feel but yet my comfort is the greatest sensation than the cold and the heat than anything that you can experience within the water. Let the water be a friend but let me be God.

Max: Thank you. Could you first share your name—as a way to translate it?

Ezra: Ezra.

Max: It sounded like Ezra.

Ezra: You may speak it any way you like.

Max: Do you mind being called Ezra?

Ezra: It is fine.

Max: Thank you for speaking. That was wonderful. At this point I will invite maybe anyone that can speak to me and . . .

Ezra: You cannot know yet. It was a pleasure to speak to you today, Max.

Max: Thank you. Come again, Ezra.

Ezra: I am surprised you enjoyed our poetry.

Max: It was wonderful, and I enjoyed seeing dolphins today. That was great too.

Ezra: We are graceful compared to humans.

Max: Yes.

Ezra: We will speak to you again.

Max: Thank you.

PERSONAL EXPERIENCES ON PLEIADIAN PLANETS

Interview with Zacariah

Zacariah Heim was born and educated on Earth, but during his early years, he lived a parallel life on Pleiadian planets. He remembers this life well, and past lives on alien worlds. Published with permission.

Max: You started the story about Armin . . .

Zacariah: Yes, the Pleiadian boy.

Max: Would you tell the whole story?

Zacariah: Yes. He doesn't like when I talk openly about his parents, so I can't discuss that now. Perhaps later, because, you know, he's still a little skittish on the whole subject. But I can talk about everything else.

Max: All right.

Zacariah: Armin is a Pleiadian boy who stays with my friend Monita. He was not "given to us," but brought to Earth to stay with Monita and I for protection. It's unfortunate, but he's, you know, an orphan. His parents died tragically in an accident that I can't explain right this minute. But in a past life, when I was in the Council of Nine as Zanzibar, I was an Arctuvian [spelled with V] and well respected in the society. I was good friends with Armin's father, Arish Narnell. And Monita, her name was Koosma, was a teenager in this life and family friends with Armin's mother. When the parents died, they basically put in the will that he would be sent to us, because they knew we were going to be placed on Earth in our next lives.

Max: Mmm-hmm.

Zacariah: So, in this life, we are taking care of and protecting Armin from those who wish to kill him. They are reptilian creatures called Saurians.

Max: Mmm-hmm.

Zacariah: They're dark workers. Because he is . . . In the original creation of our universe, there were five creator souls that came from a separate universe.

Max: Okay.

Zacariah: Well, they were created in a separate universe, and they came into ours to seed life and the creation of our universe. Armin is one of the fragments of this soul, as am I and Monita, which is why he was placed with us.

Max: Is he one of five?

Zacariah: Yes, he is one of these five.

Max: Armin, okay. Can you remind me of the two other names? How they were . . . The other names?

Zacariah: Shenshima.

Max: Uh huh.

Zacariah: Orkvine, Zanzibar, Kenowa and Koosma.

Max: Thank you.

Zacariah: He is Orkvine.

Max: Okay, and Monita is . . .?

Zacariah: Monita is Koosma.

Max: Uh-huh, thank you. So how is . . .? He's not in our dimension, not in three-D, right?

Zacariah: No, he's in the fourth, but has manifested temporarily in the third when we ask.

Max: Oh wow.

Zacariah: So this is, you know, how we have proof that he is real, because he has manifested before.

Max: Tell me more. Tell me, you know, how it looked.

Zacariah: It was actually a strange sight, and the very first time we saw him manifest was at Monita's house.

Max: Uh-huh.

Zacariah: So we were playing with a flame, we were doing pyrokinesis and flame dancing . . .

Max: Yes, uh-huh.

Zacariah: . . . and he was moving the flame around and I was like, "Okay, Armin, that's training, why don't you try manifesting yourself into our dimension?"

Max: Mmm-hmm.

Zacariah: Ten minutes later, standing in front of the TV, there was this blue little boy out of nowhere. It blew my mind and I actually freaked out a little more than I probably should have. This scared him, and he disappeared back into the fourth dimension because he couldn't hold his vibration.

Max: Uh-huh.

Zacariah: And the second time he manifested actually was in school. We were in class, and I look over at Monita's back and I see the translucent Pleiadian boy on her back, and I'm very glad that it was only for a couple of seconds because it probably would've freaked out a lot of people.

Max: Do you think only you would see that, or everybody? You don't know, right?

Zacariah: Everybody who's open to it would see it.

Max: Mmm-hmm.

Zacariah: But most people, their vision's set in this low vibration, even lower in the second dimension, so a lot of them wouldn't see him if they weren't open to it.

Max: So on fourth-dimensional Earth, are there other humans?

Zacariah: Oh yes, many. Humans exist in every single dimension of Earth's realms.

Max: Okay.

Zacariah: In the fourth dimension they are more advanced than we are, but still go through the same problems of population control, garbage disposal and stuff like that. Not as much as we, but they're ascending into the fifth and sixth dimensions right now, and look like us except they're slightly taller with less cultural diversity, meaning we're more of a global population than individual nations.

Max: So, when we move to the fourth, would we meet them?

Zacariah: No, because they would be moving into the fifth. Some souls might stay from the fourth and might not ascend because they weren't ready, so we might meet some, but won't meet the physical beings because their bodies will die.

Max: Would we see the dead bodies?

Zacariah: Possibly, there's always . . . If we're open to it, because . . . Their bodies themselves, well . . . Okay, so you have the fourth dimension, and millions of different realities.

Max: All right.

Zacariah: When we're moving into the fourth dimension, we're simply moving into a select reality there. These beings exist in another reality, so we might see them.

Max: Oh, so we wouldn't meet them.

Zacariah: We might see them.

Max: Oh, we might see them, or not.

Zacariah: If we chose . . . Yeah, might, might not, if we choose to transition.

Max: But it is the same Earth, it's kind of overlapped themes, right? It's . . . They're not overlapped but very close to each other.

Zacariah: Everything is connected, yes.

Max: Would we see their cities?

Zacariah: Yes, we would see some of their cities. We would see some of their ruins, architectural feats, technologies, but these are only the things that manifest within the reality we are viewing ourselves.

Max: I see. So you think their souls are not interchangeable with ours, that fourth-dimensional people don't incarnate in the third because they already . . .

Zacariah: Oh yeah, they do.

Max: They do.

Zacariah: They do if they want, like, if they wanna help out with the lower dimensions, help raise the vibration, they manifest lower but most of the time a higher-dimensional being won't manifest lower because that will lower its own vibration, therefore limiting its power. Because with each dimension comes a set of restrictions on what the being can do, and most want freedom so they ascend.

Max: Right, so in which house would Armin live?

Zacariah: Armin lives with Monita.

Max: No, in the fourth dimension.

Zacariah: In the fourth he lives anywhere, basically. He's with Monita's soul there, because . . . Normally he's in woods. There's a lot of nature in the fourth, a lot more there than here. He'd travel through the woods and live in trees, which is what he would do on Erra which is where he's from. He's always connected to Monita's body.

Max: Okay. Would she have a body in fourth-dimensional reality?

Zacariah: Yes, we all do. We have a different body in each dimension, and are but a soul manifesting into physicality, and with each set of vibration, each dimension, we have a different form.

Max: So you are here, and also physically there with Armin?

Zacariah: Yes.

Max: Does he have adults who watch over him over there?

Zacariah: Yes, you've spoken to Kenshin and Shensha—they watch over him from the Pleiadian Council.

Max: But not physically . . . I mean, they're not his family, they're not nearby.

Zacariah: No, they're not his family. He doesn't interact with them. Most of them are trying to kill him.

Max: What I mean is, adopted parents, other adults or . . .?

Zacariah: We are his only family.

Max: I see. Tell me about day-to-day interactions. What Monita does with him; how they communicate.

Zacariah: Communication is telepathic. I have never heard him say anything verbally, as he's in another dimension, so I don't think it would really manifest as sound in ours. So, communication is telepathic. Interaction is commonly limited to telepathic communication/channeling.

249

Normally we do exercises, help him train as a lightworker, and teach him a lot about the world. Like I'll teach him about science and history of Earth and stuff like that. Monita will teach him about health, healing abilities and other things.

Max: So you would teach him three-D life. Would you teach him something from your past life?

Zacariah: Yes, I teach him a lot about my past lives, but there really is no teaching that needs to be done, because as a Pleiadian he can just connect with me and learn everything without me having to vocalize.

Max: Ah, I understand.

Zacariah: A lot of the time he lives a normal three-D life, because in the fourth dimension he can see our TVs because he has multi-dimensional vision with his physical eyes, so when his body's in the fourth he can look into the third. He watches TV with Monita and does whatever she does.

Max: What are his favorite shows, cartoons, or movies?

Zacariah: His favourite cartoon so far is most of those on the Cartoon Network. He likes Nickelodeon, but not too fascinated by any of the news networks—he actually hates our news.

Max: Uh-huh. So far, I've spoken to extraterrestrials. None of them are, you know, can tolerate watching television for pleasure. Some will look it up just for cultural research reasons, but, you know, for them it's very difficult to watch our television.

Zacariah: Yeah. Well, the TV itself emits radiation in other dimensions, so when they watch TV there they could actually burn out their eyes, or get radiation poisoning or, you know, somehow lower their frequency.

Max: I'm talking about aliens who are far from Earth. They simply find it difficult to relate to what we do.

Zacariah: Oh, yeah. When I talk to extraterrestrials about TV they always tell me, "No, we don't watch TV, we watch *you* for entertainment."

Max: Yes, exactly, that's what Bashar typically says. Now, let's talk about your personal experiences, whatever is the brightest. I guess you spend much time on Utopia 5, and you didn't say much about it. Would you like to tell more about your personal, you know, sensations—what you see, feel?

Zacariah: When I'm on Utopia 5—I don't actually visit it much now because I don't really need to. I visit astrally occasionally when I'm bored, but Utopia 5 is love, all you feel on that planet is love, there is no fear. It doesn't exist there. I mean, they know what it is, but it's a foreign concept. I don't really know how to explain it, what it's like there. It's just an overwhelming feeling of unconditional love and acceptance. No matter what you do, no matter what you've done in your past, you are accepted there as a person.

Max: Tell me about family life there. Have you visited any families? How do they look?

Zacariah: Family life there is just like families here, you know, they coexist in the same house. Well, if you wanna call it a house. They live in trees, buildings, and don't really have houses like ours next to each other in streets and stuff, they just have individual houses anywhere.

Max: Are they multi-level?

Zacariah: They do have, yes, they do have levelled houses, not skyscrapers like we do. If you go to a city there, they're normally like San Francisco, low-rise buildings and they're not close to each other; their cities are more like our villages.

Max: Is there a cycle, like breakfast, dinner, things of that sort?

Zacariah: There really is no schedule. They do what they want when they want. If they're hungry they eat, if they're not, they don't. I don't really know how else to explain it—whatever they wanna do, they do it. They don't have specific jobs.

Max: How much technology is involved? Do they cook using technology?

Zacariah: Yes, they cook using heat induction, crystals. They have some type of crystal heating mechanism that when you place the food on it, it heats the crystal to the appropriate temperature, if you wanna call it a temperature there, and whatever they want, they have: food synthesizers, but most of the time they grow their own fruits and vegetables. They don't often eat meat.

Max: So, if you grow your vegetables, do you have, like, a fridge or something? How do you keep them?

Zacariah: Yes, they have cryo chambers, that's what they call them.

Max: Uh-huh. You grow something then collect it, do physical work, and we cannot do agriculture without physical work, so you do . . .

Zacariah: They have physical work, but there are no "jobs." You know, you don't . . . They're not assigned to do that for a certain period of time, and there is no money exchange, so you just do it because you want to.

Max: Are there robots helping? If you have to carry heavy stuff . . .

Zacariah: No, they strictly do not like robots. They view them as immoral.

Max: Do they have shovels, things for gardening, metal tools?

Zacariah: Yes, they have gardening tools and such, but don't have robotic—or AI—help.

Max: How about the tractors?

Zacariah: No, they don't have that kind of stuff either. They have machines that can move the earth simply with the press of a button. They're small and compact, then they . . . It's like a holographic display comes up, you pick your settings, and it does exactly what you want.

Max: So instead of tractor you have something which does it for you.

Zacariah: Yes, it's just like this one small cube-like thing. It's ever-changing; not a cube. Not a triangle, circle, it's just whatever shape it takes I guess. Normally that's a platonic solid, a dodecahedron, prism, sphere, you know—those types of things.

Max: Do they sleep in separate beds? Do they *have* beds?

Zacariah: Normally they don't sleep.

Max: Oh, they don't?

Zacariah: When they do, they sleep standing or in hammocks.

Max: Standing up or what?

Zacariah: Or in hammocks.

Max: Oh, hammocks. All right, so they have those.

Zacariah: Have you ever seen the movie AVATAR?

Max: Yes.

Zacariah: They're like that.

Max: Do they play sports?

Zacariah: No. They have fun and games, but no sports.

Max: Do they have cats and dogs, or any other pets?

Zacariah: They have animals, although you wouldn't call them a cat or dog. You'd probably call them "pet lizard" or something, because a lot of the animals are reptilian.

Max: Okay.

Zacariah: They do have mammals, but don't treat them as pets. They're considered as family, intelligent beings. When they treat a being as a pet it's because there's not mental development sufficient to communicate with it telepathically. They simply speak to the soul of the animal, instead of to the animal itself.

Max: How many, other than humans, animals or other creatures are around?

Zacariah: I don't have an exact number.

Max: No, percentage-wise. Here we have dogs and cats and that's about it.

Zacariah: I'd say roughly 20% humans, about 75% Pleiadians, and the rest would be animals, wildlife.

Max: Wildlife, uh-huh. Would these animals be smarter than ours, or about the same?

Zacariah: About the same.

Max: Do they hug their children?

Zacariah: Yes, on their planet they're a very loving culture, they hug their children, they hug each other when they want.

Max: Do they dance?

Zacariah: All the time. There's dancing going on all the time—I mean constant. It's like a party every day.

Max: A party; so they do parties?

Zacariah: Yes, they have parties. No alcohol; no drugs; nothing like that—but there are parties.

Max: Tell me more. What's the difference?

Zacariah: They're really colorful. Have you ever heard of the Indian festival of colors?

Max: I saw videos of Indian festivals, but not specifically of colors.

Zacariah: Okay, well, it's a lot like that. Banners all over the place; this machine that dispenses drinks and food. A lot of dancing. Their music comes from themselves. I don't know how else to explain it, except they emit a sound from their brain. Each person emits a specific sound that creates a unified musical type of structure, and they dance. Sometimes they play specific sounds composed by humans, but most of the time they're dancing to the music they generate themselves. Any type of dancing—whatever makes you happy. There is no organisation, really, on this planet.

254

Whatever you wanna do, you do it.

Max: Would the culture be similar to Indian, Indonesian, or can you compare to human dancing?

Zacariah: It looks very Hindu.

Max: Hindu. With all the mudras?

Zacariah: Yes, they do hand motions. A certain position for a percent, a certain event, word or significant time in their history. They have specific dances for specific things, but when you go to what they would call a "party," it's just to enjoy yourself.

Max: When you dance, is telepathy involved?

Zacariah: Yes. There's a lot of energy manipulation involved too. When they dance it's almost as if you're watching a rainbow move, like in a fluid motion. When somebody's, like, standing still you see their aura, but when they dance it's like this colorful abstract painting forming around them, and they send out telepathic messages to say, "Oh, hey, come dance with me," or "Hey, go over there," or, I don't know, whatever they wanna use I guess.

Max: Do any of them fly during dancing?

Zacariah: Oh yeah, there's a lot of flying going on. You fly, teleport, go underground.

Max: No, during the party, if you dance can you fly and dance in the air?

Zacariah: Yes, a lot of people do that. It just depends on your preference. Most people stand on the ground when they dance, some go up in the air, or levitate. Some morph with an object and dance. I mean, there's people making objects move, animating them in order to dance with them, like, say, a lamp.

Max: How do you morph an object? Would it become part of you?

Zacariah: Yeah, I guess. They touch it, and it becomes kind of their energy field and dances with them.

255

Max: Uh-huh. Are there performances—with an audience and a performer?

Zacariah: Not often, but yes, they do have them on rare occurrences during important festivals. Like, a remembrance of a specific day in their history.

Max: Mmm-hmm, okay. Do they have religious services?

Zacariah: No. They have temples, but they're not for worship, but for meditating and emitting love to the planet. Mainly temples that represent people in their history who did a really great thing, or a species that helped them—or the planet itself—say, another star system or another sun, or just a temple to love everything. I guess you would call them love temples.

Max: Have you been to their temples?

Zacariah: Yes, I was trained in a couple of the temples. They are pyramids, most of them.

Max: Like Egyptian?

Zacariah: Mayan.

Max: How different from Mayan?

Zacariah: I don't know, a thousand feet taller. Not made out of the same materials; and they don't have the same number of steps.

Max: But they're proportionally similar, and kind of cut at the top?

Zacariah: Yeah, there's a little room at the top, but that's for the priest. They don't have priests, but whomever's the most spiritually powerful person represented by the temple gets the top room.

Max: How does the meditation go? Anything for us to learn?

Zacariah: Nothing we don't already know.

Max: Do they sit in similar positions?

Zacariah: Yes, legs crossed, hands in mudras or different positions, and that's really all there is. Most of the time they levitate, but humans aren't at that level. Eventually we will be.

Max: Humans and Pleiadians are different in height, correct? How does it look when they dance?

Zacariah: Pleiadians can be the same size as a human, and humans can be the same size as a Pleiadian. It depends on intentionality.

Max: There's a lot of variation?

Zacariah: Yeah, a lot.

Max: Because everybody is lower in height, it is not a sign of aggression or a sign or being dominant, right?

Zacariah: Everyone's equal. There is no dominance on this planet; no one's better than the next.

Max: Do the kids grow up remembering past lives? It's a tough question, I know.

Zacariah: Yes, from the time of what you would say, maybe, from the time they're born to maybe seven years their task is to remember as many past lives as possible. From when they're, say, seven to fifteen, they're tasked with remembering and helping others with past lives. A good portion of their childhood is spent recalling past lives. Once you get out of that and become an adult, you can do whatever you want, whatever your soul is telling you to do.

Max: So, even as a baby, you possess near-adult self-awareness?

Zacariah: Yes, because they judge the soul, not the body. The body is merely a physical vessel containing the soul for experience. They judge by how old your soul is.

Max: The children behave more like adults, and the adults behave more like children?

Zacariah: I guess you could say that, yeah.

Max: Are there serious adults?

Zacariah: There are strict parents, strict adults who say, "This is how it should be. This is how you're supposed to do it," but they don't interfere with other people's beliefs or perspective, because they know that's just them. They're strict with themselves.

Max: Without doing anything negative, how would you punish your children if they misbehaved?

Zacariah: Well, as long as you have peace and love in your heart you can hit your child and it's not negative, because you're intending to show discipline, you know. Let's say your child steals from your neighbor. They'll likely get a smack on the wrist: "Don't do that again." They do have discipline, but it's not negative.

Max: They can smack the wrist.

Zacariah: Yes, they can do small punishments, but can't beat their child. They punish to teach not to do it again. Normally, though, they use mental influence; give the child an unpleasant vision or message: "Don't do that again."

Max: All right. Switching to the next topic. You say there is no money. Is there a barter system?

Zacariah: Yes, a bartering trade system.

Max: How does it work?

Zacariah: Anything of equal value. If you want something that somebody else has, you give that person something of equal value. And the equal-value thing works out, if both people agree. So, let's say one person has a crystal, and all you have are small gems. Accumulate enough gems that represent the same value as that crystal, and make the transaction. That crystal would then have the same value to you as it did to the other person.

Max: All right. Do they have specialists: doctors, healers, scientists?

Zacariah: There are healers, there are scientists. Each person has their unique task. Their "job" is simply what they most enjoy doing. If someone really, really likes healing they become a healer. If someone likes technology they become a scientist. Or if someone likes agriculture, they become a farmer for the civilisation, village or whatever.

Max: How do they get resources? Like, a scientist needs, you know, to build a sophisticated machine and also needs food and stuff for his living. How do they acquire resources?

Zacariah: From the planet itself. If they can't get that, either they synthesize the resource or go to another planet.

Max: Suppose I'm a scientist, and I want a project that requires a lot of material resources or energy, but lack those. I need people to invest resources into my project. What would I do?

Zacariah: You would go to other people who have those resources, and ask for assistance. If it fits their task, they will help. If not, they recommend others who will.

Max: Oh, sounds familiar. Do they have committees?

Zacariah: Yes, they have councils.

Max: Uh-huh, they have councils. Do they have a top council, a hierarchical system?

Zacariah: It's kind of hierarchical—higher councils and lower councils, each tasked with a specific thing. Like you might have one simply for protecting the planet, observing agriculture or healers, or, you know, what have you. It's not really this-council's-better-than-that-council; each has its own task.

Max: Sounds familiar, makes sense. Do they have news broadcasts?

Zacariah: They don't have mass media, but each person's connected to the next through a telepathic link, so they always know what's going on at all times.

Max: So, they have some sort of telepathic broadcasts, some sort of news.

Zacariah: Yeah.

Max: They have usual consciousness, family connection, and global news or something, right? Were you connected to the global news when you were there?

Zacariah: I was only a visitor, and wasn't connected with the planet itself the way the people who live there are.

Max: Okay.

Zacariah: I was connected but only temporarily, because it was a telepathic link, you know. If I wanted to link to it I could, but was also only a child. Didn't even know that any of this existed.

Max: Did you have toys?

Zacariah: Yes, they have toys for the children. Objects to entertain them. I wouldn't call them toys.

Max: Anything interesting?

Zacariah: Yeah, they have levitation toys like little spheres, and the child can play with it. Project images into the object that will be displayed like a movie in front of the child. Or, say the child wants to go to a specific part of the planet, but the parent can't make it. The object will display an image of where the child wants to go, fully immerse it in a holographic projection. This is also how they sometimes teach children—with holographic projections.

Max: Wow. Do they breastfeed their children?

Zacariah: Yes, the women do, depending on which species.

Max: Pleiadians and humans?

Zacariah: Humans do; Pleiadians often don't. Their children don't really need to be breastfed, but some Pleiadian women do do it because they think it's a necessity. Other Pleiadian women give their children over to childcare, and whoever is in charge will feed the child nutrients through a synthesiser.

Max: How many foreigners, extraterrestrial Utopians were there, like, people from other stars?

Zacariah: Many, many, many. There's much cultural diversity on the planet. It's not one select species. There are reptilians on this planet, dog-like, cat-like, fish-like species. Anything you can think of is probably there, just the majority are humans and Pleiadians because the planet itself was originally inhabited by Pleiadians, and humans brought there as slaves. There was a rebellion in their history; the humans and Pleiadians began to live in harmony, and once that happened they contacted other planets and these sent their people.

Max: I see.

Zacariah: You know the Ottoman Empire, right?

Max: Turkey, yes.

Zacariah: You know the Ottoman Empire had so many ethnic groups that it actually ended up crumbling under the revolutions that happened. Well, that's what's happening on Utopia 5, but they're aren't revolutions. There's just so much culture diversity that it's really hard to pinpoint what's there and what's not.

Max: Nice. Are you visiting it now in astral projections?

Zacariah: I do when I get bored.

Max: Can you describe what you see? How can you tell if you are on Utopia?

Zacariah: Well, I know because I know the planet mostly from the outside, but when I astral project travel through space and know what it looks like. So I know: "Oh, this is Utopia 5." Also I can tell because of the energy the planet gives off. Even if another planet looks similar, I can always tell because the world itself will tell me, "I am this planet." A living organism.

261

Utopia 5 looks Earth-like; like a really, really big Earth except it has a more greenish atmosphere because it has more carbon-based gases than oxygen and nitrogen-based gases. The water is purple, so there's a lot of that tone in the atmosphere because of reflected light. The planet resembles, say, the rainforest and Egypt. A lot like Africa, the whole planet. Forests everywhere, and deserts all over the place. There are plains, so you could say part of the planet looks like central America, and others Asia. A combination of everything. There's a North and a South pole. The North pole is slightly larger.

Max: You mean the continent on the pole, or the ice cap?

Zacariah: Yeah, the ice cap—sorry.

Max: All right. I see. So, if I happen to be on Utopia and look around, I would see green sky and the clouds would be purplish?

Zacariah: Yes, the clouds are multicolored, because of the different elements in the atmosphere. From the ground they would actually be rainbow-colored, but mainly green and purplish. I've seen red clouds, too, usually before a storm.

Max: Oh, they have storms?

Zacariah: Yes.

Max: Do they get snow?

Zacariah: Yes, they have a lot of snow, but the planet's weather is controlled telepathically. It does snow roughly once every hundred Earth-years.

Max: One hundred years, all right.

Zacariah: Yes, Earth years, because the planet itself has a weird cycle around its central star. Whenever it's farthest away—apogee—snow falls.

Max: I see. How does the star appear? Similar to our sun?

Zacariah: No, it's actually very blue and huge. You would say it's five-hundred-billion times the size of our sun.

Max: From the surface?

Zacariah: Yeah, from the surface. It's massive.

Max: Well, billion doesn't work. You know we have only so many degrees—no way it can be that big.

Zacariah: I'm just using that as an example.

Max: If you looked at our sun—Sol—you can probably cover the disc with one extended finger. There, you'd think you would need both palms. What would it take?

Zacariah: Probably three or four palms. The sun is that big.

Max: Okay. How about moons?

Zacariah: There are three.

Max: Uh-huh. Are they visible only at night, or during the day too?

Zacariah: You can see two of them during the day and one at night. Well, you see all three at night, but you see the astral one at night.

Max: Are there stars?

Zacariah: You see all the stars. Actually, if you're in the southern hemisphere, and the western, you can see a ring around the system's fourth planet.

Max: Western . . . That doesn't make sense. If the planet spins around their north-south axis every western and eastern hemisphere would see the same picture. I don't really think there can be a western or eastern hemisphere. On any part of the planet there is west and east, so it's maybe north and south see different pictures?

Zacariah: Say you take the sphere of a planet, and cut it into four parts: these two sections and those two are west and east. Then you have northwest, northeast, southwest and southeast.

263

Max: That's not how you do it on Earth, but suppose you do that.

Zacariah: Yeah, I'm saying suppose you do that, and this half of the planet will see the ringed planet, while this half won't, because the planet itself spins, but while it's spinning it's also tilting, so when it's tilting and spinning this other planet is also doing the same thing and spinning. The way it synchronizes with the other planet you don't often see it.

Max: Oh, so it's like hanging around the same spot. The planet spins and the other spins with it?

Zacariah: Yeah.

Max: Okay. So what is it, an artificial thing?

Zacariah: Yes, the planet itself is completely artificial. I mean, the planet is real, organic, but everything—rotational speed, axle speed, weather patterns, is controlled by . . .

Max: Okay, all right. And you said something I just didn't capture. You see something in the sky from the western hemisphere?

Zacariah: The ringed planet.

Max: Ring planet?

Zacariah: Yeah, it looks like our Saturn.

Max: Oh, another planet that spins around this one?

Zacariah: Yes.

Max: Wow. So there is life there too?

Zacariah: Yeah, you could say it's kind of like a binary planetary system, two planets orbiting each other, but it's not. They're simply rotating at a similar speed.

Max: Okay. I guess this is all I wanted to hear about. I mean, I've sort of covered all of my questions for Utopia 5. What do you want to do next? Do you have any stories or personal experiences, or do you want to channel?

Zacariah: I'll channel in a couple minutes, but I do have a personal experience from Utopia 5.

Max: All right.

Zacariah: I think maybe the fourth time I was brought there in this life I can remember actually being in a rain forest. The houses were built into the trees, like on Erra, and I remember walking along the forest floor and looking up and not seeing anything but trees. Being mesmerised that these trees looked like skyscrapers on our planet, if not taller. And I remember walking to the base of the tree and the Pleiadian saying, "Go in," and I looked at him and said, "But there's no door." And he said, "Silly child, we do not have doors." He gave me a shove and I phased through the tree trunk. Inside, the walls are hewn from the tree, but disproportional; bigger inside than out.

Max: I understand.

Zacariah: And when you get there, there's a spiral staircase all the way up the tree; it looks like it's alive kinda, it can morph, it can move, it can separate and connect to other things. Like . . . Have you seen Harry Potter?

Max: I'm sorry, I haven't.

Zacariah: In Hogwarts the stairs can move and connect with each other, and that's what they do on this planet. 'Cause it's a spiral staircase, the stairs can expand . . . a new set can join when they add another room. It's basically from the bottom floor to the middle what we would call retail stores. They don't have stores; they don't pay for anything, but it's where you go to get goods. And, say, from the middle to the top it's all houses.

Max: Oh, so one tree house, many families?

Zacariah: Yes.

Max: It's like a small village, or big village.

Zacariah: Yes. Each tree you could say is its own village; each tree is inhabited.

Max: When you get things from the stores, you don't pay.

Zacariah: No, you walk in, tell them what you need, and if they don't have it they synthesise it. If they can't do that they place an order, you would say, to another store that might—then they simply give it to you.

Max: That's nice to know, that's something new. So you just . . . How many people know you? How many there do *you* know? If you're a citizen, how many would you know?

Zacariah: Everybody knows everyone; they're all connected through a telepathic link. You walk down the street, and even if you've never seen the person before you automatically know them.

Max: Oh, so it's millions and millions.

Zacariah: Yeah.

Max: That's why you don't do any crime, and nothing negative, right?

Zacariah: Right. They're a peaceful planet. Personally I have five friends there still: three children, three Pleiadian. They're not adults who I grew up with there when I was visiting, because I was there only for one night, Earth-time. In their time, I was there for, like, a couple of years at once.

Max: Wow, a couple of years.

Zacariah: It's weird. Yeah, they always got me back right before my mom arrived to wake me up for school, so I was gone only for one night. There, I grew up with some kids I still talk to occasionally. I mainly talk to my trainer though, her name was Auria— A-U-R-I-A—and she's actually the queen of this planet. Well, queen of the deserts actually.

Max: Okay. Do they have problems?

Zacariah: Population control, but they don't really need to worry about it.

Max: Usual problems. A person there, would they have, you know, the level of happiness is high there apparently, but, you know, because there is duality they should be solving some sort of problem. What is their impulse

266

or motivation to grow, their challenges?

Zacariah: What do you mean?

Max: We come here to learn lessons. Do they come there to learn?

Zacariah: Yes. They don't have the same problems we do. They have . . . Okay, so humans, they would consider humans gifted because we have to go through pain and suffering, murder, rape, all of these nasty things they don't experience. So they don't get to worry about it, and they view humans as gifted. They're problems are having to deal with happiness, too much happiness, and too much is given to them so they have to, they experience that. If a human were to go there, they would be overwhelmed, then feel at peace. But if one of *them* were to come to Earth, they would feel at peace in the way that they could experience something finally, but they would feel horrible and nauseated over so much common negativity, 'cos they're so used to happiness, excessive amounts.

Max: What would be their problems? What would they worry—or get excited—about?

Zacariah: They're excited about everything. I can't put something specific on it 'cos if they talk to a plant they're excited—it's literally everything. What they worry about is negativity overtaking their planet again. Or oppression; war coming, a power that's really negative returning their planet back to the way it was before. They worry about other species coming and trying to take over the system, or about their planet dying. Over-harvesting. You know, stuff like that.

Max: Global issues.

Zacariah: Yes.

Max: So for global issues, they probably have to do something collective?

Zacariah: Yes, many, many. They have . . . I don't know if you could call them a meditation rally, but specific areas of the planet where a mass goes to meditate and heal the planet every couple years, because just like humans have a chakra system, planets have theirs.

267

Max: Yes.

Zacariah: They meditate at these chakra sites, and heal the planet.

Max: What is the difference between Utopia and Erra?

Zacariah: Right now Erra's in a state of depression; the planet itself is dying; people there are being enslaved and manipulated by another race that's trying to take over the planet. Other than that, they're almost exactly the same.

Max: The lifestyle is similar.

Zacariah: Yes, very similar, depending on which part of the planet you go to, 'cos you know, there's different species living in different parts.

Max: All right. Have you been to other planets?

Zacariah: Not physically, in this life. I've been to Erra twice that I can remember, once was just a stop, you know, just to get resources and leave. Another time I was visiting a friend of mine, and I've been to Utopia 5. Those are the only two.

Max: Tell me more about your friends on Utopia 5. How do you communicate?

Zacariah: Telepathy and astral projection.

Max: What do you talk about?

Zacariah: Oh, what do we talk about? Our daily lives. I talk about what goes on here on Earth, inform them about Earthly customs, and they inform me about what goes on there, and that's really all we talk about, and spirituality of course.

Max: Can you give me an example? What would they tell you about what's going on up there?

Zacariah: Let's say I'm talking to my friend Moslake, he's a red Pleiadian.

Max: Okay.

Zacariah: Well, say I'm talking to him, I would say, "Hello, how are you?" We'd do a formal greeting, and he would say, "Things on this planet are really good. We just got a new synthesiser so now we can feed this many more people." And I'd say, "Oh, that's great, things on Earth are doing horrible. We're going into another war, having an economic recession." And he would go, "Oh, that sucks." You know, just friendly conversation.

Max: Uh-huh. You know about the Colony project by Girk-Fitneer and the Yahyel.

Zacariah: I've heard of it from Shensha, but I don't actually know about it.

Max: They take humans, some of whom are children, and their main project is teaching humans telepathy. So right now they are very excited there are already twelve humans who are fully telepathic, and four of them are children. Now, the question to you, and you went through that, is the children do the same things that you do, they are absent from Earth for short periods of time, a few minutes, they go there for a couple weeks or one week and come back. How do you teach them to cope with human life here after becoming telepaths? Or to avoid trouble in kindergarten when they're perceived as overly intelligent?

Zacariah: They wipe your memory.

Max: No they don't.

Zacariah: Well, with me they did. I don't know if they do with other people. They wiped my memory so I wouldn't get in trouble with other children in the school, wouldn't get in trouble with adults and cause chaos in my family. And I'm assuming when they do it with these children, they're probably telling them to keep quiet about it with people they don't trust. 'Cos if they're fully telepathic they should have the ability to discern whether someone is trustworthy.

Max: Yeah, that's what they do, they keep them quiet, but I think it's not enough.

Zacariah: No, it wouldn't be enough, but I don't think they would have the need to actually keep them quiet because our planet's going through a period of ascension right now, so it's very important that each person learns about this. If anything, I would say they advertise it a little bit, you know, by *not* keeping them quiet.

Max: Yeah, it's nice but, you know, say it is a five-year-old child and he goes to kindergarten and says he speaks to aliens and travels to other . . .

Zacariah: His teachers will probably think he's making up a fantasy, and think nothing of it. And if it keeps going on they'll probably talk to the parents and tell them to seek psychiatric help.

Max: Exactly. Then they start feeding him drugs, that sort of thing.

Zacariah: Yeah. Oh my god, I hate those. I had to take ADHD medication when I was younger, and argued with my mom day in and day out to keep me off them. Finally she agreed, but I had to go through that too and it's not fun.

Max: Basically I think [inaudible] children who could live double lives, and could learn how or what they can say, and to whom. To learn discretion, and when you're questioned by negative people you have to be able to pretend you are normal. I think that's a big . . .

Zacariah: Yeah, I agree, yeah. But also the children that they're teaching, they're probably doing a complete observation to see if they're capable of doing that. So I would say there probably is not a lot of trouble or, what's the word I'm looking for? Miscommunication between the child and the teacher, the family and teacher. The child probably does everything they say without question.

Max: I would assume so. All right, so in this life you haven't been to other planets.

Zacariah: Not yet.

Max: Do you remember other planets from your past lives?

Zacariah: Yes, many of them. I was a reptilian a couple of past lives, different manifestation, and the planet, it was horrible . . . Okay, take the path that the U.S. is on right now, multiply that by about ten and then surround the whole world. That's what the planet was like. Giant fissures fracturing the mantle, black soot in the clouds, constant volcanic eruptions, tar all over the place. Murder and rape were common. You had to go outside protected or else you would be murdered or raped. Not a very nice civilisation, and I was only there for a short period of time as I was murdered. But, I've been on another planet that was the exact opposite. Extremely peaceful; there wasn't even the slightest bit of pollution. This planet was extremely advanced, I mean, if humans were to land there now, they would say there's no life on it, and that's because the life is being hidden. That's how they limit pollution, because only they live on that planet. And they use crystal technology. I think it exists in the sixth dimension, but I'm not positive. Dimensions are so hard to calculate.

Max: I see. Speaking about this reptilian planet, can you tell more about their system?

Zacariah: It was hierarchical. They use slave labor for the majority of their work. They had an economy based on a diamond-like material. It's not a diamond of course, but crystal-like, so rare they used it for currency. They also used gold, which is why they came to Earth for a short period of time to mine it, because it's not natural to their planet. They also use fossil fuels to power their technology.

Max: Oh, so it was on the level of current human technology, it wasn't that advanced.

Zacariah: Yes.

Max: Or was it?

Zacariah: Oh, it was extremely advanced. They could travel between dimensions, planetary systems, but they did it all with fossils.

Max: So they used fossil fuels for cars?

Zacariah: They didn't have cars.

Max: Oh, what did they do?

Zacariah: They walked.

Max: Oh, what, flying?

Zacariah: They could fly, yes, but only some of them. You know, there was . . . In order to fly, you have to be a really spiritually inclined person 'cos you have to flip your polarity rapidly to create a magnetic field that can sustain your own gravity. So only very powerful beings on that planet could fly. A lot of the beings just teleported. Teleportation doesn't take as much effort as flying. With flying you have to sustain your magnetic field, and then you have to sustain yourself, and in teleportation all you do is quickly change your vibration, that's it.

Max: Oh, mentally teleport?

Zacariah: No, physically teleport. All they did was change the vibration of their body in unison to everything else, and then they went somewhere.

Max: I mean, you didn't use any special technological portal for that, you just mentally commanded it?

Zacariah: Yes, they used technology for it, for the mass populous. Some of the higher-ups, the ones in power, could mentally teleport, mentally fly, but most of them used technology.

Max: Uh-huh. Do you know what planet it is, what star it orbits?

Zacariah: We would represent the star system of Draco, but it's not Draco—it's in that direction.

Max: I understand.

Zacariah: The planet itself was called Mastwooke. I think that would be the English translation.

Max: Mastwooke?

Zacariah: Yes.

Max: Excellent. You don't know the star name?

Zacariah: They called their star . . . I'm gonna have to translate it . . .

272

[inaudible] which means "great energy" in their language.

Max: Do you remember any more planets?

Zacariah: When I was an Arctuvian I actually visited Earth quite frequently, so I remember it from the ancient times. Then, I didn't live on any specific planet; I actually lived in a starship, because I was part of the Council of Nine in this life, and they don't have a planet. It's a fleet of ships that travel from planet to planet to planet.

So I visited many planets. Some were barren but still had life, and others were teeming—just like Earth, but they were smaller, different colors. One planet in particular, I don't know the name, but remember it looked like Neptune, but once you broke the atmosphere it actually looked a little bit like Earth, with continents. The water was green, with billions of microscopic organisms on the surface. The continents had, like, red grass. The terrain actually appears red. When they didn't have vegetation they resembled present-day Mars, with that flat iron-red—not as red as the grass though. That's why the grass was red, by the way. Iron deposits.

Max: I see.

Zacariah: The planet itself had crystalline cities. I'm looking at it now. If you've ever seen STAR WARS, during the . . . I don't remember which episode, but the Gungans were going against the robotic troopers, you can see in the background a crystal city behind the plasma dome, and that's what they looked like. Giant crystalline structures. They had pyramids on this planet, but they were used for power sources. They were basically giant reactors that spread wireless energy throughout the planet. You could go anywhere on the planet and find electricity.

Max: I see, like Tesla technology.

Zacariah: Yeah, a lot like it. Tesla himself was manifesting on this planet for a period of time. He wasn't called Tesla, and was there for a short period of time. I was only friends with Tesla in a past life, so don't know much of Tesla's lives. This planet, however, was extremely peaceful but it did go to war. Everything there was like utopia, but the powers that be wanted more to support their population, so they'd go to war with other

273

species to conquer other planets. So, you could say it was a more perfected form of our society now, because they had jobs, currency, all of this stuff, but it was also . . . a cross between Pleiadian and Earth society. The people there were not humanoid. We really can't describe them in our tongue. You could say they stood about eight feet tall. They normally had between four to five appendages—three arm-like limbs to grip things. Two appendages used for walking, because they were bipeds, but could also walk on all five. The reason I said four to five appendages is because they always had two legs, but sometimes two or three "arms."

Max: I see.

Zacariah: They had three to four eyes, and that's because they're ancestry was a spider-like species. Eyes positioned two here and two there; probably one in the center, depending on which version or race you're talking about. They had hair—really thick.

Max: Spiders have an exoskeleton.

Zacariah: These did. Exoskeletons grown on command. Meaning if they wanted one they willed it. They were normally formed during times of stress, war, or death. Mainly for war, because they could grow them for a period up to a week.

Max: I see.

Zacariah: They would go into a . . . kind of like what caterpillars do. A state of sleep, and grow their exoskeleton around them. That's all they'd do for that week.

Max: It's so foreign I don't really have any questions about it. It's different.

Zacariah: Extremely so. Right now it doesn't exist anymore. It was destroyed in war.

ON PLEIADIANS, DRACONIANS, REPTILIANS AND GREYS

Interview with Zacariah

Max: Remind me of the name of your twin friend.

Zacariah: Monika, also known as Juanita.

Max: Is she around?

Zacariah: She is not around. There is a different being in her body right now.

Max: Can you explain?

Zacariah: She is channeling a Pleiadian right now.

Max: Wow! To whom?

Zacariah: His name is Armin, a Pleiadian boy. He is with us physically most of the time. He likes to channel sometimes.

Max: Physically? What do you mean?

Zacariah: Well, Juanita and I . . . We had this Pleiadian boy given to us because his parents were killed. In a past life we were friends with them. So, in this life, they gave him to us to protect.

Max: Okay.

Zacariah: Yes, he stays with Juanita. He feels more connection with her; she is more like a mother figure.

Max: When you say "physical," you mean he is physically on Earth?

Zacariah: He is physical, but in a different dimension if you know what I mean. On Earth with us, but residing in the fourth dimension. Armin has come into our dimension before—it's a little harder for him to do this.

Max: Of course. I understand now. So, she's channeling him to whom, friends or visitors? Who is he talking to? Are there other people in the room?

Zacariah: No, just me and Juanita.

Max: Amazing. Say this again, the name of this boy.

Zacariah: Armin.

Max: Okay, Armin. All right. Would he like to talk with me?

Zacariah: He's saying he doesn't want to talk.

Max: All right. Does he mind if *we* continue talking?

Zacariah: No, that's fine.

Max: Great. Wherever you would like to lead your story from here is fine.

Zacariah: Another story I have could be that when I was younger, I used to speak the Light Language to my mom and she didn't know what it was. My ancestry in this life—family is predominantly Jewish—[is such that] she thought I was speaking Hebrew, but she never understood the [Light] language *because* it was similar to Hebrew, but not the same. So, she always thought I was speaking gibberish. But now that I am older, I can still speak the language I was speaking back then, but better. She understands it more now.

Max: What is that language?

Zacariah: Light language. I was speaking Arcturian and Pleiadian.

Max: Language of the light. But there are two different languages, right? The Arcturian and Pleiadian?

Zacariah: Yeah, they are different but they're one in the same. Because they are both from the Galactic Federation in order to help better communicate between species.

Max: Would it be different from [languages spoken by various] Pleiadian races?

Zacariah: Yes, each race has its own version of the Light Language, so each Pleiadian race has its own too.

Max: Okay, please continue.

Zacariah: Now that I'm older, I actually use this language and I can . . . I normally use it to heal. But I can use it also to cause better telekinesis, for better communication through telepathy. My mom burned herself the other day cooking dinner, and I actually healed her by speaking the Light Language.

Max: So she was completely healed?

Zacariah: Yes. Completely.

Max: How bad was the burn?

Zacariah: Blistered. Kind of like a small blister, and I took away that and all the pain.

Max: Very good! Anything we can use? Possibly not right? If we translated to English it wouldn't work, right? Can you translate what you said?

Zacariah: It's really hard to translate the Light Language into English because it's more a feeling than it is words.

Max: All right.

Zacariah: Like how resonance frequency works, right?

Max: Of course.

Zacariah: Yes, so that's what it is. I speak this Language; the Language holds a frequency which interacts with whatever I'm sending the Language at and raises its vibration, which is how it heals.

Max: I see. Ok, you can continue the story in any direction you like.

Zacariah: That's basically it for that story . . . I kind of just healed my mom. When I was younger I used to actually walk into walls. To me, there was a wall there. I would be walking down a hallway or something, and bump into something. But to everybody else, there was nothing there. I was actually just seeing into other dimensions and my vision was altered. I wasn't focusing on *this* dimension.

Max: I see.

Zacariah: One time . . . Oh, Juanita's back. Juanita, remember the time we were at your house and we were controlling the space ships? We were at her house and we had some Pleiadians show up in a couple craft. We were meditating on a four-wheeler, raised our hands in the air and actually controlled where the craft. We were moving them around and they were yelling at us to stop.

Max: Oh! They didn't like it, did they.

Zacariah: No, I guess we were jarring them around or something but . . .

Juanita: One fell out of the sky.

Zacariah: Oh yeah! That's right! One of them was still up in the sky and we almost crashed one by accident. That's why they were yelling at us.

Max: So, they allowed you to play but you played irresponsibly.

Zacariah: Yes, went a little far. One of the ships had Ockatu in it. Ockatu was—he's not now—but he was the King of Erra for a while. They were yelling at us for almost accidentally killing him. [laughs]

Max: Not funny!

Zacariah: It *was* funny. Because it's normal to them. If we were actually to kill him, he would just be put into another body and he'd still be King.

Max: It's not sad like it would be on Earth . . . so I see. King of what? King of which country? He was the King of some sort of planet, country or race?

Zacariah: Yes, Erra.

Max: Oh! Erra!

Zacariah: He's not now.

Max: Oh, so he's kind of a president or something?

Zacariah: Yeah, you know of Ramses, King Ramses from ancient Egypt, right?

Max: Yes.

Zacariah: Okay, that's Ockatu's bloodline. Ockatu's dad was King Ramses.

Max: Okay.

Zacariah: And Ockatu himself was put on the throne of Erra when he murdered his brother. That put him on the throne. Since he murdered his brother . . . He did it by—in secret, I guess you would say. Technically he assassinated him, and no one knew what happened. Then people started figuring it out, because Ockatu was actually dismantling the Council of Nine; getting rid of the Galactic Federation, working with dark workers, and he made alliances with the Greys and the Sorians. He was breaking up all the stuff the Pleiadians had been working for thousands of years to achieve peacefully.

Max: Okay.

Zacariah: Yeah, and he started doing it before he was King, though. Not a lot of people knew it was him. That's why he's not in power anymore.

Max: Okay, so part of the story is very ancient. You said when you were playing with the ships, he was still King, but no longer?

Zacariah: Yes, when we were playing with the ships, he was still in power but technically he wasn't King. How do I relate this on Earth terms? He was in power as if a member of the Congress, but to the people on his planet, they viewed him as President.

Max: You're saying in the really recent history. When did the assassination take place? Many thousands of years ago, was it?

Zacariah: Yes. But [keep in mind] a couple hundred years on Earth is like a couple thousand on Erra.

Max: Ahh! I understand.

Zacariah: Yeah. That's why we referred to him as "King" when we were talking to him a couple years ago. Not the same as if we were talking today.

Max: Let's go over the years, if you understand. When you played with the Pleiadians, how many years ago in Earth terms?

Zacariah: Juanita. She talks to the Pleiadians more than I do. Juanita, how many years have gone by on their planet compared to ours? [unclear background voice] Juanita says for every year we have, it's five to them.

Max: A year in five. So, suppose you played with the ships five years ago, then it would be 25 years ago in Erran time. My question: was the assassination many years ago? Ancient history?

Zacariah: Yes.

Max: And he was still in power, but they removed him when they discovered he assassinated his brother.

Zacariah: Yes, and because he was dismantling the Council of Nine. Basically creating a dictatorship.

Max: So there was a recent history—last 25 years of Erra—and last five years Earth-time.

Zacariah: Yes.

Max: I thought them very stable and advanced, but it sounds like a mess up there.

Zacariah: It is. Erra is actually at war with itself right now. [circa 2014] Civil War.

Max: Civil War?!

Zacariah: Yes, the planet itself is dying. Its death is beginning to accelerate because of what's going on. Multiple species live on Erra, and are engaged in disputes, so the Pleiadians are fighting the Saurians and the Saurians are trying to gain power over Erra. Right now, the person in control of Erra is actually a human—in power right now.

Max: What's his name?

Zacariah: His name is Kenjin.

Max: Kenjin?

Zacariah: Yes.

Max: Okay. What are the Saurians? I don't know anything about Saurians.

Zacariah: Saurians are actually a Reptilian-like race and they are not too nice. They are related to the Draconians, if you've ever heard of *them*.

Max: I've heard of the Draconians.

Zacariah: Yes, they are a subspecies.

Max: Do they have wings?

Zacariah: No. But their light bodies do. Astral bodies have light wings. But since the Saurians use dark energy, they have dark wings.

Max: I see. Can you describe them physically?

Zacariah: Depending on which version of the Saurians you're talking about, they stand between nine and ten feet tall. They can get up to ten feet, but their average is around nine.

Max: I see.

Zacariah: They're white-skinned, and are scaled. They've smallish tails, don't they? [Juanita speaks in bg.] Yeah. Some of them have small tails, some have long. Some have no tails at all. Saurians have two arms, two legs and two eyes. Their noses are reptilian-like, and kind of protrude from their slick faces.

Max: I see.

Zacariah: They have razor-sharp teeth and almost no lips.

Max: I see. Ears?

Zacariah: They have no facial hair at all. Years? They live to be about roughly 600 to 700 Earth years.

Max: I mean the physical part of the head . . . the ears.

Zacariah: Yes, some have small ears. Some have none.

Max: All right. Any other things on the top of the head? Do they wear some sort of hat?

Zacariah: They normally don't wear clothes at all. Yeah, their scales cover up anything they need to cover.

Max: They're not mammals. How would you tell apart the male and female?

Zacariah: They have genitalia, smaller than humans' though.

Max: I see. They're laying eggs, right? So, they don't . . .

Zacariah: Yes, they lay eggs.

Max: Ah-ha. So, they're not very nice. We are talking to some Reptilians in the Solar System and they say they are searchers, that they are benign. They are not aggressive. Do you know which ones?

Zacariah: Yes, the Reptilians you're speaking to are more likely to be a different species altogether because most Saurians are *not* nice at all. [laughs] I mean, they normally eat humans.

Max: They do?

Zacariah: Yes, obviously with every species, there's good and bad. So there could be good Saurians you could be speaking to, but it's very rare, if you know what I mean.

Max: Ah! What dimension are they?

Zacariah: It depends. The ones I normally communicate with are from the seventh and eighth dimensions, from our perspective, but I have come in contact with ones from dimensions higher and lower.

Max: Ah, so now we have different dimension numbers. The Pleiadians on Erra, what dimension are they in your number?

Zacariah: Five and six. Normally four, five, six, seven, eight, nine and ten. I mean the Pleiadians I speak to.

Max: And which dimensions are humans?

Zacariah: Humans? Us? Here?

Max: We on this Earth.

Zacariah: We would be in the third.

Max: Third. How . . .

Zacariah: Well, technically we're in the fourth—but that's a different story.

Max: All right. In your numbering system, how far does the physical form go? Say fourth, fifth dimension. Do they have physical bodies, and at what dimensional threshold does this cease?

Zacariah: Yes, physical bodies by my numbering system until the 20th dimension. Anything below that is very physical. Anything after is slowly beginning to get less physical. Once you enter into the 10th dimension, there is metaphysicality but it's limited.

Max: Oh. The numbering system from the people I communicate with, Lakesh and a Yahyel like Disdoo. (Lakesh is the short blue people; Disdoo the six-foot-tall Yahyel.) They both use dimensions. Where we are in the third, Pleiadians and Yahyel are in the fourth, and the seventh dimension comprises our human dead spirits. The physical body fades somewhere around the sixth dimension. Your numbering system somehow is much wider. With your numbers the physicality is gone somewhere around the 20th; my system—from Lakesh and Disdoo—defines it as vanishing in the sixth.

283

Zacariah: It also depends on the species. You know, each species is different. One may be physical in the 20th dimension, where another is completely metaphysical. In the fourth, one species may be metaphysical where another is physical, you know? Really depends on the species and the person you're talking to.

Max: All right, okay. So, Saurians fighting the Errans . . .

Zacariah: Yes, have you heard of the dark workers?

Max: Yeah.

Zacariah: That's what Saurians are. But not all dark workers are Saurians.

Max: The Reptilians I spoke to, who are visiting our Solar System, they are third-dimensional. They have the technology to get here but they're third-dimensional. All right, let's just review the exo-political situation. I think you have a lot of knowledge about this. So, let's grab the main players around humanity. Who is involved? Alien races. Who are mostly in the world right now?

Zacariah: Our Government?

Max: No. The Aliens. Extraterrestrial galactic races. Which Galactic civilizations are more involved in Earth at present?

Zacariah: Oh! Oh, okay. [laughs] There are so many it's not even funny.

Max: Let's start with the top ones—top three.

Zacariah: The very, very top are Pleiadians.

Max: All right. Pleiadians from Erra and elsewhere, right?

Zacariah: From Erra and elsewhere. Yes. Second ones on my list would have to be the Arcturians, because they're very, very active on our planet. They're more active spiritually than physically. The Greys—all 165 species.

Max: Which of the Greys are most involved?

Zacariah: The Zeta Reticula are more involved than the Yayel, but I would still put the Yahyel up there in the third.

Max: I see. Have you met any of the Zetas?

Zacariah: The Zetas? Oh yeah. All the time. They come to my house and try to abduct, or inject me—I just laugh and make them leave. It's funny to watch.

Max: Why? Are you powerful?

Zacariah: It's funny because I was a king in their society in a past life, so when they come and try to do something to me, all I have to say is "leave" and they have to listen. I can order them around. Not that I choose to . . . I don't . . . unless they're hurting me in some way. But in their old society of the Actuvians—I don't know if you've heard of this—they used to be called Actuvians, and I was an Arc in their society. Any person in their society labeled "Arc" was very highly placed. I was actually their leading engineer and advisor to the King, Arc-Mek. So, in this life, whenever they come to talk to me, I can just tell them what do because to them I'm still an Arc. That status doesn't die when you do—it stays.

Max: All right, very good. Describe to me their appearance. Actually, I may know what they look like, but briefly explain, please.

Zacariah: Okay. Zeta Reticulans. Between seven and 17 feet tall. Big black almond-shaped eyes; little to no mouth, ears, and slits for a nose; elongated skull with a very narrow chin. Very skinny. They have almost no muscle mass, and are greyish-blue in color. Depending on the clone you're looking at—they're all clones—there can be three to four fingers, sometimes five. They have two feet, and normally don't use them because they like to levitate. They have no genitalia, nipples or navels.

Max: All right. Very good. I'm worried about the height. As you described it, it's excessive and we typically . . .

Zacariah: Yes, they are huge. It's whatever they decide. The Greys can't genetically reproduce, so their cloned bodies are whatever size they desire. If they want to be 17 feet tall, they can. I've seen Greys above 20 feet, and below seven.

285

Max: A lot of abductee reports say they are below four feet tall.

Zacariah: Yes, the abductees . . . people who are abducted . . . do not interact with the Greys. This is a very common misconception. The Greys themselves are not allowed to leave their planet—they're quarantined. Sorry, I got that wrong. They're quarantined on their planet, but can get permission to leave. When they do, they don't come in contact with humans because it would create too much of a ruckus. Most abductees come in contact with drones. The Greys use these. The elite drones are between seven and 10 feet tall. Common types are about four or five feet in height. Then they have the so-called passivish drone, roughly 2 and 3 feet tall.

Max: What are the "passivish" drones?

Zacariah: Spies, basically. They send the passivish drones to anybody they need to keep an eye on. They simply sit in a corner and levitate—no use for legs. Basically dangling limbs, lingering in a corner and collecting intel. That's all they do.

Max: Are their faces the same as four-foot-tall Greys?

Zacariah: They have the same physical features, just shorter in stature, with a protruding diamond centered on the forehead—not really visible unless you look into a different dimension.

Max: I see. So much information. Excellent! Can you describe the Yahyel?

Zacariah: Which dimension?

Max: Different numbering systems . . . how about . . . ?

Zacariah: If we're in the third, which dimension from us?

Max: I don't know. Let's talk about the Yahyel we would most likely encounter, those which will enter open contact.

Zacariah: Okay. They're human-like, and don't much resemble Greys— pale skin, blonde hair and yellow eyes. Their eyes can be a range of colors. I've seen blue, pink, brown, black—doesn't really matter—but they almost always have a yellow ring around the pupil. Their chins are more elongated than ours, as is the face. Their eyes are bigger, and resemble Asian eyes. Not as in "like slits," but the angularity.

Max: Okay.

Zacariah: I told you they were really white (I think), and did I give you an average height? Okay, average height for the Yahyel—oooh, they're telling me right now—is between six and twelve feet. Seven to eight for the male. Females average six to eight feet.

Max: Tell me about your experiences with the Yahyel.

Zacariah: Okay. I was brought up in crafts with them, but mainly in this life I'm a hybrid. I was never actually a Yahyel in a past life that I remember so far . . . They just keep tabs because I have an important message in this life that they're helping me with, and because I'm one of their hybrids.

Max: What is the important message?

Zacariah: The message of light. I'm trying to send light and love to all beings, and to help with the ascension. Reach the ones who are still asleep. I have many missions in this life, which is why I can't really give you anything specific. The one that Yahyel is helping me with is the contact. I'm actually supposed to help with the contact of humans.

Max: What are the plans for full contact that you can share?

Zacariah: It will be between the years 2017 and 2023. That is, *if* humans allow them to come in. Humans have to decide; the Others don't decide anything.

Max: What form will contact take?

Zacariah: Physical. They will come down to our planet and physically communicate; come into contact with a specific set of predestined people. They will either come down and talk to them, or bring them up into a ship and give them a tour of Earth. Take them around if they haven't seen it already.

287

Max: Just came into my mind, the Draconians here on Earth.

Zacariah: Yes, the Draconians have many colonies—mostly underground, though.

Max: Do you know how many Draconians are under the Earth?

Zacariah: I can't give you a specific number . . . I'm sorry.

Max: Say, in the hundreds, the thousands . . . ?

Zacariah: Millions. [laughs] There's *a lot*.

Max: Are they all bad, or are they mixed?

Zacariah: Mixed. They also don't exist all of the time in our dimension; some reside here, some in the seventh. Others in the fourth and fifth— although not many. Mainly they're here because of a past event, the war over Earth a couple million years ago.

Max: Let's return to exo-politics. You mentioned Zetas, Yahyel, Errans, Pleiadians, Arcturians . . . who else is involved?

Zacariah: The Lyrans. I saw on your website that you spoke with a Lyran. They're in contact with our planet, but are not as yet directly interfering. There are also Apperetians, Arians, Athinians, Appolian beings from the ancient planet of Marduk. Elohim are also interacting with Earth. There are a variety of Pleiadians, and some who don't even know the relatives of Pleiadians. I can't think of the species name right now, but I'm getting an image in my head. There are a lot of nameless species interacting with our planet.

Max: Okay.

Zacariah: They have only essence; metaphysical beings. There are entities from the sixth dimension whose names, when translated, are merely symbols and clicks. There are tall blue beings that look a little like the Sirians. Oh! That's another species interacting with the planet. Yes, the Sirians. Sirius-A denizens are feline-like, and primarily the ones interacting with Earth in the fourth dimension. The beings from Sirius-B are not as active—simply observing. There are right now well over 100 different races interacting with Earth. A lot of them I haven't come in contact with.

Max: Tell me the ones you've personally met.

Zacariah: I have personally met with Lumerians—which I forgot to mention.

Max: Tell me about their appearance.

Zacariah: Male Lumerians, on average, stand between 15 and 17 feet tall. Females between 13 and 14 feet. There's obviously a range, but they have elongated skulls—crowning probably 5 to 6 inches higher than ours. They look exactly like humans except for the fact of their color—and they glow. They have skin similar to ours, normally black and white. There are also blue, red, and yellow-red Lumerians.

Max: What race do they resemble?

Zacariah: Human.

Max: Which? Asians? Africans?

Zacariah: American.

Max: Native Americans?

Zacariah: European American.

Max: Northern Europeans, you mean. Even if they are black? They would still resemble European Americans? Not Africans?

Zacariah: If they are black, they look more like Africans but still would resemble Northern Americans and Europeans as they would not have big lips, or different bone structures that come from Africa.

Max: I see. Northern Europeans. And which dimension are they?

Zacariah: Oh, that depends. They exist in every dimension. Every single being exists in every single dimension. When you ask which dimension, it's like trying to map every single being, you know what I mean?

Max: All right, okay. Tell me about your experience with them.

Zacariah: So far my experiences have been mostly craft sightings. I'll be in a meadow and they'll flash a couple of lights. I've had Lumerians show up in my room before, converse with me and leave. Mainly information exchanges . . .

Max: So, when they come into your room, how would a 15-foot-tall being fit in there?

Zacariah: They're in a different dimension, so when they arrive my house isn't there.

Max: All right.

Zacariah: They also visit me in the astral realm. So I could be in my room doing homework, but they come in astral form so it wouldn't be like actually sitting there with me.

Max: I understand, so I'm trying to grasp something tangible for myself and listeners out there. How do you know it's them? Do you see faces and forms?

Zacariah: Yes, with my third eye I see them how they wish to be seen. With my physical eyes I see their energy, feel it with my body. I can pinpoint the species by their vibrations.

Max: How do they feel?

Zacariah: Lumerians feel very loving and accepting of humans, but also— because related to humanity—share similar emotions. So, whenever I'm near a Lumerian, I feel more "at home" in this body. But I also feel negativity, because in a past life I was at war with the Lumerians. I still have some of that energy.

Max: Is that . . . uhh, which country or race?

Zacariah: I was a Martian.

Max: A Martian?!

Zacariah: Yes.

Max: Martians fighting Lumerians . . . wow.

Zacariah: Oh yes, big dispute. Martians and Lumerians hate each other with a passion.

Max: Tell me about the Martians.

Zacariah: Depending again which dimension you want to talk about, sixth-dimensional Martians are in cahoots with the dark workers. They don't really care much for Earth, so don't bother it. They do care that humans don't ascend, and want them to leave Earth so they can mine all its minerals and stuff like that. They need the water; they're running out. The Martian race in the third and fourth dimensions were completely obliterated by the Greys. Lumerians and Martians have a dispute over when the Martians came to Earth. A lot of people will tell you that the Lumerians came from another universe, and that is true. Lumerians exist in another universe, but that's because they traveled—didn't originate there. They originated from another version of Earth in the eighth dimension from our perspective, if I'm not mistaken.

When the Martians traveled to eighth-dimension Earth because they were at war with the Greys on their planet in the third and fourth dimensions, the Martians attempted to enslave and take over the Lumerians. Being peaceful, the Lumerians objected and couldn't fight back because they're pacifists. They actually went into an energy battle through psychic war. Eventually, the Yahyel entered and helped the Lumerians—the Martians were pushed away from Earth. Martian DNA remains on Earth, because they interbred.

Max: I thought the Yahyel are not as ancient as Lumerians.

Zacariah: Yes, the Lumerians are very ancient, but the Yahyel are a newer species—though quite old compared to us. The Yahyel were around with Lumerians but at the very end. They didn't see the whole civilization.

Max: I see.

Zacariah: Each timeline has a different outcome per dimension, so the

Yahyel were actually a cross between the Pleiadians and the Greys. But it wasn't the Greys as we know them, because now they're Zeta Reticulans. They are primarily biomechanical beings. But the Greys where Yahyel came from were actually called Actuvians. The Actuvians are actually another version of humans from a separate universe. They traveled into our universe because they screwed up theirs so bad they wanted to know where they went wrong. So they entered ours to see what we did to solve that similar problem. That's when they went to war with the Martians, because Yahyel and Martians had a dispute over genetic material, and they completely wiped out the Martian race.

As a result, the Actuvians were forced to genetically manipulate themselves and were quarantined on the Zeta system, which is where they remain. The Yahyel were actually a byproduct of the Actuvian and Pleiadian DNA. What happened was the Actuvians found Mars. Martians were not really a space-faring race, so when the Martians and Actuvians met, the Actuvians also met with the Pleiadians. The Pleiadians made an alliance with Actuvians. That's when their Virgin King and Virgin Princess were offered and they mated, creating the offspring of the Yahyel. The Yahyel and their genome were manipulated, and exported to another planet to grow by themselves—a common ritual among these civilizations.

While the Pleiadians and Actuvians were having an alliance, the Actuvians and Martians were still going at it for several hundred years. Eventually, the Actuvians convinced the Pleiadians to let them use their battleship, because the Actuvians didn't really have any war materials since at that time they were a more passive race. And the Actuvians used the Pleiadian battleship to blow up Mars. That's why the Pleiadians and Martians are at war since they thought it was the Pleiadians. The Martians know it was the Greys who used the Pleiadian battleship to destroy Mars. That's why they're at war with the Greys and Pleiadians. A big, vicious cycle of screw-ups.

Max: Which planet was the Yahyel's? That is, if you're allowed to tell me.

Zacariah: I can say whatever I want; it just depends whether I want to.

Max: I ask the Yahyel, Disdoo, every time and he says they will tell me— but later. So I don't want to publicize a secret if it's inappropriate at present.

Zacariah: I was going to tell you the same thing; they don't tell me where they live either. The Yahyel I am in contact with are the higher metaphysical types. I assume you're in contact with the fourth and fifth (more physical). I don't contact them as much, so I can't say where they live. But the ones in the metaphysical realm don't have a planet; they simply exist.

Max: Amazing stories. I really like what you tell me. I wish to write it down. So, the Lemurians/Lumerians are still around, and living on Earth at the time of Atlantis and Lemuria, right?

Zacariah: Yes, but when Atlantis and Lemuria sank into the ocean, they had to leave. Some left for interstellar space, the Draco system.

Max: Which are Draco's stars?

Zacariah: They're not telling me that—simply the "region" of Draco. A lot of them did die during the sinking of Atlantis. The tectonic plates under Atlantis sank into the ocean. Not only did Atlantis sink, but caused a global wipeout. Not only was Lemuria destroyed, but many civilizations experienced catastrophic flooding. This, by the way, is where the Noah's Ark story originates. Historically it did happen, but not as chronicled in the Bible. The Yahyel actually visited Earth to aid the Lumerians when they saw them in trouble. They also ended up living on Earth because they had nowhere else to go. These Yahyel—in particular a group of them—it wasn't the whole species. They had no place to live because . . . what's the word? They weren't expelled, but there was a group of them that were kicked out of their society because there were too many and not because they did anything wrong. They were kicked away from their planet and came to Earth.

They bred with the Lumerians and the Martians. This is where the Jewish— the Hebrew descent—comes from. Directly from the Yahyel. Almost anyone of Hebrew descent has original Yahyel DNA, which is why I have so much Yahyel DNA too. My family lineage derives from the Yahyel when they originally set foot on Earth. This body did not have enough DNA to lower itself onto this physical planet because my essence is a very high-metaphysical soul. In order to lower myself to this planet's frequency, I needed a higher vibratory body, so they needed to add more DNA. A

293

hybrid of Actuvians, Pleiadians and Yahyel DNA in me, though more Pleiadian than Yahyel.

Max: Is there anything you can share about alien DNA/genetics?

Zacariah: Yeah, DNA vibrates at different frequencies. The DNA that humans investigate in labs is only third-dimensional expression. DNA expression actually exists in all dimensions and is spiritual; there is DNA in the metaphysical realms. The human genome actually has up to 24 distinct molecules, if not more. I've only seen that number, so I don't know . . .

Max: Twenty-four molecules? Are you talking about chromosomes or something else?

Zacariah: No, I'm talking about the helix as we know it. Our DNA is made up of a double helix.

Max: But it wouldn't be in our dimension, would it? How many can we fit in our dimension?

Zacariah: Right now . . . we are moving up to four strands; we have two and we're moving up to four.

Max: The second two strands . . . would they be in the fourth dimension?

Zacariah: They already exist; we already have them but we're accessing them now. They are going to exist in another vibration. It is when we ascend into the higher dimension.

Max: So these additional two strands are from the fourth dimension?

Zacariah: Yes. If you do some research, the Russians—I think—discovered the quadruplex, which is the four helices. They might have discovered it. If not them, then others, but I think I remember the Russians talking about this.

Max: I doubt that . . . I really doubt that. Even if they knew that it couldn't be for real. You can't chemically analyze fourth-dimensional substance.

Zacariah: Remember, we're moving up into the fourth dimension, so some things are going to become "visible" to us.

Max: I don't think the current scientific instruments can measure anything fourth-dimensional. Lots of talk about it, but measuring it with equipment . . . I don't think so. Is there anything else on DNA you wish to share?

Zacariah: DNA is a transceiver of information—receives and gives information. Do you know what scalar waves are? DNA reads scalar waves so it can actually read different memories from other lives within this body. You're actually taking the DNA, reading the scalar waves from the universe imprinting themselves on the molecules and accessing other memories. Which is why people like me can access galactic information—'cuz I can read the scalar waves imprinting on my DNA.

Max: One of the scientific tasks (among my favorite topics) is how can you design a Reiki machine? You know Reiki, right? Healing through energy by placing hands on the body—or by vibration. Can you replace a human with that sort of machine to generate that particular energy and, if you need a conscious human, how do you create Reiki gloves to amplify energy flow and make it more efficient?

Zacariah: I'm actually designing something like that right now. I'm an engineer, and in this life I want to become a quantum physicist, and am actually designing my own advanced technologies—including a design for a machine that would do just that: raise the frequency of somebody in order to heal them. It's really complicated, because there are so many different set frequencies within the genome and the body itself that you have to actually hit specific frequencies without affecting others. So what I'm creating is a zero-point field through a boson condensation within a superfluid. This process of creating a zero-point field creates a vector field acting as a singular atom. If you were to place a body in this field, its vibration would quicken and set their entire form into one system. You then could manipulate their body using separate instruments. But I'm not sure how you would do that. Do you know anybody who, with technology, can raise the vibration of a specific chakra in the body?

Max: Nope. I follow some of the Internet trends; it's all a mess. They say a lot of words, but it's hard to do any healing experiments without a proper biophysical lab. You have to have a space where you experiment on living organisms.

Zacariah: Yeah. That's really hard in this modern day 'cuz they say, "no, respect the animals." I get that. I'm a spiritual person and I speak to animals and all that. But you have to sacrifice to have science.

Max: You can do a lot with worms. Immature worms are a perfect model; they can be grown anywhere. It's a very easy and quick model, though it requires certain techniques. It's a quick model because their lifespan is only few weeks. They grow to full size in about two to three weeks. A lot of that technology can work on the worms. You can see them even with a very cheap microscope—see them growing, control their health in many ways. Harm them and heal them.

Zacariah: I understand about not wanting to harm animals, but they're just organic vessels.

Max: The problem with using animals is that it is done in a very messy way, and the suffering is real—especially HIV experiments with monkeys. It's easier with worm and cell culture and plants, but is also a slower process. If you want a cheap technology, grow some corn and you can use the sprouts in about a week. It's possible to start experimenting in this way. But at some point, this would evolve into using mice. When justified by some experiment, I say a prayer of forgiveness for what I do with mice.

Coming back to genetics—I understand the field because it's my mainstream profession and expertise. A lot of disorders can be treated by activating and deactivating specific genes. Human science understands a lot, as we have the whole sequence of the human genome and can manipulate it in many ways. Knowing its secrets, we could possibly design a sort of instrument controlled by computer which sends a sequence of light and sound frequencies, which would be like light music—possibly holographic with a structure. Not simply the light—structured light like a computer projector and sound system directed at someone to control them. This light, sound and color frequency can be directed too at the genes. If properly coded, you can develop treatments. That's my simple-minded view. I need more sources to do it right.

Zacariah: You're on the right track, but I'm restricted from revealing certain technologies that extraterrestrials use for the main reason that they want us to figure them out for ourselves, so they cannot be responsible for anything we do after. I can tell you that many species use light and sound for DNA manipulation. It's very common; they don't always use machines, though; they use their own energy. A Pleiadian can with a glance at you activate specific DNA coding. The Zeta Greys use a combination of light, sound and biological chemicals to activate and deactivate certain human traits.

For us today, we use DNA ligase to split the nucleic basis, I think to glue genes together. They would use a combination of the ligase, light and sound. They also use chemicals, and the Greys inject you with serum to activate or deactivate your DNA.

Max: That makes sense.

DISDOO: BE BRAVE

Channeled by Jim

The way to be helpful is to be brave about matters some people may find odd: talking to aliens . . . being part of love and light, and a network of lightworkers. You must be brave and admit you are engaged with these activities. That will sometimes be a not very popular stance . . . but in order for us to "knit ourselves together" we must be brave—not pull away—because the time is coming when others will see you are standing on solid ground, and they are not. At present, though, they perceive themselves as standing solid, and you as whimsical, dreamlike or weird.

You have special values that urge others to like, or dislike, you. Positive qualities such as creative vision, music, thoughts employed to push your agenda forward—thrust your truth into the world.

ACKNOWLEDGMENTS

We thank those who helped with transcribing and editing video materials (named by names or nicknames): Ruth Tumminello, Alexander Knezhevich, Angela Speed, Carla, Casey, Christopher, Damian, Dan, Dan, David Waller, Dylan, Gisela, Heather, Indian-in-the-machine, Karl Mehler, Karyn Dolan, Laura, Laurie, Liney, Pat Hazanov, Pete Andrew, Pukli, Sabrina Arturis, Sahej Dhak, Sephira, Slava Titarenko, Chris York. We thank Kaan Demircelik (artofkaan.com), Heather Eilrich and Dahley Robertson-King for the illustrations. We thank Zacariah Heim for allowing us to use his interviews in the book.

ABOUT THE HUMAN AUTHORS OF THIS BOOK

We see a bright future and the road leading to it. We strive to bring about the Disclosure, the Open Contact, and Ascension. Our international online community Human Colony (abbreviated as Hucolo) was started in 2013 and now has thousands of followers.

James Ernest Charles started to channel in May 2013. Since then, we are doing live public webinars on YouTube every Saturday. Jim channels many aliens, angels, ancient gods, ascended masters and discarnate souls. Among them are the Pleiadians, Yahyel, Sassani, Shakani, Arcturians, Sirians, Andromedans, the Council of Nine, Archangels, a fairy, and a dolphin. Also, in nearly chronological order: Elijah, Buddha, Yeshua, Francis of Assisi, Babaji, Koot Hoomi, Helena Blavatsky, Tesla, Yogananda, Mahatma Gandhi, Neem Karoli Baba, Sathya Sai Baba, LBJ, JFK, Allen Ginsberg, John Lennon, and Terence McKenna.

James Charles is a Reiki Master and facilitates Galactic Reiki classes taught by channeled aliens.

Max Rempel is a Reiki Master and has a Ph.D. in molecular biology. Max embraces science research of DNA vibrations and metaphysics. Max has published several books about aliens and Ascension including CELESTIAL SCIENCE and WELCOME TO EARTH: A GUIDE FOR ALIENS.

We invite you to join Hucolo community online. We do weekly webinars open to the public. Our purpose is to share our knowledge and bring about the Disclosure, Open Contact and Ascension.

We announce our events on the main website http://hucolo.org

The video recordings of our webinars and Jim's channelings are posted on Hucolo TV channel on YouTube (http://youtube.com/user/HumanColonies).

Our main discussion takes place at HUCOLO PRIVATE group on Facebook (http://facebook.com/groups/hucolo). You are welcome to join!

With love,

Max and Jim

Made in the USA
Middletown, DE
28 March 2018